L2 Grammatical Representation and Processing

SECOND LANGUAGE ACQUISITION

Series Editors: Professor David Singleton, *University of Pannonia,* *Hungary* and Fellow Emeritus, *Trinity College, Dublin, Ireland* and **Associate Professor Simone E. Pfenninger,** *University of Salzburg, Austria*

This series brings together titles dealing with a variety of aspects of language acquisition and processing in situations where a language or languages other than the native language is involved. Second language is thus interpreted in its broadest possible sense. The volumes included in the series all offer in their different ways, on the one hand, exposition and discussion of empirical findings and, on the other, some degree of theoretical reflection. In this latter connection, no particular theoretical stance is privileged in the series; nor is any relevant perspective – sociolinguistic, psycholinguistic, neurolinguistic, etc. – deemed out of place. The intended readership of the series includes final-year undergraduates working on second language acquisition projects, postgraduate students involved in second language acquisition research, and researchers, teachers and policy-makers in general whose interests include a second language acquisition component.

All books in this series are externally peer-reviewed.

Full details of all the books in this series and of all our other publications can be found on http://www.multilingual-matters.com, or by writing to Multilingual Matters, St Nicholas House, 31-34 High Street, Bristol BS1 2AW, UK.

SECOND LANGUAGE ACQUISITION: 136

L2 Grammatical Representation and Processing

Theory and Practice

Edited by
Deborah Arteaga

MULTILINGUAL MATTERS
Bristol • Blue Ridge Summit

DOI https://doi.org/10.21832/ARTEAG5341
Library of Congress Cataloging in Publication Data
A catalog record for this book is available from the Library of Congress.
Names: Arteaga, Deborah, editor.
Title: L2 Grammatical Representation and Processing: Theory and Practice /
   Edited by Deborah Arteaga.
Description: Bristol; Blue Ridge Summit: Multilingual Matters, [2019] |
Series: Second Language Acquisition: 136 | Includes bibliographical
   references. | Summary: 'This book presents an array of new research on
   several current theoretical debates in the field of SLA. The studies address questions
   relating to ultimate attainment, first language   transfer, universal properties of SLA,
   processing and second language (L2) grammar, and explore a number of grammatical
   features of the L2' – Provided by publisher.
Identifiers: LCCN 2019018875 (print) | LCCN 2019022397 (ebook) | ISBN
   9781788925341 (hbk : alk. paper) | ISBN 9781788925334 (pbk : alk. paper)
Subjects: LCSH: Second language acquisition. | French
language – Grammar – Study and teaching – Foreign speakers.
Classification: LCC P118.2.L177 2019 (print) | LCC P118.2 (ebook) | DDC
   418.0071 – dc23
LC record available at https://lccn.loc.gov/2019018875
LC ebook record available at https://lccn.loc.gov/2019022397

British Library Cataloguing in Publication Data
A catalogue entry for this book is available from the British Library.

ISBN-13: 978-1-78892-534-1 (hbk)
ISBN-13: 978-1-78892-533-4 (pbk)

Multilingual Matters
UK: St Nicholas House, 31-34 High Street, Bristol BS1 2AW, UK.
USA: NBN, Blue Ridge Summit, PA, USA.

Website: www.multilingual-matters.com
Twitter: Multi_Ling_Mat
Facebook: https://www.facebook.com/multilingualmatters
Blog: www.channelviewpublications.wordpress.com

The policy of Multilingual Matters/Channel View Publications is to use papers that
are natural, renewable and recyclable products, made from wood grown in sustainable
forests. In the manufacturing process of our books, and to further support our policy,
preference is given to printers that have FSC and PEFC Chain of Custody certification.
The FSC and/or PEFC logos will appear on those books where full certification has
been granted to the printer concerned.

Typeset by Riverside Publishing Solutions
Printed and bound in the UK by the CPI Books Group Ltd.
Printed and bound in the US by NBN.

Contents

To Julia Herschensohn, for her seminal work in L2 Acquisition and for her mentoring and support of so many of us.

Contributors

Asya Achimova is a postdoc at the University of Tübingen in a Research Training Group 'Ambiguity – Perception and Production'. She got her PhD in Psychology from Rutgers University where she worked on the scopal ambiguities in questions with quantifiers. She was also involved in research on the acquisition of determiners in second language French. After her PhD, she taught courses on bilingualism and second language acquisition at the University of Leipzig. Asya now focuses on modeling the pragmatics of ambiguity resolution in conversation within the Rational Speech Acts framework.

Deborah Arteaga is Professor of Spanish at the University of Nevada, Las Vegas, where she has held a variety of administrative positions (Chair, Associate Dean, Enrollment Management Coordinator), in addition to teaching all levels of Spanish and French language and linguistics, and coordination of Spanish teaching assistants and part-time instructors. She received her MA in French at the University of Colorado, Boulder, and her PhD in Romance Linguistics at the University of Washington. Her research topics include Diachronic French Syntax, Second Language Acquisition (with Julia Herschensohn), and Teaching Social and Regional Variation in Spanish

Dalila Ayoun is Professor of French Linguistics and SLAT at the University of Arizona. Her research focuses on the second language acquisition of morphosyntax as well as French theoretical and applied linguistics from a generative perspective. Her most recent publications include a co-edited volume (Ayoun *et al.*, 2018. *Tense, Aspect, Modality and Evidentiality: Cross-Linguistic Perspectives.* Amsterdam: John Benjamins), a monograph (*The Second Language Acquisition of French Tense, Aspect and Mood and Modality.* Amsterdam: John Benjamins) and an article (2018. Grammatical gender assignment in French: Dispelling the native speaker myth. *Journal of French Language Studies* 28, 113–148).

Laurent Dekydtspotter is a Professor in the Department of French & Italian and in the Department of Second Language Studies at Indiana University Bloomington. He is also the Chair of the Department of Second Language Studies. His research mostly addresses second language sentence interpretation. His primary interests reside in the role of natural language syntax in the real-time integration of information in interpreting a second language. A string of experiments so far suggests a structural reflex in second language learners of French, challenging the notion that second language learners do not engage in real-time structural computations.

Viviane Déprez is a native of Paris, France, who grew up in German-speaking Switzerland. She went to the United States to complete her PhD in the Department of Linguistics and Philosophy at MIT. After graduating she joined the Rutgers Department of Linguistics and also became a Research affiliate of the Cognitive Science Lab at Princeton University until 1993, and subsequently an affiliate member of the Rutgers University Center for Cognitive Sciences and of the Rutgers Graduate Faculty of Psychology. She is currently a member of the CNRS Lab on Language, Brain and Cognition in Bron and the director of the Comparative Experimental Linguistics (CELL) Lab at Rutgers.

Charlene Gilbert is a PhD candidate in the Department of French & Italian as well as in the Department of Linguistics at Indiana University Bloomington. Her research interests lie in second language sentence interpretation and processing. More specifically, her dissertation work focuses on how English speakers who are learning French process various syntactic structures under anaphora resolution and in the context of long-distance dependencies. Preliminary results suggest that learners of French as a second language compute syntactic details within working memory constraints, and do not solely relying on lexical and contextual information.

Julia Herschensohn earned her doctorate in Linguistics at the University of Washington and subsequently held teaching positions at Middlebury College and Cornell University before returning to the University of Washington where she served as Professor and Chair of Linguistics for 15 years. She has published seven books and dozens of articles spanning the areas of generative syntax, second language acquisition theory, and applied linguistics, especially in the Romance languages (synchronic and diachronic). The main areas of specialization are theoretical syntax and nonnative language learning, linked in her current research dealing with language processing and age effects.

Nuria Sagarra (PhD, University of Illinois at Urbana-Champaign) researches how monolinguals and bilinguals process morphosyntax and syntax. In particular, she explores how processing is modulated by age of acquisition, language experience with the L1 and the L2, proficiency, learning context (immersion), and linguistic characteristics, such as morphological markedness, saliency, animacy, and redundancy. She also investigates whether monolinguals and bilinguals use suprasegmental cues to anticipate morphological information during word recognition, and whether anticipatory abilities are trainable. Finally, she examines processing patterns in monolingual and bilingual typically and atypically developing children. She investigates these topics using self-paced reading, eye-tracking, and ERPs.

Anne Vainikka (PhD, UMass/Amherst) was adjunct professor at the University of Delaware in Linguistics and Cognitive Science. Her PhD on Finnish syntax laid the groundwork for most subsequent work on its syntax and her continued work on Finnish was a major contribution to work on Uralic languages. During her graduate studies, she started to work on child language acquisition, and then in Germany with Martha Young-Scholten on second language acquisition. Her interest in tackling long-standing problems recently led to her Verb Company and more systematic introduction of English spelling to beginning readers including those using the Digital Literacy Instructor software Martha Young-Scholten helped develop.

Martha Young-Scholten (PhD) (University of Washington, Seattle) is professor of second language acquisition at Newcastle University. Since the 1980s she has conducted research on uninstructed adults' acquisition of German and English morphosyntax. In the early 2000s, she began to investigate acquisition of morphosyntax, phonology and development of phonological awareness and reading by adult migrants with little formal education. She has taught and presented at universities and at conferences on five continents, serves on journal editorial boards and co-edits series for de Gruyter Mouton and Narr Francke Verlag. With Julia Herschensohn, she co-edited the 2013/2018 Cambridge University Press *Handbook of Second Language Acquisition*.

Bridget Yaden, PhD, is Professor of Hispanic Studies and Director of the Language Resource Center at Pacific Lutheran University (PLU) in Tacoma, Washington. She holds a PhD and MA in Romance Linguistics (UW) and a BA in Spanish (WWU). She began her involvement in language centers during her graduate studies at the University of Washington (1995–1996, Language Learning Center) and has continued this work at PLU since 1996. Her research interests include online language programs, bilingual education, and world language teacher preparation. She has served on many professional boards, including president-elect of ACTFL, NWALL, AATSP Juan de Fuca Chapter, WAFLT, and PNCFL.

Introduction

Julia Herschensohn

Overview

From a historical perspective, theoretical approaches to second language (L2) studies can be viewed as both cyclic and innovative. Scholarship in the mid-20th century focused on contrastive analysis (Lado, 1957), the role of the native language (transfer) in acquisition of the L2, while recommending audiolingual pedagogy based on behaviorist principles (Lado, 1964). Two decades later, scholarship focused on universal properties of language and acquisition (Bailey *et al.*, 1974) while advocating communicative language teaching. From the 1980s, in both formalist Universal Grammar (UG), (White, 1989) and functionalist – sociocultural (Lantolf, 1994), cognitive (McLaughlin, 1987), and interactionist (Swain, 1985) – theoretical approaches, L2 acquisition (L2A) research expanded significantly. Interest in native transfer and concentration on universal properties have repeated cyclically over the decades, whereas theoretical innovations and empirical evidence have moved scholarship forward over many decades. The link between theory of L2A and pedagogical practice has also varied cyclically. L2 research may ignore any pedagogical implications, particularly with respect to studies of naturalistic L2A (Klein & Perdue, 1992). Likewise, Gil *et al.* (2017: 4) point out that 'the approach to second language acquisition that assumes a formal generative linguistic orientation to the properties of language has, in the bulk of its research, abstracted away from the language classroom.' In contrast, some L2 research may involve actual instruction, for example in terms of miniature language systems (Ellis & Sagarra, 2010) or it may point to a beneficial methodology (e.g. Hopp, 2016). In the same spirit, Gil *et al.* (2017) advocate for experimental classroom research based on formal generative theory, a reprise of earlier work bridging theory and practice (e.g. Arteaga & Herschensohn, 1995; Arteaga *et al.*, 2003; Whong, 2011).

The chapters in the current collection are aimed at Second Language Acquisition (SLA) researchers with interest in pedagogical implications, including scholars who use SLA expertise to assist teaching, and touch on both L2 theory and its application in pedagogical settings. The majority of the authors work in the formal generative paradigm (hence they presume some familiarity with that framework) and gather their evidence for the most part from classroom learners, with each chapter presenting a new set of empirical data. In terms of theory and practice, the chapters range from very theoretical (Chapter 4, Dekydtspotter & Gilbert) to very pedagogical (Chapter 7, Yaden), although most fall in the middle of the continuum. While the collection is not designed to be a lesson in language pedagogy, many of the chapters do address classroom applications. Arteaga and Herschensohn (Chapter 2) make concrete suggestions for teaching sociocultural pragmatic skills at beginning and advanced levels. Ayoun (Chapter 3) considers the use of certain assessment tools as measures of advanced student mastery of verbal morphology. Yaden (Chapter 7) presents a detailed picture of both overall curriculum and classroom implementation of technology in online and hybrid coursework. Finally, the Conclusion presents pedagogical implications of each study on a chapter by chapter basis, so that readers are led to consider the importance of linguistic theory to classroom L2 learning.

Currently, theoretical frameworks examining L2A continue to line up in formalist versus functionalist camps, but both share similar concerns and methodologies. Connectionist–emergentist and functionalist approaches (e.g. Ellis & Larsen-Freeman, 2009; Elman *et al.*, 1996) view language as a learned phenomenon that uses similar cognitive mechanisms as for other (animal and machine) learning, based on frequency of input and strength of activation of certain factors. Functionalist approaches are less interested in grammatical features than the role of token mastery and analogy in language learning. In contrast, formalist UG approaches (Herschensohn, 2000; White, 2003) aim to discern the properties of the interlanguage (between L1 and L2) grammar of the language learner at different stages of the L2 development. Scholarship in the UG tradition is often concentrated on a single stage in a property theory framework, but some work aims to view the developmental process in a transition theory framework (Gregg, 2003), through longitudinal or cross-sectional studies. The chapters in this collection are mainly situated in a UG framework from both property and transition perspectives. Vainikka and Young-Scholten's (Chapter 6) Organic Grammar is a transition theory noting the stages that characterize L2 development; they examine a broad range of native and second languages in providing an account of the filler words that have been documented for decades. Achimova and Déprez (Chapter 1) use a cross-sectional population to do a longitudinal investigation of L2 article mastery. Arteaga and Herschensohn (Chapter 2) and Yaden (Chapter 7) report on evaluations of L2 learners that span a year. The other studies present a snapshot of a static level of competence, from intermediate to highly advanced learners.

Within formalist theory, there are two perspectives on the role of the native language for the abstract grammatical features in the developing L2, for both grammatical representation and processing. For representation, the contrast is set in terms of the availability of grammatical features at early stages of L2 acquisition, with structure building approaches (Hawkins, 2001) assuming limited availability, and full access approaches (Schwartz & Sprouse, 1996) assuming theoretical availability of L2 grammatical features. Schwartz and Sprouse propose that at the initial stage of L2A, the learner's grammar is a full transfer of the native one, but that UG is fully accessible for the learner at all stages; this is characterized as full transfer/full access (FTFA). The learner's task is to unconsciously infer the similarities and differences between the L1 and L2 grammars based on the primary linguistic data received from the input. A number of real-life intervening factors such as age of acquisition onset (AoA), amount of input or cognitive overload may hinder the learner's acquisition or their use of the grammar in real-time processing. Subsequent research has explored such factors and built accounts for the oft-observed weaknesses in L2 morphological realization (Lardiere, 2009). In contrast to FTFA, grammatical deficit approaches (Snape *et al.*, 2009) view the morphological errors as evidence of defective syntax. The initial state of the L2 grammar may transfer lexical categories, but not functional ones, and for adults it will be difficult to acquire L2 functional categories given a critical period (late AoA) handicap. In this volume, Vainikka and Young-Scholten (Chapter 6) address the debate directly in arguing for structure building in their Organic Grammar proposal. Ayoun (Chapter 3) tests hypotheses related to morphological errors in terms of verbal tense and aspect, while Achimova and Déprez (Chapter 1) test determiner features of definiteness and specificity.

For processing, the contrast may be seen as qualitatively different (Clahsen & Felser, 2006) versus qualitatively similar (Hopp, 2013) processing strategies in both native and second language. Clahsen and Felser (2006), following in the path of fundamental difference due to critical period effects (Bley-Vroman, 1990), propose that adult L2 learners differ substantially in their parsing of the target language from child learners of the language. They propose that native speakers, in parsing the incoming language, are able to assign complex structures as they receive input, whereas L2 adults are only capable of doing 'shallow' processing (the Shallow Structure Hypothesis) that remains linear and local. In contrast, Hopp (2013) argues for fundamental similarity between L1 and L2 processing, attributing differences to factors other than AoA, such as reaction speed (L2 adults are inevitably much slower than natives) or representational lacunae (e.g. lack of knowledge of accurate gender for a given lexical item). The chapters collected here include two addressing the processing debate directly. Dekydtspotter and Gilbert (Chapter 4) set out to test very advanced speakers of L2 French and find that they actually outperform native French speakers in terms of processing subtle differences between long-distance anaphora. Sagarra (Chapter 5) looks at intermediate learners of L2 Spanish, whose processing of gender and number agreement definitely shows influence of L1 English in their greater skill with number than gender. The differences between intermediate and advanced learners is also highlighted by Achimova and Déprez (Chapter 1), who advance the hypothesis that processing load leads to differential responses between different levels of proficiency. More advanced learners, whose grammatical mastery of determiner features is better established, are better able to bring to bear this knowledge in article selection; less advanced learners, more susceptible to processing demands, show diminished performance in the same task.

All approaches have used increasingly complex and sensitive measures of assessment of language skills, exploiting offline (accuracy tests of comprehension and production) and online (real-time measures of L2 processing in comprehension and production) methodologies. While each chapter in this collection may concentrate on a small part of the L2 grammar, altogether they use real-time production and comprehension processing data to deduce the grammatical representation of the interlanguage of the L2 participants. Ranging from spontaneous production (Arteaga & Herschensohn (Chapter 2), Vainikka and Young-Scholten (Chapter 6)) to specific testing of classroom learners (Achimova & Déprez (Chapter 1), Ayoun (Chapter 3), Yaden (Chapter 7)), to online reaction time and eye tracking (Dekydtspotter & Gilbert (Chapter 4), Sagarra (Chapter 5)), the chapters use a broad selection of tools to contribute to L2A scholarship.

Chapters in this Volume

Chapter 1: Achimova and Déprez

Reexamining Ionin's Fluctuation Hypothesis, Achimova and Déprez consider the acquisition of the features of definiteness and specificity by Anglophone L2 learners of French. Definiteness indicates shared presupposition of a referent by speaker and hearer, while specificity indicates the speaker's knowledge of a unique referent in a given context. Unlike learners – such as Russian or Korean L1 speakers – whose L1 does not possess articles, Anglophones do have native articles with similar distribution to French of the two features in question, a fact that should lead to straightforward transfer. Ionin *et al.* (2004) propose that languages favor either [definite] or [specific] as the canonical morphological mark (the Article Choice Parameter), and that learners may use the incorrect morphological form as they gain mastery of the L2 differing in featural value (the Fluctuation Hypothesis). Subsequent research has shown fluctuation among learners, but some predictions of the hypothesis have not been borne out; furthermore, evidence from native speakers has shown that the Article Choice Parameter is more complex than originally stated. Achimova and Déprez carry out a cross-sectional study of French learners (low, mid and advanced college students), using an article choice task based on short situations and combining [definite] and [specific] features in both values. Although both French and English mark definiteness overtly and use specificity in a similar manner, the learners show increased article misuse in [+def −spec] and [−def +spec] contexts; that is, when the two features clash. Furthermore, errors are greater for the less proficient learners, leading the researchers to look to processing load as a factor. They argue that specificity is a pragmatic feature related to knowledge of the speaker with respect to reference. While L1 transfer facilitates article choice in the French-English pairing, cognitive pressure affects the computation of common ground in the less proficient learners. This chapter contributes to the growing evidence that knowledge of the L2 is mediated strongly by the processing load brought to bear in implementation.

Chapter 2: Arteaga and Herschensohn

Arteaga and Herschensohn use data from two advanced learners of L2 French to explore sociolinguistic competence in second language acquisition, and they then make recommendations based on their findings to enhance classroom instruction in discourse and pragmatic competence. They begin with a review of earlier work on L2 sociolinguistic competence, noting that work by Dewaele (2004), Dewaele and Regan (2002), Regan (1998), Rehner and Mougeon (1999), Rehner et al. (2003) and Armstrong (2002) has emphasized the importance of mastery of cultural knowledge and sociopragmatic appropriateness to learners of a second language. Of particular focus in terms of register in French is the appropriate use (and deletion) of negative *ne*, replacement of *nous* 'we' by *on* and the accurate deployment of second person *tu* and *vous*. First person plural is almost exclusively restricted to *on* in current spoken French, whereas *ne* deletion is a definite mark of informal register. *Tu* and *vous* use depends on a number of factors, more sociocultural than register based, but is a matter of difficulty for French L2 learners. These points are the areas of investigation in the new corpus, a collection of six interviews (three each) from two distinct profiles of language learner, 'Max' (an academic learner whose AoA is 48) and 'Chloe' (a more naturalistic learner whose AoA is 13). Both are interviewed before, during and after a year's stay in France. Max's style favors the formal, especially for *ne* deletion, whereas Chloe's style is more informal due to casual interactions with peers, diminished formal education and lower age of acquisition onset. These factors offer her fewer opportunities to switch into more formal registers. Using the data presented, the authors advocate the instruction of sociolinguistic competence by furnishing classroom students communicative activities that elicit appropriate register and interpersonal address. There are suggestions for both beginning/intermediate and for advanced learners to engage in structured communication through role play, information gap and more advanced discussions using films.

Chapter 3: Ayoun

Ayoun brings to bear her extensive research background in tense-aspect-modality (TAM) to examine short-term development of TAM mastery by fourth year college students of L2 French. She compares students with three different native languages: heritage French, heritage Spanish (with a similar TAM system to French) and English. After reviewing previous studies showing that TAM is a persistent learnability issue for L2 learners – especially the less frequent perfect tenses (e.g. pluperfect, future perfect) – she outlines three theoretical approaches to morphological feature-form mapping: the Missing (Surface) Inflection Hypothesis, the Prosodic Transfer Hypothesis and the Interface Hypothesis. She notes the following points of difficulty for Anglophones learning L2 French: abstract features of aspect and their correlation to surface forms (e.g. *passé composé* versus *imparfait, être en train de* progressive) and the mood differences between indicative and subjunctive. The semester-long study (with a post-test after completion of the term) investigated longitudinal changes in the ability of the students to produce target verb forms in a cloze test format. Classroom pedagogy included communicative methodology, audiovisual materials, recasts and interpersonal involvement in a course that used movies as the launching point for the study of the corresponding novel that the students discussed over a period of weeks. The results indicated quite a bit of variability among the students, with disproportionate mastery of present tense over others and of stative over telic and activity verbs. There was also no advantage in TAM for French and Spanish heritage learners (despite their advantage in the initial general proficiency test). Ayoun concludes that cloze tests are not a good instrument for testing students, because they produce quite varied results for the native speaker controls, who sometimes scored but half of the targeted forms (yet were appropriate). She suggests that explicit instruction and corrective feedback may be more effective than implicit instruction and recasts, whose 'correction' may be missed by the student.

Chapter 4: Dekydtspotter and Gilbert

Dekydspotter and Gilbert investigate the relationship of grammatical knowledge (representation) and its implementation in real-time processing while comparing native speakers (NSs) and nonnative speakers (NNSs) on two tasks involving long distance anaphora. They consider Clahsen and Felser's (2006) Shallow Processing Hypothesis – which holds that L2 learners use only superficial parsing, whereas native speakers employ detailed grammatical representations in their parse – and the possibility that shallow processing may become more detailed under environmental circumstances (e.g. living in L2 target environment or performing a task focused on grammaticality). Their area of investigation is long distance anaphoric dependencies in multiply embedded sentences in French, contrasting selected complement (1) versus nonselected modifier (2).

(1) Quelle décision à propos de lui$_i$ est-ce que Paul$_i$ a dit que Lydie avait rejetée [*quelle décision à propos de lui*] sans hésitation? 'What decision about himself did Paul say that Lydie had rejected without hesitation?'
(2) Quelle décision le$_i$ concernant est-ce que Paul$_i$ a dit que Lydie avait rejetée [*quelle décision*] sans hésitation? 'What decision concerning him did Paul say Lydie had rejected without hesitation?'

The anaphor *lui* in (1) is syntactically bound in the embedded position and raised with its head noun to matrix Complementizer Phrase (CP); in contrast, *le* in (2) gains coreference through discourse semantics, not syntax. The referential chain of (1) should reduce processing load and increase speed of parsing compared to that of (2). The contrast permits the authors to design an experiment that will test the hypothesis for both NSs and NNSs. Using a moving window design, they compare reading times (RTs) and accuracy of the two groups, finding that the NSs and NNSs are comparable on both criteria. They also address the issues of environment (their subjects are not in a target environment) and grammaticality (the tasks focus on meaning and reference, not grammaticality). The comparability of the native and nonnative groups lead them to conclude that the noun-complements with matching embedded clause subjects induced the advanced L2 learners to read the verb generally more quickly than NP-modifiers did (see Chapter 4, p. 87), thus supporting their contention that NNSs are capable of processing as do NSs and that anaphoric chains facilitate syntactic parsing.

Chapter 5: Sagarra

Sagarra gives fresh perspectives on the well-explored area of second language difficulties with gender agreement, considering the influence of learner characteristics, morphological markedness and experiment design. Drawing from the extensive L2 literature of the past 25 years, she reviews the competing representational and processing accounts. The former propose either that post-critical period learners are morphologically impaired if their native language does not have gender agreement, or that factors other than age of acquisition onset cause L2 agreement difficulties. Some morphology-based models propose that default (e.g. masculine, singular) forms are more available to L2 learners than marked (feminine, plural) ones in both comprehension and production. The latter attribute processing factors such as cognitive load, input frequency or morphological transparency as the source of L2 agreement problems. The author points out that the conflicting results obtained in earlier studies can be in part attributed to the experiment designs' using explicit (requiring more cognitive resources) rather than implicit tasks and noncumulative presentation. Her investigation studies intermediate Anglophone L2 Spanish learners' perception of agreement/disagreement of adjectives with respect to gender and number, asking two research questions: (1) do L2 learners process gender agreement/disagreement as do native speakers of Spanish? and (2) does morphological markedness affect native and L2 processing? A corollary question is whether experimental design may have an impact on results. Using eye tracking of self-paced reading (an implicit, cumulative methodology that is cognitively facilitative), she tests native and L2 reading responses in terms of reaction time and cumulative eye movement. Her results indicate that L2 learners are slower than native speakers, but that the processing of agreement and disagreement of adjectives is qualitatively similar for both groups, and that morphological markedness is not a factor in processing for either native speakers or for L2 learners. She also finds a distinction for both groups in processing gender versus number, which she convincingly explains in the discussion.

Chapter 6: Vainikka and Young-Scholten

Working within a Universal Grammar framework, Vainikka and Young-Scholten elaborate their model of Organic Grammar (OG) as a theoretical account of L2 acquisition. OG is a theory of transition that accounts for the evolving grammar of the learner at different stages of acquisition. In this chapter, they particularly focus on the use of what they call placeholders as a stage in the development of the morphosyntax of Tense Phrase (TP). The authors first outline the two theoretical 'camps' in developmental L1 and L2 acquisition: those who maintain that functional projections are absent in the earliest grammars (e.g. Radford, 1995 for L1A, Hawkins, 2001 for L2A) and those who argue that functional projections are present but unrealized (e.g. Lust, 2006 for L1A, Lardiere, 2009 for L2A). For both L1 and L2, production from the earliest stages is devoid of inflectional morphology, function words and accurate syntactic order. The authors belong to the first camp and have built their framework over decades for both L1 and L2; the current chapter contributes to the ongoing elaboration of their theory. Learners begin with only lexical projections, not functional ones, and in the case of L2A they start with their L1 directionality bias. OG is based on four assumptions: (1) a master tree is the backbone of syntactic structure, containing all functional projections for a given language; (2) inflectional morphology mirrors syntax; (3) acquisition is constrained by UG; and (4) development of grammar proceeds from lowest to highest functional projection. In intermediate stages, the authors argue that learners substitute placeholders – closed class items that are not target-like, yet are functional not lexical items – to transition to the correct target morphosyntax. Examples from L2 German,

Dutch and English demonstrate the placeholder substitutions used to fill in projections within the Inflectional Phrase (namely Aspect Phrase, Asp; Negative Phrase, NegP, NP; TP, Agreement Phase, AgrP). Vainikka and Young-Scholten see placeholders as evidence for UG in L2A, concluding because it takes a while 'for learners to figure out exactly what fills that head, they could well recruit non-target functional elements' in the same or in another functional category (see Chapter 6, p. 134). In further fleshing out OG, they also provide an account for the long observed appearance of consistent non-target functional morphology at intermediate levels of L2 development.

Chapter 7: Yaden

Yaden concentrates on an instructed environment in discussing the exploitation of online resources to create and implement a new L2 Spanish curriculum. She notes that liberal arts colleges have often been resistant to online courses, believing that computer-based learning is incompatible with small classes using interpersonal communication among students and teacher. However, an increasing body of research points to multiple advantages of online and hybrid (online plus classroom) language courses, advantages that Yaden tests in her case study. Students' schedules (often including extracurricular work) can be easily adapted to online coursework and homework. Physical presence is no longer limited to a given classroom and time, making enrollment much more flexible (with increasing numbers of students and decreasing costs). Finally, the availability of rich resources enhances the amount of input and interaction possibilities for the students. In order to implement the new curriculum at the institution in question, involved faculty participated in workshops designed to train them in the technical aspects of online instruction, and in the means of 'transferring this campus experience to the online experience' (see Chapter 7, p. 144). The first and second year Spanish courses that Yaden describes in detail provide a formula for curriculum development as well as a wealth of specific online resources. The two-year pilot program confirmed the advantages of schedule and enrollment flexibility; the student evaluations were enthusiastic; and the online, hybrid and classroom-only students all achieved comparable proficiency and knowledge of Hispanic culture.

Conclusion

This collection highlights a number of innovative findings. Achimova and Déprez (Chapter 1) make use of psycholinguistic theory of processing load to inform their discussion of the L2A of specificity and definiteness by Anglophone learners of L2 French. Arteaga and Herschensohn's chapter (Chapter 2) studies two profiles of more mature L2 speakers that are quite distinct from earlier sociolinguistic reports on college students in more formal instructional environments. Ayoun (Chapter 3) pioneers the study of heritage French and Spanish learners in her study of TAM in advanced L2 French. Dekydtspotter and Gilbert (Chapter 4) reexamine the differences between native and near-native speakers in terms of both representation (accuracy) and processing (reaction time) for a task involving very complicated anaphoric relations. Sagarra (Chapter 5) looks at processing of number and gender as diagnostics of native influence in L2 parsing. Vainikka and Young-Scholten (Chapter 6), in further elaborating their theory of OG, provide an explanation of the well-documented L2 'placeholders'. Finally, Yaden's report (Chapter 7) on the initiation of the online curriculum in L2 Spanish furnishes the track record of this advance as well as a detailed template for implementing it.

The persistent themes of native language transfer and universal properties of L2A are explored through the chapters in this volume, with special emphasis on L2 French and Spanish. The exploration of grammatical features of the L2 – tense, aspect, modality, specificity, definiteness, gender, number, anaphora – is complemented by the study of pragmatic competence in sociocultural aspects of register use. Finally, the chapters elicit pedagogical considerations from the macro curricular level to the micro cloze assessment.

References

Armstrong, N. (2002) Variable deletion of French *ne*: A cross-stylistic perspective. *Language Sciences* 24, 153–173.

Arteaga, D. and Herschensohn, J. (1995) Using diachronic linguistics in the language classroom. *Modern Language Journal* 79, 212–222.

Arteaga, D., Gess, R. and Herschensohn, J. (2003) Focusing on phonology to teach morphology form in French. *Modern Language Journal* 87, 58–70.

Bailey, N., Madden, C. and Krashen, S. (1974) Is there a 'natural sequence' in adult second language learning? *Language Learning* 24, 235–243.

Bley-Vroman, R. (1990) The logical problem of foreign language learning. *Linguistic Analysis* 20, 3–49.

Clahsen, H. and Felser, C. (2006) How nativelike is non-native language processing? *Trends in Cognitive Science* 10, 564–570.

Dewaele, J-M. (2004) The acquisition of sociolinguistic competence in French as a foreign language: An overview. *Journal of French Language Studies* 14, 301–320.

Dewaele, J-M. and Regan, V. (2002) Maîtriser la norme sociolinguistique en interlangue française: Le cas de l'omission variable de 'ne'. *Journal of French Language Studies* 12, 123–148.

Ellis, N.C. and Larsen-Freeman, D. (eds) (2009) *Language as a Complex Adaptive System*. Boston: Wiley-Blackwell.

Ellis, N.C. and Sagarra, N. (2010) The bounds of adult language acquisition: Blocking and learned attention. *Studies in Second Language Acquisition* 32, 553–580.

Elman, J.L., Bates, E.A., Johnson, M.H., Karmiloff-Smith, A., Parisi, D. and Plunkett, K. (1996) *Rethinking Innateness: A Connectionist Perspective on Development*. Cambridge MA: MIT Press.

Gil, K-H., Marsden H. and Whong, M. (2017) The meaning of negation in the second language classroom: Evidence from 'any'. *Language Teaching Research*, https://doi.org/10.1177/1362168817740144.

Gregg, K. (2003) The state of emergentism in second language acquisition. *Second Language Research* 19, 95–128.

Hawkins, R. (2001) *Second Language Syntax: A Generative Introduction*. Oxford/Malden, MA: Blackwell.

Herschensohn, J. (2000) *The Second Time Around: Minimalism and L2 Acquisition*. Amsterdam/Philadelphia: J. Benjamins.

Hopp, H. (2013) Grammatical gender in adult L2 acquisition: Relations between lexical and syntactic variability. *Second Language Research* 29, 33 56.

Hopp, H. (2016) Learning (not) to predict: Grammatical gender processing in second language acquisition. *Second Language Research* 32, 277–307.

Ionin, T., Ko, H. and Wexler, K. (2004) Article semantics in L2 acquisition: The role of specificity. *Language Acquisition* 12 (1), 3–69.

Klein, W. and Perdue, C. (1992) *Utterance Structure: (Developing Grammars Again)*. Amsterdam/Philadelphia: J. Benjamins.

Lado, R. (1957) *Linguistics Across Cultures: Applied Linguistics for Language Teachers*. Ann Arbor, MI: University of Michigan Press.

Lado, R. (1964) *Language Teaching: A Scientific Approach*. New York: McGraw Hill.

Lantolf, J.P. (ed.) (1994) Socio-cultural theory and second language learning. Special issue of *The Modern Language Journal* 78 (4).

Lardiere, D. (2009) Some thoughts on the contrastive analysis of features in second language acquisition. *Second Language Research* 25, 173–227.

Lust, B.C. (2006) *Child Language – Acquisition and Growth*. Cambridge: Cambridge University Press.

McLaughlin, B. (1987) *Theories of Second Language Learning*. London: Arnold.

Radford, A. (1995) Children: Architects or brickies? In D. MacLaughlin and S. McEwen (eds) *BUCLD 19 Proceedings* (pp. 1–19). Somerville, MA: Cascadilla Press.

Regan, V. (1998) Sociolinguistics and language learning in a study abroad context. *Frontiers: The Interdisciplinary Journal of Study Abroad* 4, 61–91.

Rehner, K. and Mougeon, R. (1999) Variation in the spoken French of immersion students: To *ne* or not to *ne*, that is the sociolinguistic question. *The Canadian Modern Language Review* 56, 124–154.

Rehner, K., Mougeon, R. and Nadasdi, T. (2003) The learning of sociolinguistic variation by advanced FSL learners: The case of *nous* versus *on* in immersion French. *Studies in Second Language Acquisition* 25, 127–157.

Schwartz, B.D. and Sprouse, R. (1996) L2 cognitive states and the full transfer/full access model. *Second Language Research* 12, 40–72.

Snape, N., Leung, Y-k.I. and Sharwood Smith, M. (eds) (2009) *Representational Deficits in SLA: Studies in Honor of Roger Hawkins*. Amsterdam/Philadelphia: J. Benjamins.

Swain, M. (1985) Communicative competence: Some roles of comprehensible input and comprehensible output in its development. In S. Gass and C. Madden (eds) *Input in Second Language Acquisition* (pp. 235–253). Rowley, MA: Newbury House.

White, L. (1989) *Universal Grammar and Second Language Acquisition*. Amsterdam: J. Benjamins.

White, L. (2003) *Second Language Acquisition and Universal Grammar*. Cambridge: Cambridge University Press.

Whong, M. (2011) *Language Teaching: Linguistic Theory in Practice*. Edinburgh: Edinburgh University Press.

1 Specificity Affects Determiner Choice Even When Definiteness Transfers

Asya Achimova and Viviane Déprez

1 Introduction

Specificity and definiteness, Ionin *et al.* (2004) argued, are two features that parametrically determine article lexicalization choice in the languages of the world. To account for the characteristic specificity effect that describes errors that second language (L2) learners have been observed to make in their determiner uses, Ionin *et al.* (2004) proposed that second language learners with determiner-less first language (L1) access the Article Choice Parameter available from Universal Grammar (UG) and initially fluctuate between its definiteness versus specificity settings. After an initial fluctuation phase, L2 learners fix the parameter, settling on the appropriate value, so that specificity driven misuse disappears. Second language research on the acquisition of determiners has subsequently been concerned with the question of whether the article parameter remains accessible to L2 learners.

In this chapter, we argue that specificity effects on determiner acquisition, unlike definiteness effects, are not due to fluctuating access of a parametrized universal semantic feature system, as they appear to occur even in cases of predicted transfer, when the L1 and L2 both feature the same parameter setting. Here, we look at the acquisition of L2 French by native speakers of English. Both languages have articles that mark definite versus indefinite noun phrases (NPs). We explore the possibility of full transfer of the article system from the L1 to the L2. However, as we show, the acquisition data also reveal an effect of specificity in some contexts. The rest of the paper is structured as follows. In Sections 1.1 and 1.2, we review the Article Choice Parameter hypothesis and related second language acquisition studies. Section 2 introduces our experimental techniques, followed by results in Section 3 and a discussion of the possible source of the observed specificity effect in Section 4. In Section 5, we conclude that specificity should be viewed as a pragmatic notion rather than a grammaticalized parameter.

1.1 The Article Choice Parameter

Acquisition of determiners is a well-known challenge for speakers of languages that lack overt articles. Such L2 learners have been observed to overuse the definite article in [+specific, –definite] contexts (Huebner, 1983; Master, 1987; Parrish, 1987; Thomas, 1989), and overuse the indefinite article in [–specific, +definite] contexts (Ionin *et al.*, 2004; Leung, 2001). Ionin *et al.* (2004) developed an account that traces these two types of errors to the same source: learners initially fluctuate between the two settings of the Article Choice Parameter and therefore sometimes use the definite determiner to mark [+definite] and sometimes [+specific] NPs. In the developing L2 grammars, the indefinite determiner marks either [–definite] or [–specific] NPs. This view of early stages of language acquisition became known as the Fluctuation Hypothesis.

Ionin *et al.* (2004) conceptualize definiteness and specificity as semantic features that they informally define as follows (Ionin *et al.*, 2004: 5) (for formal definitions, see Heim, 1982):

- If a determiner phrase (DP) of the form [D NP] is [+definite], the speaker and the hearer presuppose the existence of a unique individual in the set denoted by the NP.
- If a DP is the form [D NP] is [+specific], the speaker intends to refer to a unique individual in the set denoted by the NP, and considers this individual to possess some noteworthy property.

In English, the definite determiner *the* marks definite NPs, independent of whether these NPs are specific (1a) or nonspecific (1b) (examples from Ionin *et al.*, 2004: 8). As the following examples show, the definite article *the* is used to encode uniqueness whether or not the referent is known to the speaker with a noteworthy property.

(1) a. I'd like to talk to *the winner of today's race* – she is my best friend!

    b. I'd like to talk to *the winner of today's race* whoever that is; I'm writing a story about this race for the newspaper.

Unlike English, languages such as Samoan, according to Ionin *et al.* (2004), have determiner systems based on specificity. Thus, the Samoan article *le* marks specific singular DPs, while the article *se* appears with nonspecific singular DPs (Mosel & Hovdhaugen, 1992). Plural DPs are not marked.

Nevertheless, the validity of this classification is questioned by Tryzna (2009). She conducted an experiment to find out whether the article *se* in

Samoan could appear in definite nonspecific contexts. If Samoan lexicalizes articles based on their specificity values, *se* is predicted to be able to occur in nonspecific definite and indefinite contexts, and *le* in specific definite and indefinite contexts. Tryzna (2009) created a data-elicitation questionnaire. The test sentences in Samoan contained DPs in four contexts: specific definite, specific indefinite, nonspecific definite, and nonspecific indefinite ones. The Article Choice Parameter (Ionin *et al.*, 2004) predicts that *se* should appear in definite nonspecific contexts. However, as Tryzna (2009) shows, the nonspecific definite context requires the article *le*, as in (2). The article *se* only appears in nonspecific indefinite contexts.

(2)   A'fai   'ete mana'o 'e   tautala i*se/le malo   fa'atali se'i uma
      If   you want you   speak to ART winner   wait till over

      le   tautuuna.
      ART   race.

'If you want to talk to the winner, stay until the race is over.'
(Tryzna, 2009: 72)

The author proposed the following system of articles in Samoan (see Table 1.1) (Tryzna, 2009: 71).

Additional evidence that questions the status of specificity as a grammaticalized feature come from typological studies. Contrary to early accounts of the article systems in French-based Creoles, recent studies (e.g. Déprez, 2011) show that definite articles encode familiarity – that is, presupposed unique existence by speaker and hearer – rather than specificity, and that indefinite determiners can be used in both specific and nonspecific contexts (see also Déprez, 2013, 2016).

Ionin *et al.* (2009) addressed this cross-linguistic evidence by modifying their original Fluctuation Hypothesis. They argued that the article system in Samoan is more complex than initially assumed. Samoan uses the article *se* to mark NPs in nonspecific indefinite contexts, while *le* appears with specific indefinites and all definite NPs (specific and nonspecific). Drawing

Table 1.1 Specificity and definiteness interaction in Samoan

Context type	An example of a test sentence (target DP in bold)	The corresponding Samoan DP
1. Nonspecific indefinite	I'm looking for **a hat** to go with my new coat.	**se polou**
2. Specific indefinite	I'm looking for **a hat**. I must have left it here yesterday.	**le polou**
3. Specific definite	I want to talk to **the winner** of the race. She is a good friend of mine.	**le malo**
4. Nonspecific definite	If you want to talk to **the winner**, wait until the end of the race.	**le malo**

from typological work on other topics, Ionin *et al.* (2009) showed that a similar division is relevant in a number of domains. Thus, specific indefinite and definite NPs require the same marker in Spanish, for example, the dative preposition *a* 'to' (Aissen, 2003; Leonetti, 2004; Torrego, 1998) receive accusative case marking in Turkish (Enç, 1991; Kelepir, 2001), and trigger the appearance of an initial vowel in nominals in Luganda (Ferrari-Bridgers, 2004). Ionin *et al.* (2009) note that in their 2008 experiments (Ionin *et al.*, 2008), L1 Russian speakers acquiring L2 English made more specificity-related errors with indefinites than with definites. The authors attribute the larger number of errors with indefinites to the natural language pattern described above: specificity distinguishes between different classes of indefinites. Here the specific indefinites pattern with definites and appear with the definite article, and nonspecific indefinites are marked with a separate article (the indefinite one).

In sum, the updated version of the Fluctuation Hypothesis (Ionin *et al.*, 2008) makes a different set of predictions. If L2 learners have access to the semantic features in UG, they should make errors with specific indefinites, namely manifest overuse of the definite *the* in [-definite, +specific] contexts – as this is an option available in natural languages, such as Samoan. At the same time, errors with nonspecific definites should not occur, since, according to Ionin *et al.* (2009), no known language makes an article distinction between specific and nonspecific definite NPs. In fact, Ionin *et al.* (2009) discovered that children made more specificity-related errors with indefinites, while adults made such errors both with indefinites and definites. The authors argue that the adults' data may show the effect of explicit strategies that adult learners apply in choosing an article.

Further studies on the acquisition of articles show that there are other factors that may influence article choice in L2 learners of languages, such as English. Ionin *et al.* (2012) examine how speakers transfer the semantics of demonstratives into their L2. For example, native speakers of Korean learning L2 English show different preferences in choosing between the definite article *the* and a demonstrative *that*, possibly reflecting the influence of their L1 that only has demonstratives and lacks overt articles.

1.2 Second language acquisition studies

According to Ionin *et al.* (2004), speakers of article-less languages should fluctuate between definiteness and specificity-based article systems at the initial stages of L2 acquisition; however, not all studies have found evidence in support of the fluctuation hypothesis. Tryzna (2009) examined the acquisition of English determiners in L1 speakers of Mandarin and Polish. Both languages lack determiners, so the Fluctuation Hypothesis predicts that speakers should alternate between using the definite article *the* to mark definite or specific NPs. In a forced choice elicitation task, participants had to complete the dialogues where determiners were missing.

The results appeared more complex than predicted by the Fluctuation Hypothesis alone. Chinese L1 speakers either adopted the target 'definiteness' setting or showed a fluctuation pattern. Polish speakers, on the other hand, showed a greater variety of strategies. While 21% of the advanced learners followed the fluctuation pattern, 26% showed optional use of *the* both with specific indefinites and definites. In the intermediate group, none of the speakers adopted the 'specificity' setting, with 11% following the fluctuation pattern and 53% using *the* optionally with all NPs. Tryzna (2009) concluded that the expected overuse of *the* in specific indefinite contexts was by far not the only pattern of errors.

Tryzna (2009) also made a proposal about the nature of specificity as a semantic feature. Since L2 learners do not overuse *the* with nonspecific indefinite NPs, they must have access to the specificity value; otherwise, we would expect no difference in the overuse of *the* with specific versus nonspecific DPs. Consequently, she views specificity as a universal semantic feature available to L2 learners regardless of their L1. The latter conclusion, however, seems to make incorrect predictions. If both specificity and definiteness are universal semantic features available to the learner, why is it that only some learners fluctuate between these settings in developing an L2 determiner system?

In another study, Jaensch (2009) looked at L3 acquisition of German by L1 speakers of Japanese and L2 learners of English. She found that Japanese speakers did not fluctuate between the settings of the Article Choice Parameter. Speakers did not successfully transfer their L2 article system into L3, and frequently omitted the articles, especially in the oral production task. Thus, this study provides only partial evidence in favor of the Fluctuation Hypothesis. As the updated Fluctuation Hypothesis (Ionin *et al.*, 2009) predicts, learners in Jaensch (2009) behaved in a more target-like manner in definite contexts than in indefinite ones. Specificity had an effect on the article misuse, but only in definite contexts: when the NP was nonspecific there was a higher rate of the indefinite article used.

The studies reviewed above focus on the acquisition of articles by speakers of article-less languages. We would now like to turn to situations where a speaker of an L1 with articles acquires an L2 with an article system. Such studies can shed light on the problem of transfer: do semantic features transfer to L2? Sarko (2009) examined L2 English acquisition by native speakers of French and Syrian Arabic. Both languages have articles, yet French is different from English as French requires overt articles for both singular and plural definites and indefinites. The article system of Syrian Arabic is also different from English, as Arabic lacks an overt article for indefinites singular and plural. In a forced choice elicitation task, Arabic speakers picked an incorrect article *the* in indefinite specific contexts (count singular nouns: 31% in the intermediate group, 23% in the advanced group), while the French speakers did not (5% and 3% respectively). Sarko (2009) attributes these errors to L1 transfer and interprets the findings as evidence in favor of the Full Transfer Full Access Hypothesis (Schwartz & Sprouse, 1994). According to this hypothesis, L2 learners have full access to the possible parameters of any grammatical feature in a language. At the same time, learners do not start L2 acquisition from scratch; instead they bring the values of the parameters from their L1. According to this hypothesis, L1 speakers of French learning L2 English should not fluctuate between the definiteness and specificity values of the Article Choice Parameter (Ionin *et al.*, 2004). As expected, the French speakers did not differ from native speakers of English in their choice of determiners for singular nouns.

However, other studies report conflicting results. Déprez *et al.* (2011) tested Dutch and Arabic speakers acquiring L2 French with a task adapted from Ionin *et al.*'s (2004) work. Their results showed that, unexpectedly, both groups of beginning L2 learners manifested specificity driven errors. Dutch learners of French overused the indefinite determiner *un/une* in definite nonspecific contexts 45% of the time, and the definite determiner *le* in indefinite specific contexts 68% of the time. The Full Transfer Hypothesis would predict a straightforward transfer from L1 to L2. Since Dutch is a definiteness based language, the 'specificity effect' should not arise in such cases. Similar error types found in child article acquisition were previously argued to stem from a child's egocentric perspective biasing the computation of the domain of reference toward a speaker center perspective (Maratsos, 1974; Schaeffer & Matthewson, 2005; among others). This explanation was rejected for adult L2 acquisition by Ionin *et al.* (2004) on the assumption that pragmatically mature adults no longer manifest such developmental pragmatic bias. However, Keysar *et al.* (2003) experimentally demonstrated that an egocentric computation of the domain of reference, favoring a speaker-centered perspective over a shared common ground is not just a developmental child strategy, but also arises with adults under cognitive pressure.

Keysar *et al.* (2003) used an experimental paradigm based on Horton and Keysar (1996), in which subjects, whose visual access to referent objects was distinct from that of a director, are instructed by this director to move objects in a grid. The question investigated was whether subjects would take into account the different visual access of the director to compute a referent based on the common ground or, on the contrary, rely on their own visual access and egocentric perspective, despite clear awareness of the difference. For clarity, let us consider an example of Keysar *et al.*'s (2003) task. At the onset of the experiment, a participant hid an object in a paper bag, say a large cup, and then placed it in a slot of the grid, crucially, occluded and hence invisible for the director but visible to the participant. Other slots of the grid, visible to both the participant and the director, contained two additional cups: a mid-size one and a small one. The director then instructed the participant to 'move the large cup'. A participant taking into account the visual map common to both the director and themselves (the common ground) is expected to move the mid-sized cup, as this one counts as the largest one visible to all, given that the director only sees two cups, the mid-size one and the small one. A participant who considers the cups visible to themselves only (egocentric perspective) would move the cup previously hidden in the paper bag, the largest one from their perspective, since the participant sees three cups. Strikingly, in 30% of trials, participants moved the object previously hidden in the bag, even though they knew it was visible only to them, but not to the director. About 70% of the participants moved the previously bagged cup at least once, and 46% did it half the time or more. Results showed that under cognitive pressure (increased time pressure), adult subjects behaved like children and sometimes failed to take into account the director's perspective.

Keysar *et al.* (2003) concluded that speakers were not able to fully employ their interlocutor's perspective, failing to take their interlocutor's knowledge into consideration. In other words, participants behaved egocentrically, taking only their own perspective into account and not the common ground for the calculation of a referent object, even though they knew that the director had a different vision of the grid than their own. The authors argued that while adults have a fully developed theory of mind and can consciously reflect upon others' beliefs, in real time, they sometimes fail to use it efficiently under cognitive pressure. As Keysar *et al.*'s (2003) study suggests, adults may behave egocentrically and ignore their interlocutor's perspective when they are performing demanding cognitive tasks.

Based on these results, Déprez *et al.* (2011) propose to attribute the 'specificity effect' they witnessed to such pragmatic considerations. They hypothesize that under the processing load of a second language, speakers tend to consider their own speaker perspective first, and do not always take into account the common ground. As a result, they overuse the definite determiner when the referent is speaker known and overuse the indefinite determiner when the referent is speaker unknown (Kagan, 2011).

As we have seen, the data on the status of the 'specificity effect' are conflicting. In this chapter, we take another look at the French/English language pair with L1 English speakers acquiring L2 French. As Table 1.2 illustrates, English and French both mark NPs with different articles depending on whether the NPs are definite or indefinite. The French

Table 1.2 Articles in English and in French

	English		French	
	Singular	Plural	Singular	Plural
Indefinite	a(an)	—	un/une	des
Definite	the	the	le/la	Les

indefinite article has three forms: masculine singular *un*, feminine singular *une*, and a plural *des*. The definite article also comes in three forms: *le*, *la* and *les*. English lacks a plural form for indefinites, has a number neutral definite determiner and makes no distinction based on the grammatical gender of the nouns.

Our experiment focused on masculine singular nouns where the English and French systems are most comparable to avoid independent problems that L2 learners encounter with gender marking in the French determiners. If specificity is indeed one of the two possible values of the Article Choice Parameter, a full transfer of the definiteness-based article system of English into L2 French with no specificity effect is expected. In contrast, if, as some studies suggest, specificity reflects a pragmatic priority to the speaker perspective when the processing load is affected, we may see an increased number of article misuse in situations where the values of these two features clash, namely in [+definite −specific] and [−definite +specific] contexts. If speakers are at least sometimes driven by notions of 'speaker knowledge', that is, speaker known or speaker unknown rather than the common ground for the computation of the reference domain, in the cases named above, they may pick the wrong article.

2 Methods

We tested L1 speakers of English acquiring L2 French. One hundred and one native speakers of English completed the test; 10 subjects were eliminated from the analysis because they either failed to rate how well they understood the dialogues or rated their understanding below four on a seven-point scale. Thus, data from 91 participants were obtained from three proficiency levels: 36 low-intermediate (131 course), 42 intermediate (132 course) and 13 advanced speakers (200+ course). Participants self-rated their language proficiency also (see Table 1.3). Self-reported proficiency ratings have been shown to correlate with objective measures of language proficiency (Blanche & Merino, 1989; Shameem, 1998).

The participants had to complete dialogues with an appropriate choice of articles. We limited the choice of nouns to masculine singular to avoid added difficulty owing to gender choice. There were four types of contexts: [+definite −specific] (3), [+definite +specific] (4), [−definite

Table 1.3 Self-reported proficiency and comprehension assessment

Question	Average rating level 131	Average rating level 132	Average rating level 200
How well would you rate your level of French?	4.73	5.29	5.66
How well did you understand these dialogues?	5.08	5.77	6.35

+specific] (5) and [–definite –specific] (6). The task was to insert *le, un, de* or nothing into the gap.

(3)   [+definite –specific] *Dans une classe:*
La maîtresse: La plante de la classe a disparu. Savez-vous qui l'a prise?
Un élève: Non, madame, on cherche ____ voleur, mais on ne sait pas encore qui c'est!

In a classroom:
The teacher: The plant of the class disappeared. Do you know who took it?
A student: No, miss, we are looking for ____ thief, but we do not yet know who that is.

(4)   [+definite + specific] *Dans une école:*
Un enfant: Papa que fait-on dans cette école?
Son père: Je passe voir ____ directeur. C'est un ami à moi.

In a school:
A child: Daddy, what are we doing in this school?
Father: I am going to see ____ director. He is a friend of mine.

(5)   [–definite +specific] *Dans un restaurant:*
Le serveur: Bonjour! Je prends votre commande, ou est-ce que vous attendez quelqu'un ?
Le monsieur: Donnez-moi une minute s'il vous plaît, je vais manger avec ____ copain. Il va arriver bientôt.

In a restaurant:
The waiter: Hello, can I take your order or are you waiting for someone?
The customer: Give me one minute, please. I will be eating with ____ friend. He is arriving soon.

(6)   [–definite –specific] *Avant les contrôles:*
Un étudiant: Je commence à angoisser et du coup j'ai trop faim.
Sa copine: Tu veux manger quelque chose?
L'étudiant: Oui, j'aimerais bien ____ sandwich pour calmer ma faim.

Before exams:
A student: I am starting to be nervous and so I am starving.
His girlfriend: Do you want to eat something?
The student: Yes, I would love to eat ____ sandwich to ease my hunger.

Each of the four conditions had 16 dialogues, with a total of 64 items; one item was dropped from the analysis owing to a coding error. We initially tested the experiment with six native speakers of French, who performed as expected: they picked the definite determiner in definite contexts and the indefinite determiner in indefinite contexts, regardless of whether these contexts were specific or not.

3 Results

Two types of analyses were performed. First, to test whether specificity and definiteness were factors that affected article choice in L2 French, we fitted a binomial logistic regression model with subjects and items as random intercepts. The independent variables were definiteness and specificity, and the dependent variable was the article choice. Definiteness clearly turned out to be a significant predictor of correct article choice ($\beta = 4.739$, SE $= 0.555$, $p < 0.01$). But neither specificity by itself ($\beta = -0.735$, SE $= 0.55$, $p = 0.181$) nor its interaction with definiteness ($\beta = 0.62$, SE $= 0.778$, $p = 0.425$) were significant factors in this model. These results indicate that learners successfully transferred definiteness as a determining feature of an article system in their L2. As predicted by the Full Transfer Hypothesis, they generally appropriately used *le* to mark NPs in definite contexts, and *un* to mark indefinite NPs both in specific and nonspecific contexts. This result provides additional evidence that definiteness is a grammaticalized feature that is susceptible to transfer.

In the second type of analysis, we looked at the accuracy of the article choice in different conditions (Figure 1.1) and focused on article misuse. Recall that four conditions were tested, crossed for definiteness and specificity. The Full Transfer Hypothesis predicts that specificity should not affect article choice in any of the conditions, since the L1 English does not grammaticalize the specificity value in its article system. Since the full model with a three-way interaction of definiteness, specificity and proficiency level did not converge, we performed separate analyses for definite and indefinite contexts, and adjusted the p-values for multiple comparisons. In definite contexts, we saw no effect of specificity ($\beta = 1.237$, SE $= 1.039$, $p = 0.234$) or specificity by proficiency level interaction ($\beta = -0.003$, SE $= 0.006$, $p = 0.605$) on the amount of article misuse. In other words, participants did not choose *un* more often in [+definite –specific] contexts (3) compared to [+definite +specific] contexts (4). The amount of errors decreased as proficiency increased ($\beta = 0.015$, SE $= 0.006$, $p < 0.05$).

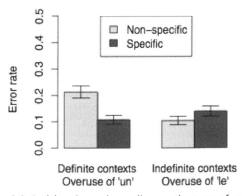

Figure 1.1 Article misuse depending on the type of context

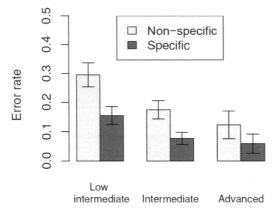

Figure 1.2 Overuse of *un* in definite contexts

However, when we looked at the error rates in definite contexts more closely, a tendency for an increase in the number of errors when the definiteness and specificity features clash (Figure 1.2) was observed. Even though the differences in error rates did not reach statistical significance owing to item variability, speakers at all proficiency levels made more errors in nonspecific definite contexts than in specific definite contexts. In other words, participants possibly driven by speaker-related pragmatic considerations used *un* to mark nonspecific NPs where the referent was speaker unknown as in examples such as (3), missing the fact that the context called for the definite article *le* based on the uniqueness of the referent.

In indefinite contexts, a different picture emerged (Figure 1.3). Here, again, we saw a decrease of the amount of errors with the growth of proficiency ($\beta = 0.016$, SE $= 0.007$, $p < 0.05$). There was also a marginally significant effect of specificity ($\beta = 2.284$, SE $= 1.092$, $p = 0.07$). The analysis also revealed a significant interaction between specificity and proficiency

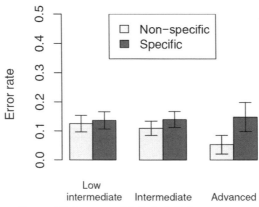

Figure 1.3 Overuse of *le* in indefinite contexts

level ($\beta = -0.018$, SE = 0.007, $p < 0.05$), suggesting that the effect of specificity is not the same for all proficiency levels. And, indeed, in Figure 1.3 we see that this effect is partly driven by the most advanced group, who shows a reduced amount of errors in indefinite nonspecific contexts as compared to less advanced speakers and to indefinite specific contexts. It is not quite clear why only the most advanced group displayed an apparent specificity effect. This might be due to the smaller number of participants (i.e. 13) in this group and its greater heterogeneity with students having quite diverse self-reported levels of proficiency (SD = 1.85 as compared to SD = 1.12 for the low intermediate and SD = 1.36 for the intermediate group).

One final note concerns the cases of specificity-based errors that are the most expected from a theoretical standpoint. If, like Ionin *et al.* (2009) suggest, languages of the world group together specific indefinites with definites, participants would be expected to make more errors picking *le* to mark specific indefinite NPs. However, Figures 1.2 and 1.3 suggest that this was not the case in our experimental data. The differences in error rates between specific and nonspecific NPs are more apparent in the overuse of *un* in definite contexts than in the overuse of *le* in indefinite contexts.

4 Discussion

In this chapter, we tested whether specificity affects article misuse in an L2 acquisition situation where transfer is possible. There is conflicting evidence concerning the effect of transfer. While some studies argued for full transfer to L2 if L1 had the relevant features, other studies suggested that the transfer may not be the only factor that affects determiner use by L2 learners. Here, we provide evidence in favor of the Full Transfer Hypothesis: our participants clearly mainly relied on definiteness when choosing an appropriate article in L2 dialogues. At the same time, we saw some effect of specificity. There was a tendency for an increased number of errors in definite contexts that were nonspecific, with some subjects overusing the indefinite article *un*.

The presence of some specificity effect in the use of L2 French determiners by English learners, and the lack of typological evidence for a specificity-based article system in the languages of the world, suggests that the status of specificity as a semantic feature parametrically available in UG may need revisiting. Some studies reviewed in Section 1.2 (e.g. Déprez *et al.*, 2011) argued that specificity, rather than a semantic feature, should be viewed more as a pragmatic strategy related to speaker-perspective taking with respect to the domain of reference. Our data provide some evidence in favor of this pragmatic view, and suggest that specificity affects L2 determiner acquisition, independently of the L1. Transfer from L1, when possible, clearly facilitates article choice in L2, and therefore makes specificity effects less pronounced in learners who have definiteness-based articles in both their L1 and L2.

The explanation for the L2 determiner errors advocated here relates to the view of egocentricity (failure to take the interlocuter's perspective into account) in language acquisition suggested in Déprez *et al.* (2011). In our tasks, the specificity-driven errors could arise from participants failing to fully take into consideration the common ground in the speaker's and the hearer's perspective as the relevant domain of reference. The definite article in French marks a familiar or unique referent in a common ground, and hence its appropriate use involves computing the common ground that the speaker and the hearer share and in which uniqueness can be established. What some learners appear to do instead is to base their choice of articles on speaker identifiability – when an entity is known to them – or perhaps rather the lack of such identifiability, differently marking an entity that is unknown them. If the referent is unknown to them, learners tend to overemploy the indefinite article. Kagan (2011) refers to such NPs as antispecific. She views specificity as a pragmatic notion, rather than as a semantic notion affecting the truth conditions. Unlike the parametric view of specificity (Ionin *et al.*, 2009), the pragmatic approach (Kagan, 2011) predicts that L2 learners can make errors both in definite and indefinite contexts.

It has been argued that performing a task in a foreign language may place additional processing costs on the subjects (e.g. Hyönä *et al.*, 1995; Roussel *et al.*, 2017), which could lead them to fail to fully take into account the hearer's perspective and hence the common ground. That is, while under the added cognitive pressure of speaking a foreign language, a learner may choose to prioritize their own perspective rather than the common ground. We refer to this behavior as specificity-driven: learners tend to mark speaker-known NPs with the definite determiner and speaker-unknown NPs with the indefinite determiner, failing to fully take into account the common ground that is shared with their interlocutor in their determiner use.

5 Conclusion

Our data show that while an L1 definiteness system transfers into L2, specificity can also affect the choice of articles in second language learners, although less so than in languages without article systems. This, we speculate, may be in part due to how computational load could affect the calculation of the common ground by speakers. The learners sometimes choose between an indefinite and a definite determiner based on whether the referent is known or not known to them. If the referent is speaker-unknown (antispecificity for Kagan, 2011), as in (3) above, the overuse of *un* increases in contexts that call for a (nonspecific) definite. If the referent is speaker-known, we see some overuse of *le* in contexts that call for an (specific) indefinite. The lack of parallelism for the two types of errors in our results suggests that the concept of antispecificity (i.e. being unknown to the speaker) may be of stronger relevance to L2 learners for whom definiteness transfer is available.

We interpret these facts as evidence for a pragmatic view of specificity. On this view, learners rely on their own knowledge of the referent when they cannot establish whether the referent is unique or familiar within a common ground domain or are under added cognitive pressure. As demonstrated by Keysar *et al.* (2003), calculating what is in the speaker's perspective is easier than calculating what is both in the speaker and the hearer's common ground. This could be why an adult learner under an increased cognitive load resorts to a domain that is more immediately accessible – the speaker domain – and mainly uses articles to mark what they know or, perhaps more strongly, do not know (antispecificity). It could be that using *un* is a strategy of caution: if speakers are not sure that the referent is unique or familiar in the common ground or if speakers are under cognitive pressure when calculating reference, they use *un* when a referent is unknown to them, failing to consider whether uniqueness could be established in a different way.

In order to be able to use the definite article correctly, a speaker needs to establish the uniqueness or familiarity of a referent for both the speaker and the hearer. When under pressure, a learner may take a shortcut by choosing an article on the basis of speaker's familiarity or lack thereof. When doing so, the indefinite article may serve as a default marker as it poses fewer requirements on its felicity conditions. In order to test this hypothesis, we could further look at the plurals in L2 French. We would predict that English speaking learners of French would make more article omission errors with nonfamiliar definites than with familiar definites, as familiarity provides additional cues in establishing the uniqueness of a referent.

References

Aissen, J. (2003) Differential object marking: Iconicity vs. economy. *Natural Language & Linguistic Theory* 21 (3), 435–483.

Blanche, P. and Merino, B. (1989) Self-assessment of foreign language skills: Implications for teachers and researchers. *Language Learning* 39 (3), 313–338, http://dx.doi.org/10.1111/j.1467-1770.1989.tb00595.x.

Déprez, V. (2011) Specificity and definiteness in French based creoles and L2 French. Invited paper presented at the Workshop on Creole Grammars and Linguistic Theories, University Diderot, Paris, France, 23 June.

Déprez, V. (2013) Nominal reference in L2 and French based creoles. Invited paper presented at the Workshop on Origins of Temporal, Spatial and Nominal Reference. Center of Experimentation on Speech and Language, and Laboratory of Speech and Language, Aix en Provence, France, 29 November 2013.

Déprez, V. (2016) Definiteness and specificity in L2 and Creole languages: A comparative study. Invited paper at the University of Nice-Sophia Antipolis, France, 12 May.

Déprez, V., Sleeman, P. and Guella, H. (2011) Specificity effects in L2 determiner acquisition: UG or pragmatic egocentrism. In M. Pirvulescu, M.C. Cuervo, A.T. Pérez-Leroux, J. Steele and N. Strik (eds) *Selected Proceedings of the 4th Conference on Generative Approaches to Language Acquisition North America (GALANA 2010)* (pp. 27–36). Somerville, MA: Cascadilla Press.

Enç, M. (1991) The semantics of specificity. *Linguistic Inquiry* 22 (1), 1–25.

Ferrari-Bridgers, F. (2004) The semantics-syntax interface of Luganda initial vowel. Paper presented at the 35th Annual Conference on African Linguistics (ACAL), Harvard University, Boston, Massachusetts. 2–4 April 2004.

Heim, I. (1982) The semantics of definite and indefinite noun phrases. PhD thesis, Massachusetts Institute of Technology.

Horton, W.S. and Keysar, B. (1996) When do speakers take into account common ground? *Cognition* 59 (1), 91–117.

Huebner, T. (1983) *A Longitudinal Analysis of the Acquisition of English*. Ann Arbor, MI: Karoma Publishers.

Hyönä, J., Tommola, J. and Alaja, A.M. (1995) Pupil dilation as a measure of processing load in simultaneous interpretation and other language tasks. *The Quarterly Journal of Experimental Psychology Section A*, 48 (3), 598–612.

Ionin, T., Ko, H. and Wexler, K. (2004) Article semantics in L2 acquisition: The role of specificity. *Language Acquisition* 12 (1), 3–69.

Ionin, T., Zubizarreta, M.L. and Maldonado, S.B. (2008) Sources of linguistic knowledge in the second language acquisition of English articles. *Lingua* 118 (4), 554–576.

Ionin, T., Zubizarreta, M.L. and Philippov, V. (2009) Acquisition of article semantics by child and adult L2-English learners. *Bilingualism: Language and Cognition* 12 (3), 337–361, https://doi.org/10.1017/S1366728909990149.

Ionin, T., Baek, S., Kim, H., Ko, H. and Wexler, K. (2012) *That's* not so different from *the:* Definite and demonstrative descriptions in second language acquisition. *Second Language Research* 28 (1), 69–101.

Jaensch, C. (2009) Article choice and article omission in the L3 German of native speakers of Japanese with L2 English. In M.D.P. Garcia Mayo and R.D. Hawkins (eds) *Second Language Acquisition of Articles: Empirical Findings and Theoretical Implications* (pp. 233–263). Amsterdam: John Benjamins.

Kagan, O. (2011) On speaker identifiability. *Journal of Slavic Linguistics* 19 (1), 47–84.

Kelepir, M. (2001) Topics in Turkish syntax: Clausal structure and scope. PhD thesis, Massachusetts Institute of Technology.

Keysar, B., Lin, S. and Barr, D.J. (2003) Limits on theory of mind use in adults. *Cognition* 89 (1), 25–41.

Leonetti, M. (2004) Specificity and differential object marking in Spanish. *Catalan Journal of Linguistics* 3 (1), 75–114.

Leung, Y.-K.I. (2001) The initial state of L3A: Full transfer and failed features. In X. Bonch-Bruevich, W.J. Crawford, J. Hellermann, C. Higgins and H. Nguyen (eds) *The Past, Present and Future of Second Language Research: Selected Proceedings of the 2000 Second Language Research Forum* (pp. 55–75). Somerville, MA: Cascadilla Press.

Maratsos, M.P. (1974) Preschool children's use of definite and indefinite articles. *Child Development*, 446–455.

Master, P.A. (1987) A cross-linguistic interlanguage analysis of the acquisition of the English article system. PhD thesis, University of California, Los Angeles.

Mosel, U. and Hovdhaugen, E. (1992) *Samoan Reference Grammar*. Oslo: Scandinavian University Press.

Parrish, B. (1987) A new look at methodologies in the study of article acquisition for learners of ESL. *Language Learning* 37 (3), 361–384, http://dx.doi.org/10.1111/j.1467-1770.1987.tb00576.x.

Roussel, S., Joulia, D., Tricot, A. and Sweller, J. (2017) Learning subject content through a foreign language should not ignore human cognitive architecture: A cognitive load theory approach. *Learning and Instruction* 52, 69–79, https://doi.org/10.1016/j.learninstruc.2017.04.007.

Sarko, G. (2009) L2 English article production by Arabic and French speakers. In M.D.P. Garcia Mayo and R.D. Hawkins (eds) *Second Language Acquisition of Articles: Empirical Findings and Theoretical Implications* (pp. 37–66). Amsterdam: John Benjamins.

Schaeffer, J. and Matthewson, L. (2005) Grammar and pragmatics in the acquisition of article systems. *Natural Language & Linguistic Theory* 23 (1), 53–101.

Schwartz, B.D. and Sprouse, R. (1994) Word order and nominative case in nonnative language acquisition: A longitudinal study of (L1 Turkish) German interlanguage. In T. Hoekstra and B.D. Schwartz (eds) *Language Acquisition Studies in Generative Grammar* (Vol. 31) (pp. 317–368). Amsterdam: John Benjamins.

Shameem, N. (1998) Validating self-reported language proficiency by testing performance in an immigrant community: The Wellington Indo Fijians. *Language Testing* 15 (1), 86–108.

Thomas, M. (1989) The acquisition of English articles by first- and second language learners. *Applied Psycholinguistics* 10 (03), 335–355.

Torrego, E. 1998. *The Dependencies of Objects.* Cambridge, MA: MIT Press.

Tryzna, M. (2009) Questioning the validity of the article choice parameter and the fluctuation hypothesis. In M.D.P. Garcia Mayo and R.D. Hawkins (eds) *Second Language Acquisition of Articles: Empirical Findings and Theoretical Implications* (Vol. 49) (pp. 67–86). Amsterdam: John Benjamins.

2 What Can Acquisition Studies Contribute to the Instruction of Register? A Case Study of French

Deborah Arteaga and Julia Herschensohn

1 Introduction

The recognition and production of speech in context is a crucial component of second language acquisition (L2A); language users need grammar as well as learned knowledge about cultural norms in order to judge the social situation correctly and produce socially appropriate speech in response (cf. Coveney, 1996, 2000; DeWaele, 2004; Dewaele & Regan, 2002; Etienne & Sax, 2006; Harley *et al.*, 1990; Howard, 2004; Lyster, 1994; Regan, 1995, 1996, 1997, 1998; Rehner & Mougeon, 1999; Rehner *et al.*, 2003; Valdman, 2000). A component of communicative competence, this kind of proficiency includes the ability to adapt speech both to circumstances and to listeners; it requires mastery of register and variety, and may elude even the most advanced students (Howard, 2004; Regan, 1998).

Given the importance of sociolinguistic competence, the question arises as to whether it should be (or can be) explicitly taught or whether learners are able to acquire it in a naturalistic setting. An examination of these questions requires that we take into account a variety of fields, as argued by Beacco and Porquier (2001: 5):

> Les enseignements de langues sont régulièrement amenés à faire le point sur leurs relations avec les disciplines non didactiques qui les nourissent et les fondent. C'est particulièrement le cas pour les relations entre la grammaire (devenue description 'traditionnelle'), les sciences du langage (qui proposent des descriptions argumentées, sans visée pédagogique) et l'enseignement de la langue.[1]

Indeed, relations among theoretical linguistics, acquisition studies, applied linguistics and pedagogical applications have been complex, oscillating between collaboration and mutual exclusion.

A distinction intersecting with these research paradigms is the environ-ment of L2 learning, that is, naturalistic versus instructed. In the 1980s, acquisition researchers favored the examination of data from unguided L2A (cf. Klein, 1986), and subsequent researchers adopted the opinion that data from spontaneous learning was the only evidence that should be used in theory building (Vainikka & Young-Scholten, 1998). Such approaches exclude consideration of pedagogical applications of research results. On the other hand, a range of other studies supports the importance of guidance for L2A and sees instructed learning as a different mode with the same end results (Arteaga *et al.*, 2003; Doughty, 2003; Doughty & Williams, 1998; Lee & Valdman, 2000; Long, 1991). Approaches that evaluate outcomes of instructed learners versus noninstructed learners (as opposed to naturalistic research) may or may not offer pedagogical advice, although in many cases, it is implicit from the study.

In this chapter, we bring together issues of pedagogy and L2A research in considering the acquisition of sociolinguistic competence by two advanced L2 learners of French, Max and Chloe. As French is a highly stratified language, we argue that it provides an ideal test case for acqui-sition of formal versus informal register. We begin by presenting an over-view of vernacular French, followed by a discussion of the importance of communicative competence and a review of previous studies of sociolin-guistic ability in L2 French. We next present our data, which include the context appropriate use of *on* for *nous* and the use of vernacular negation (*ne* deletion) by our learners, and the correct use of *tu* versus *vous*, second person forms of address whose usage varies according to the relationship between the speaker and listener. We infer that both learners generally have command of the appropriate register with respect to the use of *on* and the deletion of *ne*, although they are at ceiling from the beginning with respect to the proper use of the second person forms of address, *tu* and *vous*. The expected difference between male and female speech, as reported by Armstrong (2002), is not seen in our data. The final section draws inferences from our case study for the French classroom, suggesting specific ways in which the acquisition research could inspire French cur-riculum and classroom techniques within a communicative methodology.

2 Background

For sociolinguistic competence, learners must approximate the native use of informality markers. Dewaele (2004) argues that L2 learners are initially 'monostylistic', meaning that they overgeneralize a single register, typically the formal register. The gender of L2 learners has been argued to play a role, with females preferring a more formal register (Armstrong, 2002).

L2 learners may learn through authentic interactions to extend their stylistic range and acquire an approximate native pattern of variation.

Previous L2 studies have stressed the importance of immersion environments for the development of this kind of pragmatic competence,
although immersion alone does not guarantee the development of sociolinguistic competence (Howard, 2004; Regan, 1998). We begin this section
with a summary of characteristics of vernacular French; we then consider
the importance of sociolinguistic ability in the acquisition of L2 French
and review earlier studies on this topic.

2.1 Vernacular French

Variation in French is highly stratified, with phonological, lexical and
morphosyntactic markers of formality. Joseph (1988) describes 11 characteristics of 'New French,' or vernacular French, which include in situ
questions, lack of impersonal *il* 'it', and use of prepositions as adverbs;
examples are shown in (1)–(3):[2]

(1) *Tu vas où?* (cf. *Où est-ce que tu vas?*) 'Where are you going ?'

(2) *Faut manger.* (cf. *Il faut manger*) 'It is necessary to eat.'

(3) *J'y vais avec.* (cf. *J'y vais avec elle*) 'I'm going with her.'

In this chapter, we focus on two of the characteristics given in Joseph
(1988), namely the replacement of *nous* by *on* (4), and the elimination of
ne, negation particle (5); we further include the correct use of *tu* and *vous*,
informal and formal second person pronouns:

(4) use of *on* for *nous*

    a. *Nous sommes contents* 'We are content'

    b. *On est contents.* 'We are content'[3]

(5) *ne* deletion

    a. *Il ne voit pas Marie* 'He doesn't see Mary'

    b. *Il voit pas Marie* 'He doesn't see Mary'

The sociolinguistic status of the two informal markers, *on* for *nous* and *ne*
deletion, is not identical. The former is more common, and is considered to be
mildly informal only. In fact, L1 French speakers prefer *on* almost exclusively
in all registers over *nous* (96–98.4%, depending on their dialect), according to
Rehner *et al.*, 2003).

On the other hand, negative *ne* deletion is considered by native speakers to be highly informal. Its deletion shows variability according to both
age and gender (Armstrong, 2002), with older females the least likely to
delete *ne*. The omission rate for *ne* is 64% to 88.6% for natives in the informal register, although it can reach 100% in Canadian French (Sandy, 1997).
This rate drops sharply, to 50%, with the use of a formal register in French.

Given the diffusion of *on* for *nous* and *ne* deletion in informal speech, it is clear that L2 learners should adopt these informality markers in informal contexts. Moreover, they also need to understand the appropriateness of use of the informality markers (i.e. morphosyntactic markers which indicate informal speech), especially *ne* omission, which is more sociolinguistically marked (i.e. less common in the language, having more striking connotations). In order for L2 learners to approximate L2 speech, *on* should be used for *nous* extensively in all registers (i.e. level of formality of speech), while *ne* should be omitted only in the informal register.

With respect to the pronouns *tu* and *vous*, L2 learners should know in which contexts to use which form. Broadly speaking, *tu* is used when there is solidarity, equality of social position and similarity of age when the discourse is informal. *Vous*, on the other hand is used to establish sociological distance, when the discourse is formal. The examples below in (6) and (7) illustrate this use of *tu* and *vous*:[4]

(6) *Pierre, tu veux quoi?* 'Peter, what do you (informal) want?'

(7) *Bonjour, Madame. Comment allez-vous?* 'Hello, Ma'am. How are you (formal)?'

We next turn to the role of pedagogical instruction in the acquisition of French L2 sociolinguistic competence.

2.2 Pedagogy and sociolinguistics

In an article that set an agenda for a line of research to be followed in the next decade, Long (1991: 41) addresses the 'tension between the desirability of communicative use of the [foreign language] in the classroom, on the one hand, and the felt need for a linguistic focus in language learning, on the other.' He provides evidence that a focus on form (i.e. emphasis on grammar, presented in context, inductively) can speed up rate of learning, improve accuracy and raise the ultimate level of attainment (i.e. the ceiling at which L2 learners arrive). Numerous articles and books (e.g. Doughty & Williams, 1998; Lee & Valdman, 2000; Lyster, 2004) develop the focus on form pedagogy, which emphasizes communicative language learning, systematic staging (i.e. sensitivity to the developmental stage of L2 learners) and targeted instruction (i.e. instruction focused on the grammatical problems L2 learners are experiencing). The techniques recommended by these approaches include reactive feedback in error correction (i.e. explicit metalinguistic correction or recasts at the time of utterance by the L2 speakers), meaningful contextualization of classroom activities, inductive presentation of grammar, input flooding (i.e. a presentation which focuses on the grammar point in question) and focus on a particular form.

Recognizing the importance of developing communicative ability in an L2, subsequent approaches to language pedagogy see two advantages to instructing the language as it is spoken in real situations, namely encouragement of communicative competence and acknowledgment of native speaker norms (Arteaga & Herschensohn, 1998). 'The mandate to teach language for communication requires that the curriculum acknowledge sociolinguistic and pragmatic factors as well as grammatical prescription' (Arteaga & Herschensohn, 1998: 608). Variation in language use relates to register (formal/informal), medium (written/spoken) and peer group (e.g. age, social class).

While French native speakers gain sensitivity to these distinctions at an early age, L2 learners are disadvantaged both by their native sociolinguistic preconceptions, and by their tendency to prioritize structural properties of the L2 grammar and lexicon over the more subtle meanings implied by language usage. For this reason, Valdman (1989, 2000) advocates presenting variability at early stages of instruction to make students aware of 'multinorm' usage (i.e. sensitivity to context regarding the level of formality). Magnan (1991) also recognizes the importance of making students aware of variability, but she warns that inexperienced learners are better equipped with a formal rather than informal register. For example, L2 use of formal *vous* 'you' with a young child can be amusing, not offensive, to native speakers of French, whereas use of informal *tu* with a superior would be highly inappropriate. Etienne and Sax (2002) make a similar point in their article advocating instruction of stylistic variation in French. It is clear that some introduction to sociolinguistic variability is necessary even for beginners of French, and more explicit training is required at higher levels of instruction; we return to this topic in Section 4 of this chapter.

2.3 L2 French studies: *on* for *nous*, *ne* deletion, *tu* versus *vous*

As we have seen, in L1 French, the use of *on* for *nous* is quite pervasive, occurring 96% (European) to >98% (Canadian) of the time, in all registers. L2 speakers, on the other hand, typically underuse *on*. For example, Rehner *et al.* (2003) find that Canadian Anglophone immersion students of French use *on* for *nous* only 56% of the time. They argue that increased input of L1 French, including TV and conversation, leads to an increased use of *on* for *nous*. Among L2 speakers, the use of *on* is more frequent than *ne* deletion.

Previous studies have shown no significant difference between formal and informal settings for instructed L2 learners with respect to *ne* deletion. For example, Regan (1998), in a longitudinal study of Irish students who spent a year in France, found an increase in the L2 speech of students during year abroad of *ne* deletion (from 38% to 65%); this use of *ne* deletion was retained one year after return. However, the L2 students did not show sensitivity to registers, and even tended to overgeneralize *ne* in some cases.

Similarly, Rehner and Mougeon (1999), in a study of 40 English L1 students in immersion contexts in Ontario, found lower *ne* deletion rates for L2 speakers, at 28%, than for L1 French speakers. They claimed that extracurricular contact with French L1 speakers contributes to a higher incidence of *ne* deletion. They also found evidence that *ne* deletion was overgeneralized by some L2 learners.

Finally, the correct use of *tu* versus *vous* is essential for the L2 learner, as argued by Kinginger and Belz (2005), among others. In a study of the L2 learner 'Bill', Kinginger and Belz reported that in a pretest, he scored well regarding general understanding of the difference between these forms; however, his speech showed errors, such as using *vous* to address an intimate friend (Kinginger & Belz, 2005: 410). The authors further argued that study abroad, while it provides authentic input in the usage of forms of address, does not always lead to developed pragmatic competence in the L2.

3 Present Study

In the present study, we consider the use of these sociolinguistic markers by two advanced L2 speakers of French, Max and Chloe. Max and Chloe were both interviewed before, during and after an extended time abroad; our study therefore gives a longitudinal view of register acquisition. Each of the three interviews included informal discussion on a variety of topics, as well as a role play which required the use of the formal register.

Max was mostly exposed to structured French, first learning French at the age of 48 through self-instruction, and was 59 at the time of the interview. Self-instruction continued and has taken the form of reading, discussion and watching TV in French. He also regularly received French tutoring by a native speaker. In addition, he was exposed to naturalistic input during frequent vacations to France and an immersion experience in Paris and Lyon for 7 months. In short, Max mirrors the learners discussed in Regan, as they are all instructed, but this instruction has been followed by an extensive time abroad. For this reason, Max's instruction in sociolinguistics/pragmatics had been incidental and not systematic, before his time abroad. In our view, he would have benefited from the types of exercises presented below in the last section of this chapter (see Section 4).

Chloe, who was age 22 at the time of the interview, first began French study at the age of 13. In addition, she had experienced several periods living abroad, including a 6-month period of immersion in France at the age of 16 and then again at 20, in addition to 9 months as an *assistante d'anglais* or 'English instructor', at the age of 22, in the French overseas department of Réunion. At the time of the interview, Chloe's input had been mainly naturalistic, although she had received formal instruction in the language as well.

Max and Chloe, as advanced L2 speakers of French, use a broad range of vocabulary, with infrequent lexical errors. Their verbal syntax is similarly varied, and shows high accuracy with respect to inflection marking (somewhat less so with tense and aspect). Within the noun phrase, they consistently assign the correct gender to nouns, with occasional errors, and generally correctly place adjectives within the determiner phrase (DP). Their most frequent error with respect to nominal syntax is gender concord.

For the purposes of this study, we focused on the sociolinguistic markers of the use of *on* for *nous*, *ne* deletion and the appropriate use of *tu* and *vous*. Our goal was to determine whether these advanced L2 speakers, whose syntax and lexicon were varied and highly accurate, showed a similar command of sociolinguistic registers, or whether they were instead monostylistic, as suggested by previous studies. Moreover, we sought to determine if there was evidence of a male/female difference in use of sociolinguistic markers between our two L2 learners. Finally, we looked for a longitudinal progression with respect to sociolinguistic register.

3.1 Formal versus informal register: Max

Native speakers, as we have seen, prefer *on* almost exclusively in all contexts, and delete *ne* 50% of the time in the formal register. For Max, formal interview contexts included role-playing on the following topics: sports in American education, introducing a keynote speaker and resolving a problem at a dry cleaner's. The use of *on* for *nous* in native French is quite widespread, as discussed above. In his formal speech, however, Max uses no tokens of the first person plural, so that we can draw no conclusions regarding *on* versus *nous*.

In contrast to the use of *on* for *nous*, *ne* deletion is considered to be highly informal, although native speakers delete *ne* in 50% of cases in the formal register. Max is even more conservative than native speakers in this respect, retaining *ne* in every case in the formal register except one instance in the third interview. An example of *ne* retention by Max in formal interview contexts is given in (8) and (9); additional examples are given in Appendix 1.

(8) *En Amérique il n'y a pas de système éducatif centralisé.* (Interview I)
'In America, there is no centralized educational system.'

Max's only token of *ne* deletion in formal speech, which occurs in Interview III, is given below in (9).

(9) *Il y a pas mal de gens.* (Interview III) 'There are quite a few people.'

Table 2.1 summarizes Max's use at the formal register of the two sociolinguistic markers, *on* for *nous* and *ne* deletion.

Table 2.1 Tokens of sociolinguistic markers, Max, formal register

Interview	1pl TOC	On	Nous	ne TOC	ne deleted	ne retained
I	N/A	N/A	N/A	5	0, 0%	5, 100%
II	N/A	N/A	N/A	2	0, 0%	2, 100%
III	N/A	N/A	N/A	4	1, 25%	3, 75%

Note: TOC, total obligatory contexts.

Most of the discussion in the three interviews was in the informal register. In his informal speech, for the first person plural, Max exclusively prefers *on*, as in Example (10).

(10) *On a fait une petite promenade* (Interview I) 'We went for a little walk.'

Max's use of *on* for *nous* is in sharp contrast to his lack of *ne* deletion. Indeed, even in the informal register, Max retains *ne* most of the time (86%, Interview I, 80%, Interview II and 90%, Interview III). Example (11) illustrates Max's retention of *ne*:

(11) *On ne prend presque rien* (Interview I) 'We take almost nothing.'

Examples of his infrequent *ne* deletion are given in (12) and (13):

(12) *Ça nous conviendrait pas* (Interview I) 'That wouldn't meet our needs.'

(13) *J'ai pas grand' chose* (Interview II) 'I don't have a lot.'

Table 2.2 summarizes Max's use of sociolinguistic markers in informal speech.

Max correctly alternates between *tu* and *vous*, as illustrated by Examples (14) to (16); further examples are given in Appendix I:

(14) *Mais je ne comprends pas pourquoi tu ris* (Interview III) 'But I don't understand why you (informal) are laughing.'

(15) *Oh là là, qu'est-ce que vous avez fait ?* (Interview III) 'Oh, my, what have you (formal) done ?'

(16) *Vous l'avez fait, vous m'avez dit* (Interview III) 'You (formal) did it, you (formal) told me so.'

We next turn to a summary of Max's command of sociolinguistic markers.

Table 2.2 Tokens of sociolinguistic markers, Max, informal register

Interview	1pl TOC	On	Nous	Ne TOC	ne delete	ne retain
I	14	9, 64%	5, 36%	21	3, 14%	18, 86%
II	5	5, 100%	0, 0%	25	5, 20%	20, 80%
III	1	1, 100%	0, 0%	40	4, 10%	39, 90%

Note: TOC, total obligatory contexts.

3.2 Use of sociolinguistic markers in French: Max

In the formal register, Max produces no first person plural token; he produces relatively few tokens of the first person plural in the informal portions of the three interviews (9, 6 and 1, respectively). In his first interview, Max is more conservative than native speakers in his use of *on* (64%), but the second and third interview show an exclusive preference for *on*, slightly higher than native speakers at 100%. Therefore, although we can draw no conclusions regarding the use of *on* in formal speech, we can conclude that in informal speech, Max does eventually reach native-like levels of the use of *on* for *nous*, which increases in his speech longitudinally (Interview I, 57%; Interview II, 100%; Interview III, 100%).

However, Max's apparent longitudinal mastery of *on* is in contrast to his lack of progression in *ne* deletion, which ranges from 14% (Interview I), to 20% (Interview II) and then to 10% (Interview III). Indeed, with respect to *ne* deletion, Max is far below the native target in all three interviews of 50% of the time in formal contexts and +88% of the time in informal situations. In contrast, Max rarely uses *ne* deletion in the formal register (Interview I, 0%; Interview II, 0%; Interview III, 25%). Interestingly, *ne* deletion in the informal register is even less frequent for Max by his third interview (Interview I, 14%; Interview II, 20%; Interview III, 20%), and shows no longitudinal development. Indeed, where *ne* deletion is concerned, Max appears to prefer the formal register.

Nevertheless, as indicated in Table 2.2, Max did delete *ne* in one instance where he was in a formal role play, using *vous*, in the third interview. In all other formal contexts in that interview, he correctly retained *ne*.

In summary, while Max appears to have mastered the use of *on* for *nous*, he fails to show native-like use of *ne* deletion, no longitudinal progression with respect to negation is seen in his speech. Further, as he is at ceiling (i.e., has perfect accuracy) from the beginning, there is no longitudinal development with *tu/vous*, either. We next turn to Chloe.

3.3 Formal versus informal register: Chloe

Chloe's three interviews also included informal discussion as well as role play requiring a formal register. For Chloe, formal role plays included the following: reporting an accident, returning shoes to shoe store and a formal discussion of the role of sports in American education. In the formal register, Chloe produces only one token, in the third interview, of the first person plural in formal speech. Her sole example of the first person plural, which she expresses as *on*, is given in Example (17):

(17) *On ne perte [=perd] pas notre temps aux Etats-Unis5* (Interview III)
     'We don't waste our time in the USA.'

With respect to *ne* deletion in the formal register, Chloe exceeds the rate seen in L1 speech by the third interview (67% for Chloe, compared to 50% for L1 speakers of French). An example of *ne* retention in her formal speech is given in Example (18); additional examples are given in Appendix 2.

> (18) *Je n'aime pas du tout les styles* (Interview II) 'I don't at all like the styles.'

Despite these isolated examples of *ne* retention, however, Chloe typically deletes *ne*, even in the formal register, as illustrated by Example (19):

> (19) *J'espère pas* (Interview I) 'I hope not.'

Chloe's use of *on* for *nous* and *ne* deletion in formal speech is summarized in Table 2.3.

Table 2.3 Tokens of sociolinguistic markers, Chloe, formal register

Interview	1pl TOC	On	Nous	Ne TOC	ne delete	ne retain
I	N/A	N/A	N/A	4	1, 25%	3, 75%
II	N/A	N/A	N/A	14	8, 57%	6, 43%
III	1	1, 100%	0, 0%	9	6, 67%	3, 33%

Note: TOC, total obligatory contexts.

As in the case of Max, the context of most of Chloe's three interviews was informal. Chloe produces more tokens of first person plural in the informal register than Max, especially by the third interview (56 tokens); in all cases, she uses *on* for *nous*. Example (20) illustrates Chloe's use of *on* in the informal register:

> (20) *On est à la Réunion* (Interview II) 'We are on Reunion Island.'

As in the formal register, Chloe rarely retains *ne* in informal speech, although there are a few isolated examples, as in (21):

> (21) *Ils ne peuvent pas travailler* (Interview II) 'They cannot work.'

Chloe typically deletes *ne* in the informal register; her *ne* deletion ranges from 14% in Interview I to 77% in Interview II, to 60% in Interview III. *Ne* deletion in Chloe's informal speech is illustrated in Example (22) below:

> (22) *Je suis pas si choquée* (Interview III) 'I am not so shocked.'

Table 2.4 summarizes Chloe's use of sociolinguistic markers in informal French.

Table 2.4 Tokens of sociolinguistic markers, Chloe, informal register

Interview	1pl TOC	On	nous	Ne TOC	ne delete	ne retain
I	1	1, 100%	0, 0%	14	2, 14%	12, 86%
II	3	3, 100%	0, 0%	31	24, 77%	7, 22%
III	56	56, 100%	0, 0%	53	32, 60%	21, 40%

Note: TOC, total obligatory contexts.

Table 2.5 Proper use of forms of address, Chloe

Interview	tu/te TOC	tu/te SOC	% correct	vous/vous TOC	vous/vous SOC	% correct
1	0	0	N/A	0	0	N/A
II	9	9	100	1	1	100
III	12	12	100	1	1	100

Note: TOC, total obligatory contexts; SOC, suppliance in obligatory contexts.

With respect to *tu* versus *vous* dichotomy, Chloe again excels. Her use of these pronouns is summarized in Table 2.5.[6]

We next turn to a summary discussion of the sociolinguistic markers in Chloe's speech.

3.4 Use of sociolinguistic markers in French: Chloe

Chloe produces only one token of the first person plural (*nous* or *on*) in the portions of the interviews requiring the formal register, for which she uses *on*. However, in informal speech, Chloe makes extensive use of the first person plural, particularly in the third interview (56 tokens); she uses *on* exclusively in all three interviews, which is slightly higher than L1 levels (96–98%). Given the wide diffusion of *on* in L1 speech, it is difficult to determine whether she is monostylistic, but she has clearly mastered the use of *on*. There is no longitudinal development to speak of in this regard, as she is already at ceiling in the first interview in informal speech.

Unlike Max, Chloe shows clear longitudinal development with respect to *ne* deletion at the formal register, although she deletes *ne* at a higher rate than native speakers in the last two interviews during formal speech (Interview I, 25%; Interview II, 57%; Interview III, 67%). For the informal register, Chloe's *ne* deletion is below L1 levels (L1 88%) at 14% for Interview I, 77% for Interview II and 60% for Int III. By the third interview, she also appears to be monostylistic; however, unlike Max, she prefers the informal register. Like Max, Chloe shows complete mastery of the *tu* versus *vous* dichotomy, reaching 100% in all interviews.[7]

While both Max and Chloe have had extensive immersion experience, they nonetheless began their studies of French in a canonically traditional classroom setting; for example, Max's self-instruction and tutoring is didactic, while Chloe's immersion experience is complemented by some coursework – their sociolinguistic tendencies partially reveal their overall input. Although Max has had ample exposure to colloquial French in movies, television and (basically informal) tutor interaction, his style heavily favors the formal, at least for *ne* deletion. Chloe, on the other hand, has favored the informal, since her interactions with peers, coupled with lack of formal instruction of French, did not afford her the opportunity of switching into more formal registers. Tracing the command of register variation (i.e. adapting their speech to the level of formality) of these two learners to their long term input, we will suggest in the next section how instruction can facilitate recognition of sociolinguistic variation.

4 Pedagogical Implications

Particularly relevant to the enhancement and structuring of focused input is the contextualization of instruction in realistic language settings. VanPatten (2000) argues that learners pay more attention to meaning than to form, so that presentation of a given structure should be embedded in a meaningful (hence affectively attractive) context. Using the retrospective insight of our advanced learners' use of sociolinguistic variables, in this section we will explore possible curricular and methodological extensions of sociolinguistic instruction within a communicative framework. In accordance with focus on form approaches, we consider this question from three perspectives – adequacy of input, meaningful contextualization and reactive feedback in error correction – for two classroom levels, beginning/intermediate and advanced post-immersion. This is particularly important for L2 learners without immersion experience. We begin by discussing such learners.

4.1 Beginning/intermediate learners

Two important components of the idea of focus on form are the necessity of using the L2 as much as possible, and targeting the focused form through input flooding. How might one implement a form-focused lesson aiming to induce an understanding of *ne* deletion or *on* for *nous* in L2 French? Bérard (1995) illustrates the complex interaction of a coalition–communicative model of language which draws on complementary *Activités d'automatisation* and *Activités de repérage*, activities focused on automaticity of response. His schema has interdependent components that respond to the pedagogical points raised earlier – it takes primary linguistic data as the point of departure, coupling a focus on form (*repérage*) with automatization (*automatization*). These early steps must necessarily be reinforced by the development of a grammatical and sociolinguistic awareness, the conceptualization that leads to generalization of the systematic nature of the L2.

Previous studies of L2 French sociolinguistic phenomena by instructed learners (cf. Dewaele, 2004) have focused on the development of this competence as a somewhat accidental result of instruction. Generally speaking, the French classroom furnishes sociolinguistic instruction mainly through communicative activities and grammatical rules of thumb such as 'Use *tu* in informal situations and *vous* in formal ones.' In our view, beginning students need to be exposed to register variation in the classroom first from instructor input and second from the materials and activities employed. The instructor – who presumably maximizes use of the target language – would naturally vary the use of *ne*, deleting it 50% of the time or more in formal contexts. As for *on*, that pronoun has virtually replaced *nous* in most contexts of all but the most formal speech among native speakers. The instructor can easily exploit the classroom setting to speak of what 'we' do, using adequate examples of the use of *on*, while relating it to its explicit first plural counterpart.

Classroom activities that encourage use of the L2 in a meaningful context might include role play (Flament-Boistrancourt, 2001), information gap tasks (Gass & Varonis, 1994) or structured interaction (Naughton, 2006). These studies show that structured communication foster more extended interlanguage discourse and increased opportunities for spontaneous production by learners. They are directly relevant to the development of sociolinguistic competence, as they involve manipulation of different registers.

Naughton (2006: 171–172) outlines the following interactional routines: follow-up instructor questions and clarifications, requests to the student for help and recasts. The encouragement of such discourse strategies for beginning students serves them immediately in the task at hand (e.g. information gap), but also constitutes a pattern that can aid them in later interactions. These methods of reactive feedback are not limited to the instructor, but become one of the tools in classroom interaction. These strategies can be implemented by students interacting with the instructor or with each other in role plays that target different levels of formality: asking a stranger for directions or purchasing something in a store would require a certain distance, whereas if the role play involved close friends or family, the register would be informal. Once the students had been alerted to those differences, they could engage interactional routines focused on formality markers.

The actual production of colloquial forms by beginning students is most probably unlikely at an early stage, since they focus much more on the standard textbook variety than register variation. Like Max, they will tend to establish the formal variants, even if they hear informal examples in the input; classroom discourse, while not terribly formal, nevertheless is more so than casual conversation among university students. Interactions between target language input and classroom activities can engage learners to put emerging competence to work in actual communication.

4.2 Advanced post-immersion learners

Unlike beginning learners who need to be exposed to naturalistic register variation and to be encouraged to use the language in meaningful communication, post-immersion learners have in principle had rich exposure to the spoken language in the target culture context. We have found, however, from personal classroom experience with post-immersion students, that they often – as in the case of Chloe – favor colloquial patterns without understanding the need to master both informal and formal register. For this reason, we believe that they need to focus in a more metalinguistic way on the formal/informal differences. The same recommendations for naturalistic input, meaningful contextualization and reactive feedback suggested above also hold for more advanced learners, but the discourse level should be much more sophisticated. Role play, for example, should vary more complicated situations of formality versus informality so that students have experience with both (and in so doing, expand the situational contexts they may have encountered in a year abroad). In responding to student miscalculations, instructors may use recasts to model appropriate target behavior (Ayoun, 2001, 2006; Loewen & Philp, 2006). For example, if a student uses *on* in a very formal context (e.g. introducing someone to the president of the university), the instructor may recast the sentence with *nous* to emphasize its formality. Another source of feedback may be peer review by other students, if, for example, the role plays are performed for the whole class. Tasks such as information gap activities may be raised to a more advanced level by incorporating films or literature as the frame for coursework (Alkhas, 2006). For example, Paesani (2006) provides rich suggestions for use of Malle's *Zazie dans le Métro*, while Etienne and Sax (2006) generalize the instruction of register to a broader group of films.

5 Conclusion

In this chapter, we have shown that L2 research provides us with insight concerning register variability and its translation into L2 competence. In keeping with this tradition, we have presented new sociolinguistic data from two advanced L2 speakers of French, Max (age of onset, 48) and Chloe (age of onset, 13). Both speakers confirm previous L2 studies, in that they appear to be monostylistic, in a general sense; however, the expected gender difference is not seen, as Max favors the formal register, while Chloe's speech is highly informal in both formal and informal contexts. Specifically, both of our subjects appear to have mastered the use of *on* for *nous*, while Max shows rates of *ne* deletion below native levels, particularly for informal speech. Finally, both subjects have mastered the complex sociolinguistic dance involved with respect to the second person forms of address, *tu* and *vous*.

By applying sociolinguistic insights to classroom curriculum and methodology, we believe that it is possible to better target instruction, providing adequate input with meaningful contextualization, and giving reactive feedback in error correction.[8]

Notes

(1) 'Language instruction regularly needs to align its relationship to the more theoretical disciplines that are at its foundation. This is especially the case for relationships among traditional grammar, descriptive linguistics without pedagogical intent and language teaching.'
(2) The complete list of the characteristics of New French, according to Joseph (1988), are given in Appendix 1.
(3) As noted by Lang and Pérez (2004: 39), 'If *on* clearly refers to and feminine and/or plural noun, adjectives or past participles referring to the noun must agree with the noun. The verb remains singular.' The examples that Lang and Pérez (2004: 39) give are the following: 'On est contentes, les petites? Are we all happy, girls? On est devenus bons copains. We have become good friends.'
(4) Note the word order, as discussed for (1).
(5) Chloe's utterance contains a lexical error, **perte* for *perd*, the third singular of the verb *perdre*, 'to lose'.
(6) The pronoun *te* is the informal object pronoun that corresponds to the subject pronoun *tu*; the corresponding formal object pronoun is *vous*.
(7) While the longitudinal development is uneven for these speakers, it was nonetheless necessary, in our view, to investigate it for purposes of thoroughness.
(8) This is a revised version of papers presented at the 2004 Association of French Language Studies conference (Aston University) and the 2006 Second Language Research Forum held at the University of Washington.
(9) (1) I come from Nancy [me]. (2) Where are you from? (3) We are content. (4) It's raining. (5) He will arrive. (6) He doesn't like Mary. (7) It is necessary to eat. (8) You saw. (9) I'm coming with [you]. (10) My brother's car. (11) the man I'm talking about.

References

Alkhas, A. (2006) DVD for dummies: Lessons in technology from le dîner de cons. *French Review* 79, 1252–1264.
Armstrong, N. (2002) Variable deletion of French ne: A cross-stylistic perspective. *Language Sciences* 24, 153–173.
Arteaga, D. and Herschensohn J. (1998) Diachronic perspectives on the teaching of new French. *French Review* 71, 607–620.
Arteaga, D., Gess R. and Herschensohn, J. (2003) Focusing on phonology to teach morphological form in French. *Modern Language Journal* 87, 58–70.
Ayoun, D. (2001) The role of negative and positive feedback in the second language acquisition of the passé composé and imparfait. *Modern Language Journal* 85, 226–243.
Ayoun, D. (2006) The effectiveness of written recasts in the second language acquisition of aspectual distinctions in French: A follow-up study. *Modern Language Journal* 88, 31–55.
Beacco, J-C. and Porquier, R. (2001) Présentation: Grammaire d'enseignants et grammaires d'apprenants de langue étrangère. *Langue Française* 131, 3–6.
Bérard, E. (1995) La grammaire encore... et l'approche communicative. *ELA Revue de Didactologie des langues-cultures* 100, 10–19.
Coveney, A. (1996) *Variability in Spoken French*. Exeter: Elm Bank Publications.

Coveney, A. (2000) Vestiges of nous and the 1st person plural verb in informal spoken French. *Language Sciences* 22, 447–481.

Dewaele, J-M. (2004) The acquisition of sociolinguistic competence in French as a foreign language: An overview. *Journal of French Language Studies* 14, 301–320.

Dewaele, J-M. and Regan, V. (2002) Maîtriser la norme sociolinguistique en interlangue française: Le cas de l'omission variable de 'ne'. *Journal of French Language Studies* 12, 123–148.

Doughty, C. (2003) Instructed SLA: Constraints, compensation, and enhancement. In C. Doughty and M. Long (eds) *The Handbook of Second Language Acquisition* (pp. 256–310). Malden/Oxford: Blackwell.

Doughty, C. and Williams, J. (eds) (1998) *Focus on Form in Classroom Second Language Acquisition*. Cambridge: Cambridge University Press.

Etienne, C. and Sax, K. (2006) Teaching stylistic variation through film. *French Review* 79, 934–950.

Flament-Boistrancourt, D. (2001) Jeux de rôle et évaluations sur le vif en Belgique néerlandophone. Analyse d'un double bind ordinaire. *Langue Française* 131, 66–88.

Gass, S. and Varonis, E. (1994) Input, interaction and second language production. *Studies in Second Language Acquisition* 16, 283–302.

Harley, B., Cummins J., Swain, M. and Allen, P. (1990) The nature of language proficiency. In B. Harley, J. Cummins, M. Swain and P. Allen (eds) *The Development of Second Language Proficiency* (pp. 7–25). Cambridge: Cambridge UP.

Howard, M. (2004) Sociolinguistic variation and second language acquisition: A preliminary study of advanced learners of French. *SKY Journal of Linguistics* 17, 143–165.

Joseph, J. (1988) New French: A pedagogical crisis in the making. *Modern Language Journal* 72, 31–36.

Kinginger, C. and Belz, J.A. (2005) Sociocultural perspectives on pragmatic development in foreign language learning: Case studies from telecollaboration and study abroad. *Intercultural Pragmatics* 2, 369–421.

Klein, W. (1986) *Second Language Acquisition*. Cambridge: Cambridge University Press.

Lang, M. and Pérez. I. (2004) *Modern French Grammar: A Practical Guide*. London: Routledge.

Lee, J. and Valdman, A. (eds) (2000) *Form and Meaning: Multiple Perspectives*. Boston: Heinle and Heinle.

Long, M. (1991) Focus on form: A design feature in language teaching methodology. In K. de Bot, R. Ginsberg and C. Kramsch (eds) *Foreign Language Research in Cross-cultural Perspective* (pp. 39–52). Amsterdam: J. Benjamins.

Loewen, S. and Philp, J. (2006) Recasts in the adult English L2 classroom: Characteristics, explicitness, and effectiveness. *Modern Language Journal* 90, 536–556.

Lyster, R. (1994) The effect of functional-analytic teaching on aspects of French immersion students' sociolinguistic competence. *Applied Linguistics* 15, 263–287.

Lyster, R. (2004) Research on form-focused instruction in immersion classrooms: Implications for theory and practice. In F. Myles and R. Towell (eds) *The Acquisition of French as A Second Language* (Special Issue). *Journal of French Language Studies* 14, 321–342.

Magnan, S. (1991) Social attitudes: The key to directing the evolution of grammar teaching. In J. Alatis (ed.) *Georgetown University Roundtable on Languages and Linguistics* (pp. 323–334). Washington DC: Georgetown University Press.

Naughton, D. (2006) Cooperative strategy training and oral interaction: Enhancing small group communication in the language classroom. *Modern Language Journal* 90, 169–184.

Paesani, K. (2006) A process-oriented approach to Zazie dans le Métro. *French Review* 79, 762–778.

Regan, V. (1995) The acquisition of sociolinguistic native speech norms: Effects of a year abroad on L2 learners of French. In B. Freed (ed.) *Second Language Acquisition in a Study Abroad Context* (pp. 245–267). Amsterdam/Philadelphia: J. Benjamins.

Regan, V. (1996) Variation in French interlanguage. In R. Bayley and D. Preston (eds) *Second Language Acquisition and Linguistic Variation* (pp. 177–201). Amsterdam/ Philadelphia: J. Benjamins.

Regan, V. (1997) Les apprenants avancés, la lexicalization et l'acquisition de la compétence sociolinguistique: Une approche variationniste. In I. Bartning (ed.) *Les apprenants avancés. Acquisition et Interaction en Langue Etrangère* 9, 193–210.

Regan, V. (1998) Sociolinguistics and language learning in a study abroad context. *Frontiers: The Interdisciplinary Journal of Study Abroad* 4, 61–91.

Rehner, K. and Mougeon, R. (1999) Variation in the spoken French of immersion students: To ne or not to *ne*, that is the sociolinguistic question. *The Canadian Modern Language Review* 56, 124–154.

Rehner, K., Mougeon, R. and Nadasdi, T. (2003) The learning of sociolinguistic variation by advanced FSL learners: The Case of *nous* versus *on* in immersion French. *Studies in Second Language Acquisition* 25, 127–157.

Sandy, S. (1997) L'emploi variable de la particule négative ne dans le parler des Franco-Ontariens adolescents. Unpublished MA thesis, York University.

Vainikka, A. and Young-Scholten, M. (1998) Morphosyntactic triggers in adult SLA. In M. Beck (ed.) *Morphology and its Interfaces in Second Language Knowledge* (pp. 89–113). Amsterdam/Philadelphia: J. Benjamins.

Valdman, A. (1989) Classroom foreign language learning and language variation: The notion of pedagogical norms. In M. Einstein (ed.) *The Dynamic Interlanguage* (pp. 262–278). New York: Plum.

Valdman, A. (2000) Comment gérer la variation dans l'enseignement du français langue étrangère aux Etats-Unis. *French Review* 73, 648–666.

VanPatten, B. (2000) Processing instruction as form-meaning connections: Issues in theory and practice. In J. Lee and A. Valdman (eds) *Form and Meaning: Multiple Perspectives* (pp. 43–68). Boston: Heinle and Heinle.

Appendix 1: New French Characteristics, Joseph (1988)

Table A2.1 Characteristics of New French[9]

Morphosyntactic characteristic	Modern French structure	New French structure
(1) Right dislocation	a. *Je viens de Nancy.*	b. *J'viens de Nancy moi.*
(2) *In situ* questions	a. *D'où viens-tu?*	b. *Toi tu viens d'où?*
(3) Replacement of *nous* by *on*	a. *Nous sommes contents.*	b. *On est contents.*
(4) Use of *ça* as generic impersonal	a. *Il pleut.*	b. *Ça pleut.*
(5) Analytic verb forms	a. *Il arrivera.*	b. *Il va arriver.*
(6) *ne* deletion	a. *Il n'aime pas Marie.*	b. *Il aime pas Marie.*
(7) Lack of impersonal. *il*	a. *Il faut manger.*	b. *Faut manger.*
(8) Reduction of subject pronouns	a. *Tu as vu.*	b. *T'as vu.*
(9) Use of prepositions as adverbs	a. *Je viens avec vous.*	b. *Je viens avec.*
(10) Generalization of possessive *à* 'to'	a. *la voiture de mon frère.*	b. *la voiture à mon frère.*
(11) Generalization of relative *que* 'that'	a. *l'homme de qui je parle.*	b. *l'homme que je parle.*

Appendix 2: Examples of Sociolinguistic Markers: Max

(1) *Ce n' est pas une question très importante.* (Interview II) 'It isn't a very important question.'

(2) *Il n' y a pas de problème.* (Interview III) 'There is no problem.'

(3) *On est arrivés mi-septembre.* (Interview II) 'We arrived in mid-September.'

(4) *On avait des conversations un peu bizarres.* (Interview III) 'We had rather strange conversations.'

(5) *Il n'y a pas de coussin.* (Interview II) 'There are no cushions.'

(6) *Je ne suis pas trop au courant.* (Interview III) 'I'm not very up to date.'

(7) *qu'ils veulent pas.* (Interview II) 'that they don't want'.

(8) *Tu vas rire notre dîner traditionnel, les pintades, les pintades au limon, citron.* (Interview I) 'You are going to laugh about our traditional dinner, game hens, game hens with lemon.'

(9) *Mais je je te parie que ça ça sera le Sénégal.* (Interview II) 'But I bet you that it, it will be Senegal.'

(10) *Je suis très content de te voir.* (Interview II) 'I'm very happy to see you.'

(11) *Sans plus d'hésitation, je vous présente M. le Bourreau.* (Interview II) 'Without a moment further of hesitation, I am pleased to present M. Bourreau.'

(12) *Comme tu pourrais imaginer.* (Interview III) 'As you may well imagine.'

Appendix 3: Examples of Sociolinguistic Markers: Chloe

(1)   *Donc, je ne crois pas.* (Interview I) 'Thus, I don't believe.'
(2)   *On ne voit pas la musique.* (Interview III) 'We don't see music.'
(3)   *Je savais pas.* (Interview II) 'I didn't know.'
(4)   *C'est pas.* (Interview III) 'It's not.'
(5)   *On a étudié.* (Interview I) 'We studied.'
(6)   *On a traversé le centre ville.* (Interview III) 'We crossed the city center.'
(7)   *Mais je ne suis pas du tout sûre.* (Interview I) 'But I'm not at all sure.'
(8)   *On ne dit pas ça quoi.* (Interview III) 'We don't say that, for sure.'
(9)   *Il y a pas beaucoup de monde là.* (Interview I) 'There aren't a lot of people there.'
(10)   *Je ne suis pas exactement sûre des mots tu vois.* (Interview II) 'I'm not exactly sure of the words, you see.'
(11)   *Tu pensais à Bashak.* (Interview II) 'You were thinking of Bashak.'
(12)   *Parce que déjà cette paire de chaussures sont les plus petites que vous avez.* (Interview II) 'Because already this pair of shoes is the smallest that you have.'
(13)   *Depuis que je suis arrivée, tu veux dire?* (Interview III) 'Since I arrived, you mean?'
(14)   *Tu vois, vous voyez ce qui prend tout la journée, c'est le repos entre midi et deux.* (Interview III) 'You [fam] see, you [formal] see, what takes all the time, it's the break between noon and two PM.'

3 The L2 Acquisition of French Morphosyntax by Anglophone Learners: Refocusing on the Input

Dalila Ayoun

1 Introduction

There is almost an embarrassment of riches with respect to the research of second language (L2) acquisition of tense, aspect, mood/modality (TAM) systems by L2 French learners in instructed (e.g. Ayoun, 2013 and references therein) and immersion settings (e.g. Lyster, 2004), as well as in study abroad programs (e.g. Duperron, 2006; Howard, 2005), but much more rarely with heritage speakers (Kupisch *et al.*, 2014 being one notable exception). This is because the development of TAM systems is crucial to L2 learners' overall progression toward the target language as it touches upon almost all aspects of a language (i.e. morphology, syntax, semantics and their interfaces, both internal and external). However, it is fraught with learnability difficulties, particularly for Anglophone learners who need to transition from an L1 modal system to an L2 mood/mode system. Although French uses modal verbs (e.g. *devoir, pouvoir, vouloir*), they behave similarly to lexical verbs in that they are fully inflected for TAM properties contrary to English modal auxiliaries which are morphologically defective, but polysemous. For instance, *devoir* may correspond to 'must', 'had to', 'should have' or 'was supposed to', depending on the verbal inflection it is used with, as illustrated in Example (1)[1]:

(1) a. *Je dois*-IndPres *partir sans tarder*
    'I must leave without delay'

  b. *Je devais*-IMP *partir avec lui*
    'I was supposed to leave with him'

c. *J'aurais dû*-CondPast *partir plus tôt*
'I should have left sooner'

d. *J'ai dû*-PC *partir à midi*
'I had to leave at noon'

Other important cross-linguistic differences include a well-developed mood system in French (e.g. alternation between the indicative and the subjunctive and the use of the present and past conditional where English would require various modal auxiliaries). French also displays a much richer morphology compared to the English verbal morphology, which is limited to *–ed* or *–ing*, for instance. This may lead to difficulties in mapping abstract features to morphological forms, as will be further discussed below.

The present study is part of a larger longitudinal study in the L2 acquisition of French morphosyntax in instructed settings by English native speakers (NSs), some of whom were heritage speakers of French or Spanish, with a particular focus on the specific linguistic and classroom input to which the participants were exposed during the course of an academic semester.

Although empirical research in L2 acquisition has long been aware of the importance of the input (e.g. Gass, 1997; see Mitchell & Myles, 2004 for a review), as recently reiterated for empirical research from a generative perspective as well (e.g. Rankin & Unsworth, 2016; Slabakova *et al.*, 2014), it does not figure as prominently as it should in the information presented about the L2 learners as participants in a given study. The present study carefully controlled the input that the instructed learners received over the course of an academic semester, in order to probe the impact it could have on their performance. It is detailed below.

2 Literature Review

A review of the literature led Ayoun (2013: 88–89 and references therein) to note that the majority of L2 French studies from a nongenerative perspective have focused on past temporality and the aspectual distinction expressed by the *passé composé* ([+perfective]) and the *imparfait* ([–imperfective]), as well as iterative and durative. The former emerges earlier and is more robust, while other past tense forms (e.g. *plus-que-parfait*) are rarely produced, nor is the subjunctive in the few studies that investigated it (e.g. Ayoun, 2013; Howard, 2008; McManus & Mitchell, 2015). Several studies focusing on future temporality (e.g. Ayoun, 2014; Howard, 2012, 2015 for the most recent) suggest that L2 learners acquire various morphological forms from the indicative present to the simple future and the periphrastic future, but that they struggle with the future perfect. Present temporality in French can be indicative present or subjunctive present and has not yet been thoroughly investigated. A few studies indicate high accuracy for the indicative present, but not the subjunctive present (e.g. Ayoun, 2013; Herschensohn & Arteaga, 2009; Howard, 2008, 2012; Lealess, 2005).

In a longitudinal case study of Billy, an Anglophone instructed learner of French, focusing on the indicative and subjunctive present, Ayoun (2015) found that his interlanguage grammar displayed contrasts and systematicity between different temporalities and with the indicative-subjunctive alternation. However, his accuracy percentages for inflectional verbal morphology were noticeably higher on production tasks than on some elicitation tasks, which may suggest a few residual difficulties and/ or a strong task effect.

Few studies have focused on the entire TAM system that L2 learners develop as they progress toward French as a target language. Herschensohn and Arteaga (2009) is an exception as a longitudinal study with three advanced L2 French learners, along with Myles (2005), Howard (2012) and Ayoun (2013). A few L2 studies from a generative perspective produced mixed findings. The beginning and advanced L2/L3 French learners (Vietnamese monolingual and Cantonese-English bilingual learners) in Leung (2002, 2005) obtained near native-like performance on agreement, adverbs and finiteness with written production and preference tasks in support of the Full Access/Full Transfer Hypothesis (i.e. adult learners can successfully acquire the functional features and categories present in the L2).

In Ayoun (2005), a longitudinal study on L2 morphosyntax, the personal narratives of instructed English-speaking learners at three different proficiency levels displayed well-formed sentences with appropriately inflected morphological forms, indicating they had acquired the functional categories associated with strong features; they also displayed various semantic contrasts, but not uniformly so across the different lexical classes. They did not perform as well on the cloze tests, which revealed significant differences between groups across all aspectual classes.

In a similar longitudinal study with Anglophone learners of L2 French at beginning, intermediate and advanced proficiency levels, who completed production and sentence completion tasks as well as cloze tests, Ayoun (2013) found that participants were accurate but limited to a few morphological forms on production tasks; clear proficiency and lexical class differences emerged on the cloze test and sentence completion tasks. Modals and the indicative/subjunctive alternation turned out to be particularly difficult (e.g. even the advanced group's performance depended on the type of semantic/syntactic triggers).

Izquierdo and Collins (2008) compared the performance of Anglophone ($n = 15$) and Hispanophone ($n = 17$) learners of L2 French on a 68 item cloze test with a balanced number of imperfective and perfective obligatory contexts. The Hispanophone learners outperformed the Anglophone learners only for the appropriate use of imperfective morphology, and findings reveal lexical class effects as well. The follow-up retrospective interviews indicate that the Hispanophone learners were aware of similarities between Spanish and French and that their L1 Spanish may have had a facilitative effect for some of the participants. However, Child (2014) did not find a facilitative effect for Spanish heritage speakers learning L3 Portuguese in the distinction of indicative/subjunctive mood alternation.

Herschensohn and Arteaga (2009) report that three advanced Anglophone learners of L2 French used a variety of morphological forms (i.e. *passé composé*, *imparfait*, present conditional) with nearly perfect accuracy as measured by oral and written production tasks as well as grammaticality judgment tasks. The authors conclude that their findings provide evidence against impairment hypotheses such as the Failed Functional Features Hypothesis, according to which the grammar of adult L2 learners is permanently impaired leading to incomplete L2 acquisition (e.g. Hawkins & Chan, 1997; Hawkins & Liszka, 2003). Indeed, it appears that most studies show an improvement in performance with proficiency levels, suggesting that adult L2 learners do eventually acquire temporal systems. However, they face numerous learnability difficulties, to which we now turn.

3 Learnability Issues and Research Questions

The difficulties that L2 learners experience in mapping abstract features to morphological forms have been explained by various hypotheses, including the following: the Missing Inflection Hypothesis (Haznedar & Schwartz, 1997), the Missing Surface Inflection Hypothesis (Prévost & White, 2000), the Prosodic Transfer Hypothesis (Goad *et al.*, 2003) and the Interface Hypothesis (Sorace, 2011). The first three hypotheses propose that the difficulties L2 learners have in appropriately mapping abstract features such as [±perfective] – expressed in French by the *passé composé* and the *imparfait* – are due to surface morphological problems rather than to syntactic problems (e.g. Ayoun & Rothman, 2013). The last hypothesis – the Interface Hypothesis – takes into account the complexity of TAM properties that are relevant to both internal interfaces (i.e. interaction between at least two grammar modules such as morphology and syntax or syntax-semantics) and external interfaces (i.e. interaction between a grammar internal module and cognition such syntax and discourse-pragmatics).

From a minimalist perspective, the task of Anglophone learners is to acquire the following: (1) the strong features of functional categories such as aspect phrase; (2) the perfective-imperfective aspectual distinction expressed by a complex morphosyntax (i.e. the inflectional paradigms for *passé composé* and *imparfait*); (3) the appropriate mapping of the formal feature [+perfective] with *passé composé* morphology, and the feature [–perfective] with *imparfait* morphology, which is complicated by the fact that French verbs display a rich morphology; (4) the three aspectual values of the *imparfait* (durative, imperfective, iterative); (5) the lexical idiom *être en train de* ('to be doing something') for the progressive, which is not grammaticalized in French; and (6) the indicative/subjunctive alternation.[2]

Based on the learnability issues and the findings of the previous research reviewed above, the present study addresses the following research questions:

(1) Will a controlled, targeted input with repeated exposure make a difference in the L2 acquisition of the French TAM system by instructed learners as measured by cloze tests?
(2) Can L2 French learners acquire a well contrasted TAM system as measured by cloze tests?
(3) Will there be an L1 effect? There may be a facilitative effect for the L1 French heritage speakers as well as the L1 Spanish speakers whose TAM system is closely related to the French TAM system.
(4) Will there be a morphological form effect? In other words, will the participants perform better on some forms than others (e.g. contrasting the *passé composé* and the *imparfait* or the indicative and subjunctive present)?
(5) Will there be a lexical class effect? The stimuli were classified by lexical class (states, activities and telic) to test the Lexical Aspect Hypothesis (e.g. Robison, 1990, 1995), also known as the Redundant Marking Hypothesis (e.g. Shirai & Kurono, 1998). It claims that the early stages of L2 acquisition are characterized by a verbal morphology encoding inherent aspectual distinctions rather than tense or grammatical aspect.
(6) If there is a gain over time, will it be retained as measured by the delayed post-test?

The data were collected over the course of a regular semester (16 weeks) – at the beginning, the middle, and the end of the semester, as well as a month after the end of the semester for the delayed post-test – allowing us to track any potential gain over time (see Table 3.1).

4 Methodology

4.1 Participants

The participants were instructed learners of L2 French who were enrolled in a 4th-year course at a major North American university. Their background information appears in Table 3.2.

Most of the participants were English NSs ($n = 9$), but a few were heritage speakers either in French ($n = 4$) or in Spanish ($n = 3$), a language whose TAM system is much closer to the French system than to

Table 3.1 Study design

	Task 1	Task 2	Task 3
Session 1 at beginning semester	Background information questionnaire	General proficiency test (as well as TAM and gender agreement)	Grammatical judgment test (GJT)
Session 2 at mid-semester	Grammatical gender assignment test	GJT/correction (gender and number agreement)	Cloze test (various TAM)
Session 3 at end of semester	Grammatical gender assignment test	GJT/correction (gender and number agreement)	Cloze test (various TAM)
Session 4 delayed post-test, 1 month later	Grammatical gender assignment test	GJT/correction (gender and number agreement)	Cloze test (various TAM)
Every 3 weeks throughout semester	6 essays written at home		

Table 3.2 Participants' background information

	L1 English	L1 French	L1 Spanish
Participants	$n = 9$	$n = 4$	$n = 3$
Age	21 (20–22)	22 (20–24)	21.7 (20–23)
Status	Undergraduate	Undergraduate	Undergraduate
Major	French ($n = 5$)	French ($n = 2$)	French ($n = 3$)
Age of onset	15–17	0	15–17
Setting	Instructed	Home/instructed	Instructed
French-speaking parents	No	Yes	No
Francophone country stay	No ($n = 6$) Yes ($n = 4$) 6 weeks to a year	Yes ($n = 3$) 4–12 years	No ($n = 3$)
Motivation	Very to extremely motivated	Very to extremely motivated	Very to extremely motivated

the English system, allowing us to track a potential L1 effect. The French heritage speakers were born and raised in France (at least one of their parents was a French NS), and they had moved to the USA before the age of 5. Therefore, they were French-English bilingual speakers, but they had never been schooled in France and had never received formal instruction in French until they started taking French classes in college in the USA. The Spanish heritage speakers were born and raised in the USA by Mexican parents. They were thus Spanish-English bilinguals. All the participants were undergraduate students, most of them were majoring in French ($n = 10$), and they all indicated being very to extremely motivated to learn French. A group of French NSs ($n = 16$) living in France completed the cloze tests as well.

4.2 Procedure and tasks

The present study is part of a larger longitudinal study in the L2 acquisition of French morphosyntax that also investigated the acquisition of grammatical gender as well as gender and number agreement. The study design is summarized in Table 3.1.

Participants were asked to complete three different tasks during four sessions held at the beginning, middle and end of the semester and 1 month after the end of the semester as a delayed post-test. All tasks were written and available online. The participants accessed them from a computer on campus. During the first session, they filled out a background information questionnaire and were administered a general proficiency test as an independent measure of proficiency (see Ayoun, 2013, 2015). Then, during each subsequent session (Sessions 2, 3 and 4), the participants first completed two grammatical gender assignment and number tasks; the third task was about the cloze tests that will be discussed here. Participants also wrote six essays at regular intervals during the course of the semester; the findings of these essays will be reported elsewhere.

All of the students enrolled in the class were invited to participate in the study as foreign language learners. They were not given any details about the linguistic focus of the study; they were simply told that it was about learning French as a foreign language. All agreed to participate.

The class in which the participants were enrolled met three times a week for 50 minutes each time and it was organized as follows: five novels made into movies had been selected as course materials. The participants would first watch the movie at home to get acquainted with the storyline, the characters and the social-historical context. They were then asked to read about 20 to 30 pages at a time at home so that they could come to class prepared to discuss the story and the characters, as well as share their opinions and reactions during instructor-led interactions. The focus was on the content of the novels. Recasts were used to implicitly indicate that a form was not target-like without interrupting the flow of the interaction, but there was no explicit focus on form.[3] However, if participants asked for a grammatical clarification or explanation, it was given explicitly.

The instructor thus led class discussions of the novels for about three weeks for each novel, thereby providing the participants with controlled, repeated input. The fact that the cloze tests were about three novels with very similar themes contributed to that repeated exposure. All three novels are set during World War II and recount the horrors of the Holocaust and the work of the Résistance from the very personal perspective of the characters. The fact that they recount true stories allowed the instructed learners to identify with the characters.

The cloze test for Session 2 was based on *Un secret* (by Philippe Grimbert); it was composed of 34 verb tokens (12 states, 8 activities, 14 telics). The cloze test for Session 3 was based on *Elle s'appelait Sarah* (by Tatiana de Rosnay); the 39 verb tokens were divided among 11 states, 4 activities and 24 telics. The last cloze test, administered for Session 4 as a delayed post-test, 1 month after the end of the semester was a summary of three novels (*Un secret, Elle s'appelait Sarah, Les enfants de la liberté* by Marc Levy, the last novel to be read and discussed in class). It was composed of 30 verb tokens (5 states, 7 activities, 18 telics). The number of tokens per lexical class was not balanced because it was deemed important to have an authentic text with a solid internal cohesion.

The participants were instructed to read the entire text before providing the inflected form of the verbs given in parentheses at the infinitive (i.e. the base form of French verbs such as *penser* 'to think') given the context. The texts were controlled for vocabulary and although the storylines took place in the past, they were designed to elicit a variety of morphological forms, as we will see below.

5 Findings

5.1 Pre-test

The results of the pre-test – a grammaticality judgment task testing various morphosyntactic properties – indicate that there was a significant difference between groups. The L1 French group obtained the highest accuracy means (80.5%), followed by the L1 Spanish group (69.8%) and the L1 English group (60.1%).

5.2 Overall findings

Table 3.3 presents the overall findings in terms of accuracy percentages per group and for each of the three sessions (the statistical analyses are displayed in Table 3.3(b)). The column with '% correct' indicates the participants' accuracy in producing the targeted forms. Both the participant and NS groups performed poorly in that they rarely produced the

Table 3.3. (a) Overall findings

% correct	Session 2	Session 3	Session 4	Average
L1 English	46.2%	48.5%	65.0%	53.2%
L1 French	42.2%	56.4%	51.1%	54.1%
L1 Spanish	52.9%	53.8%	62.2%	56.3%
French NSs	59.9%	56.9%	40.2%	52.3%

(b) Overall findings: statistics

	Pearson χ^2	df	Significance (2-sided)
Session 2	21.622	3	0.000
Session 3	7.186	3	0.066
Session 4	50.436	3	0.000

targeted forms, but for very different reasons, as we will see below. Their performance varied with the cloze test, so there is a task effect as well as a time effect. The L1 Spanish group performed slightly better than the L1 French group, even though the L1 French participants were born and raised in France until the age of 5. One would therefore expect the L1 French group to have a facilitative advantage, which is not borne out by the data.

5.3 Findings by lexical classes

The findings by lexical classes are displayed by session in Tables 3.4 to 3.6. Session 2 targeted five morphological forms: the *passé composé* (PC), the *imparfait* (Imp), the indicative present (IndPres), the *plus-que-parfait* (PQP) and the subjunctive present (SubjPres). The statistical results are significant for all lexical classes and groups except for the L1 French group for states (Pearson $\chi^2 = 3.686$, df = 3, $p = 0.297$) and telics (Pearson $\chi^2 = 3.750$, df = 3, $p = 0.290$).

The L2 learners almost always failed to produce the PQP and the SubjPres. Their performance on morphological forms depended on the lexical classes. For instance, they encoded states with the Imp (a prototypical use) more often than activities or telics. As we will see below, the French NS group rarely produced the PC, opting for the *passé simple* (PS) instead.

In addition to PC, Imp, PQP and IndPres, Session 3 also targeted conditional present (CondPres), conditional past (CondPast) and future (Fut). Again, the statistical results are significant for all lexical classes and groups except for the L1 Spanish group for activities (Pearson $\chi^2 = 4.00$, df = 3, $p = 0.135$). The participants did not produce the PQP or the SubjPast (but

Table 3.4 Findings by lexical classes: Session 2

Session 2		L1 English	L1 French	L1 Spanish	French NSs
States (*n* = 12)	PC	50.0%	33.3%	85.5%	21.9%
	Imp	66.0%	60.0%	66.7%	78.8%
	IndPres	80.0%	50.0%	50.0%	37.5%
	SubjPres	12.5%	25.0%	8.3%	89.1%
	Average	52.1%	42.1%	52.6%	56.8%
Activities (*n* = 8)	Imp	56.7%	56.6%	66.7%	64.6%
	PQP	0%	0%	0%	22.9%
	IndPres	100%	100%	100%	81.3%
	Average	52.2	52.2%	22.2%	84.3%
Telics (*n* = 14)	PC	64.0%	33.5%	80.0%	22.5%
	Imp	32.5%	50.0%	66.7%	85.9%
	PQP	0%	16.7%	0%	56.3%
	SubjPres	10%	0%	0%	93.8%
	Average	26.6%	25.1%	36.7%	64.6%

Table 3.5 Findings by lexical classes: Session 3

Session 3		L1 English	L1 French	L1 Spanish	French NSs
States (*n* = 11)	PC	80.0%	33.3%	33.3%	12.5%
	Imp	60.0%	85.7%	66.7%	94.6%
	PQP	0%	0%	0%	43.8%
	IndPres	100%	100%	100%	100%
	CondPres	40.0%	33.3%	33.3%	62.5%
	CondPast	0%	33.3%	0%	39.6%
	SubjPast	0%	0%	33.3%	12.5%
	Average	40.0%	40.8%	38.1%	52.2%
Activities (*n* = 4)	Imp	80.0%	100%	66.7%	93.8%
	PQP	0%	0%	0%	6.3%
	CondPres	35.0%	66.7%	66.7%	93.8%
	Average	38.3%	55.6%	44.5%	64.6%
Telics (*n* = 24)	PC	87.8%	51.9%	88.9%	28.5%
	Imp	45.0%	100%	50.0%	65.6%
	PQP	0%	25.0%	16.7%	32.8%
	CondPres	43.3%	77.8%	44.4%	89.6%
	Future	50.0%	66.7%	100%	68.8%
	Average	45.2%	64.3%	60.0%	57.1%

Table 3.6 Findings by lexical classes: Session 4

Session 4		L1 English	L1 French	L1 Spanish	French NSs
States (*n* = 5)	PC	60.0%	66.7%	66.7%	18.8%
	Imp	70.0%	88.9%	66.7%	62.5%
	IndPres	50.0%	0%	66.7%	6.3%
	Average	60.0%	51.8%	66.7%	29.2%
Activities (*n* = 7)	PC	75.0%	50.0%	58.3%	53.1%
	IndPres	42.5%	0%	50.0%	40.6%
	Average	58.7%	25.0%	54.1%	46.8%
Telics (*n* = 18)	PC	80.8%	69.2%	79.5%	30.8%
	PQP	25.0%	50.0%	0%	71.9%
	IndPres	30.0%	0%	33.3%	37.5%
	Average	45.3%	39.7%	37.6%	46.7%

neither did the French NSs, indicating it was not obvious). The learner groups did well with the PC, while the French NSs continued to produce the PS instead.

The last cloze test was administered a month after the end of a semester as a delayed test; it targeted fewer forms (PC, Imp, IndPres, PQP). The participants' accuracy varied greatly depending on the morphological form and the lexical class. The statistical results are significant for all lexical classes and groups except the L1 English group and states (Pearson $\chi^2 = 1.389$, df = 2, $p = 0.499$) as well as the L1 Spanish group and states (Pearson $\chi^2 = 0.000$, df = 2, $p = 1.00$) and activities (Pearson $\chi^2 = 0.168$, df = 1, $p = 0.682$). The activities encoded with the IndPres were nonprototypical, which may explain why the accuracy percentages are so low. The L1 English and L1 French groups, but not the L1 Spanish group, eventually encoded some verbs with PQP.

5.4 Findings by targeted forms

The data were also analyzed to see what morphological forms the participants produced when they failed to produce the targeted forms. They are presented by session and group.

Table 3.7(a–c) shows the responses by L2 learner group for Session 2. They indicate that participants produced up to five different morphological forms instead of the targeted forms. IndPres and Imp were often used instead of PC; Imp and IndPres were used instead of PQP.

The French NS group produced up to 10 different morphological forms. PS, which has the same aspectual value as PC, was produced instead of PC, contra claims that it has fallen into disuse (e.g. Labeau, 2015); it is even produced instead of Imp (8.9%) and mostly PQP (23.8%). The French NSs also tended to use Imp instead of PQP like the L2 learner groups. The most striking difference between the NS group and the L2 learner groups is the use of the SubjPres (90% of the NSs produced it, while very few L2 learners did).

Table 3.8(a–c) displays the L2 learner groups' responses to the targeted forms for Session 3. All the statistical results were significant for all groups and lexical classes for this session, as well. The L1 English and L1 Spanish groups performed better for PC (87.0% and 83.3%, respectively), but not the L1 French group (only 50.0% for PC, but 10% for PS), who produced Imp (26.7%) or PQP (13.3%). All groups did very well with IndPres (100%) and relatively well with Imp (from 59.0% for L1 English to 90.0% for L1 French). They failed to produce CondPres, CondPast or SubjPast.

Table 3.8(d) shows that the French NSs continued to produce a variety of forms. They produced PS (59.4) much more frequently than PC (26.9%); they did so instead of PQP as well (34.4% versus 30.2%). Contrary to the L2 learner groups, they produced CondPres (83.0%), but not CondPast (39.6%) or SubjPast (12.5%), preferring instead SubPres (50.0%) or SubjImp (31.3%).

Table 3.9(a–c) displays the morphological forms L2 learners produced for the last and delayed session, Session 4. Although this cloze test targeted only four forms, participants produced as many as six different forms. The statistical results are significant for all groups and lexical classes. They did

Table 3.7 (a) L1 English group's responses to targeted forms: Session 2

L1 English	Targeted forms – Session 2				
Responses	PC	Imp	PQP	IndPres	SubjPres
PC	60.0%	22.5%	28.0%		18.0%
Imp	12.9%	52.5%	50.0%		30.0%
IndPres	22.9%	24.2%	20.0%	92.0%	38.0%
SubjPres			2.0%	8.0%	12.0%
CondPres	4.5%				2.0%
SubjPast		0.8%			

(b) L1 French group's responses to targeted forms: Session 2

L1 French	Targeted forms – Session 2				
Responses	PC	Imp	PQP	IndPres	SubjPres
PC	33.3%			13.3%	14.7%
Imp	4.8%	55.6%		20.0%	25.5%
IndPres	61.9%	44.4%	80.0%	46.7%	52.9%
SubjPres			20.0%	20.0%	5.9%

(c) L1 Spanish group's responses to targeted forms: Session 2

L1 Spanish	Targeted forms – Session 2				
Responses	PC	Imp	PQP	IndPres	SubjPres
PC	81.0%	25.0%	53.3%		
Imp		66.7%	40.0%		66.7%
IndPres	19.0%	5.6%		80.0%	20.0%
SubjPres				20.0%	6.7%
CondPres		2.8%	6.7%		
Future					6.7%

(d) French NS group's responses to targeted forms: Session 2

French NSs	Targeted forms – Session 2				
Responses	PC	Imp	PQP	IndPres	SubjPres
PC	22.3%	2.6%	8.8%		
Imp	6.3%	77.6%	28.8%	16.3%	
PQP	10.7%	7.3%	36.3%		
IndPres		3.1%	2.5%	63.8%	
SubjPres		0.5%		20.0%	90.0%
CondPres	6.3%				
CondPast	0.9%				
PS	50.0%	8.9%	23.8%		
SubjImp					10.0%
Future	3.6%				

moderately well for the PC (from 64.8% to 74.1%), and performed better for the Imp (from 66.7% to 88.9%). A few participants among the L1 French and L1 English groups finally produced PQP, but none of the L1 Spanish heritage speakers did, which is a bit surprising since that form is instantiated in Spanish as well. The participants' accuracy percentages for IndPres were much lower on this session than on the previous sessions,

Table 3.8 (a) L1 English group's responses to targeted forms: Session 3

L1 English group	Targeted forms – Session 3							
Responses	PC	Imp	PQP	IndPres	CondPres	CondPast	SubjPast	Future
PC	**87.0%**	35.0%	76.7%		14.3%	16.7%	50.0%	
Imp	13.0%	**59.0%**	21.7%		27.1%	30.0%	40.0%	
PQP					1.4%			
IndPres		4.0%	1.7%	**100%**	10.0%	16.7%		50.0%
CondPres		2.0%			**40.0%**	36.7%	10.0%	
CondPast								
SubjPres					2.9%			
Future					4.3%			**50.0%**

(b) L1 Spanish group's responses to targeted forms: Session 3

L1 Spanish group	Targeted forms – Session 3							
Responses	PC	Imp	PQP	IndPres	CondPres	CondPast	SubjPast	Future
PC	**83.3%**	26.7%	66.7%			22.2%		
Imp	16.7%	**63.3%**	22.2%		4.8%		66.7%	
PQP			11.1%					
IndPres		6.7%		**100%**	4.8%	33.3%		
CondPres		3.3%			**47.6%**	44.4%		
SubjPres							33.3%	
Future					42.9%			**100%**

(c) L1 French group's responses to targeted forms: Session 3

L1 French group	Targeted forms – Session 3							
Responses	PC	Imp	PQP	IndPres	CondPres	CondPast	SubjPast	Future
PC	**50.0%**	3.3%	22.2%					
Imp	26.7%	**90.0%**	33.3%		33.3%	33.3%	100%	
PQP	13.3%		**16.7%**					
IndPres		6.7%		**100%**				33.3%
CondPres					**61.9%**	33.3%		
CondPast						33.3%		
PS	10.0%		22.2%					
Future			5.6%		4.8%			**66.7%**

(d) French NS group's responses to targeted forms: Session 3

French NS group				Targeted forms – Session 3				
Responses	PC	Imp	PQP	IndPres	CondPres	CondPast	SubjPast	Future
PC	**26.9%**	1.9%	8.3%		0.9%			
Imp	6.9%	**88.8%**	24.0%		9.8%	37.5%		
PQP	6.9%	3.1%	**30.2%**				6.3%	
IndPres				**100%**				12.5%
SubjPres					2.7%		50.0%	
CondPres		0.6%	1.0%		**83.0%**	4.2%		
CondPast						**39.6%**		
SubjPast					1.8%	18.8%	**12.5%**	
PS	59.4%	5.6%	34.4%					
SubjImp					1.8%		31.3%	
Future								**68.8%**
FutPro								18.8%

probably because these IndPres tokens were nonprototypical, such as the use of the historical present in a text set in the past. As shown in Table 3.9(d), most of the French NSs failed to produce them as well. It seems that they overused PQP, producing it also when Imp, PC and to a lesser extent, IndPres, were targeted.

To summarize the findings, the L2 learner groups' performance varied greatly depending on the session, the lexical classes and the morphological forms. They performed well with IndPres, except on the nonprototypical tokens of the last session.

6 Discussion

We can now address our research questions. The first one asked whether a controlled, targeted input with repeated exposure would make a difference in the L2 acquisition of the French TAM system by instructed learners as measured by cloze tests. Previous studies found that L2 learners performed better on production tasks than on cloze tests and the present study confirms that L2 learners do not do well on cloze tests. Their accuracy was even lower than found previously (e.g. Ayoun 2013, 2015). So, it appears that the input to which they were exposed in a controlled and repeated manner did not lead to a better performance.

The second question asked whether L2 French learners would acquire a well contrasted TAM system as measured by cloze tests. Their TAM system does display contrasts in that they produced different morphological forms in different contexts, but their accuracy varied so much that it is difficult to claim that they have acquired a well contrasted system. They acquired certain forms faster than others, but their TAM system remains quite unbalanced.

Table 3.9 (a) L1 English group's responses to targeted forms: Session 4

L1 English	Targeted forms – Session 4			
Responses	PC	Imp	PQP	IndPres
PC	**78.3%**	26.7%	60.0%	45.7%
Imp	6.7%	**70.0%**	15.0%	12.7%
PQP	2.8%		**25.0%**	
IndPres	11.7%	3.3%		**40.0%**
SubjPres				1.4%
CondPres	0.6%			

(b) L1 French group's responses to targeted forms: Session 4

L1 French	Targeted forms – Session 4			
Responses	PC	Imp	PQP	IndPres
PC	**64.8%**	11.1%		28.6%
Imp	11.1%	**88.9%**	33.3%	52.4%
PQP	13.1%		**50.0%**	
IndPres	1.9%			
PS	9.3%		16.7%	19.0%

(c) L1 Spanish group's responses to targeted forms: Session 4

L1 Spanish	Targeted forms – Session 4			
Responses	PC	Imp	PQP	IndPres
PC	**74.1%**	22.2%	100%	33.3%
Imp	5.6%	**66.7%**		14.4%
PQP	1.9%			
IndPres	18.5%	11.1%		**47.6%**
PS				4.8%

(d) French NS group's responses to targeted forms: Session 4

French NS	Targeted forms – Session 4			
Responses	PC	Imp	PQP	IndPres
PC	**35.1%**	4.2%	6.3%	12.5%
Imp	4.5%	**62.5%**	12.5%	29.5%
PQP	27.8%	31.3%	**71.9%**	3.6%
IndPres	6.6%			**34.8%**
PS	24.7%	2.1%	9.4%	17.0%
Future	1.4%			2.7%

The third question was about a potential facilitative effect for the French heritage speakers, as well as the L1 Spanish speakers whose TAM system is closely related to the French TAM system. Once again, it depended on the lexical class and the morphological class. The L1 French speakers did produce two forms which the other groups never produced, PS and CondPast; they also used SubjPres and PQP much more often, but the accuracy percentages for these forms remain low. The L1 Spanish group did not seem to benefit from TAM similarities between French and Spanish, such as the aspectual difference between perfective and imperfective, or the common use of the SubjPres and SubjPast (only 33.3% in Session 3), also found in Spanish.

The answer to the fourth and fifth research questions is positive: there was definitely a morphological form effect with the participants performing better on some forms than others (e.g. IndPres), and there was a definite lexical class effect with a better performance on states than on telics or activities.

Since there was not really a gain over time from the second to the third session, the last research question about whether it was retained as measured by the delayed post-test is moot. In addition, the strong lexical class and morphological class effects obscure any potential gains. Lexical class effects are similar to those found in previous studies: states are most often appropriately encoded with Imp than PC, but activities were also successfully encoded with Imp in Session 3, for instance. The L1 French group was accurate in encoding telics with Imp, but the L1 English and L1 Spanish groups were not. Figures 3.1 to 3.3 show the strong lexical class and group effects across sessions.

Accuracy percentages were averaged across morphological forms (as displayed in the tables above). Keeping in mind that there was a strong morphological form effect, we can nevertheless observe that the L2 groups' performance varied quite a bit with respect to the sessions and lexical classes. They were similarly affected by the sessions for states (best

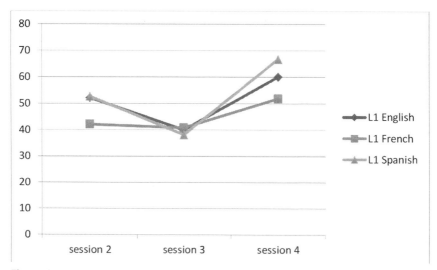

Figure 3.1 L2 learner groups on states by session

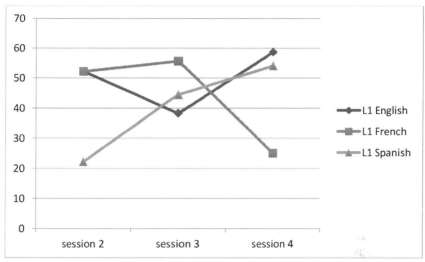

Figure 3.2 L2 learner groups on activities by session

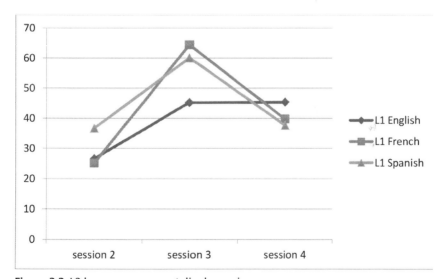

Figure 3.3 L2 learner groups on telics by session

performance on Session 4, worst on Session 2), but the L1 French group underperformed the other groups on Sessions 2 and 4 for telics. Activities show the most differences among sessions; groups all performed almost erratically from session to session. These figures underscore again the finding that there was no facilitative effect for L1 French or L1 Spanish, as previously found (Child, 2014; Izquierdo & Collins, 2008).

It is important to note a major difference between the performance of the L2 learner groups and the NSs. When the L2 learner groups did not produce the targeted forms, they produced forms that were inappropriate for the context, such as PC instead of Imp, whereas NSs always produced forms that were appropriate for the context and were consistent with the way they encoded all the verbal tokens within a given cloze test. However, NSs interpreted the text differently than the way it was intended, for instance when they used the historic present to recount past events. The NSs variation underscores the difficulty of cloze tests as an empirical task. Although the L2 participants were very familiar with the content of the cloze tests since they were about novels they had read and discussed extensively, they had to adopt the viewpoint of the narrator and if they missed or misunderstood a contextual cue, then they mis-encoded predicates. Another difficulty about these cloze tests is that they may have targeted too many different forms (four for Session 4, five for Session 2 and eight for Session 3). The participants may have performed better if the cloze tests had targeted fewer different morphological forms and if the texts had been shorter, perhaps presented as paragraphs. However, the participants had been repeatedly exposed to all the targeted forms during the course of the semester while reading and discussing the novels, so better performance was expected.

The present study suffers from a few limitations, such as the relatively small number of participants (counterbalanced by the large amount of data over a long period); a larger and more even number of participants per group would have been desirable. Moreover, a greater effort should have been made to balance the number of tokens per lexical class while also preserving the internal cohesion of authenticity of the text. The uneven number of tokens per lexical class (total of 19 activities, 28 states and 56 telics for all cloze tests combined) may have adversely affected the participants' performance (and hence the findings).

7 Conclusion

The present study addressed the importance of input in the L2 acquisition of the French TAM system by Anglophone and Hispanophone learners. Unfortunately, it does not appear that a specific, targeted input with repeated exposure made a positive difference, as measured by cloze tests, since strong lexical and form effects were found along with overall low accuracy in obligatory contexts. However, it is important to continue to focus on the input to which participants are exposed: the more we know about their particular input, the more we should be able to make predictions about their progression toward the target language and adjust pedagogical approaches.

Future studies with instructed learners may want to investigate whether different pedagogical approaches would lead to a more positive outcome. In the present study, a communicative approach favored implicit negative feedback in the form of recasts, which were previously shown to be effective with the aspectual distinction between *passé composé* and *imparfait* (e.g. Ayoun, 2001, 2004), but recent meta-analyses have found that explicit instruction is overall more effective than implicit instruction (Spada & Tomita, 2010). In particular, combining oral and written treatment was found to be significantly more effective than written treatments alone in either implicit or explicit conditions (Norris & Ortega, 2015). Similarly, Shintani (2015) found that production-based instruction was more effective to processing instruction when both treatment groups received the same explicit information.

In the case of L2 French, explicit instruction may be useful for difficult aspectual distinctions, mood alternations and less frequent forms (i.e. PQP, future perfect), as well as less morphologically salient forms (e.g. subjunctive forms of all verbs ending in *–er*) and nonprototypical forms, as previously suggested (e.g. Ayoun, 2013; Blyth, 2005). Yang and Lyster (2010) provided Chinese-speaking learners of L2 English with either corrective feedback (i.e. metalinguistic cues, repetition, clarification request, elicitation) or prompts or recasts (i.e. the instructor would reformulate a nontarget-like utterance with or without encouraging the participate to rephrase with a correction). The results of pre-tests, immediate post-tests and delayed post-tests revealed that prompts led to greater accuracy in producing regular past tense forms, while prompts and recasts had comparable effects on the accuracy of irregular past tense forms. But Yang and Lyster (2010) used production tasks, not cloze tests. It would be helpful for future studies to continue investigating the L2 acquisition of TAM systems with a combination of written and oral elicitation tasks such as cloze tests, narratives, preference and grammaticality judgment tasks.

Notes

(1) The following abbreviations are used: IndPres for indicative present; IMP for *imparfait*; CondPast for conditional past; PC for *passé composé*.
(2) See Ayoun (2013) for a more detailed account.
(3) A recast reformulates an erroneous utterance, but implicitly, without interrupting the communicative flow of an interaction (e.g. Ayoun 2001, 2004). A focus on form is an explicit focus on the erroneous production of a learner and may be accompanied with a metalinguistic explanation.

References

Ayoun, D. (2001) The role of negative and positive feedback in the second language acquisition of *passé composé* and *imparfait*. *The Modern Language Journal* 85 (2), 226–243.
Ayoun, D. (2004) The effectiveness of written recasts in the second language acquisition of aspectual distinctions in French: A follow-up study. *Modern Language Journal* 88 (1), 31–55.
Ayoun, D. (2005) The acquisition of tense and aspect in L2 French from a Universal Grammar perspective. In D. Ayoun and R. Salaberry (eds) *Tense and Aspect in Romance Languages: Theoretical and Applied Perspectives* (pp. 79–127). Amsterdam: John Benjamins.

Ayoun, D. (2013) *The Second Language Acquisition of French Tense, Aspect, Mood and Modality*. Amsterdam: John Benjamins.

Ayoun, D. (2014) The acquisition of future temporality by L2 French learners. *Journal of French Language Studies* 24 (2), 181–202.

Ayoun, D. (2015) There's no time like the present: a longitudinal case study in L2 French acquisition. In D. Ayoun (ed.) *The Acquisition of the Present* (pp. 87–113). Amsterdam: John Benjamins.

Ayoun, D. and Rothman, J. (2013) Generative approaches to the L2 acquisition of temporal-aspectual-mood (TAM) systems. In R. Salaberry and L. Comajoan (eds) *Research Design and Methodology in Studies on Second Language Tense and Aspect* (pp. 119–156). Berlin: Mouton de Gruyter.

Blyth, C. (2005) From empirical findings to the teaching of aspectual distinctions. In D. Ayoun and R. Salaberry (eds) *Tense and Aspect in Romance Languages* (pp. 211–252). Amsterdam: John Benjamins.

Child, M. (2014) Cross-linguistic influence in the L3 Portuguese acquisition: Language learning perceptions and transfer of mood distinctions by three groups of English-Spanish bilinguals. PhD dissertation, University of Arizona.

Duperron, L. (2006) Study abroad and the second language acquisition of tense and aspect in French: Is longer better? In S. Wilkinson (ed.) *Issues in Language Program Direction* (pp. 45–71). Boston: Heinle.

Gass, S. (1997) *Input, Interaction and the Second Language Learner*. Mahwah, NJ: Lawrence Erlbaum Associates.

Goad, H., White, L. and Steele, J. (2003) Missing inflection in L2 acquisition: Defective syntax or L1-constrained prosodic representations? *Canadian Journal of Linguistics* 48 (3/4), 243–263.

Hawkins, R. and Chan, C. (1997) Partial availability of Universal Grammar in second language acquisition: The failed formal features hypothesis. *Second Language Research* 13 (3), 187–226.

Hawkins, R. and Liszka, S. (2003) Locating the source of defective past tense marking in advanced L2 English speakers. In R. van Hout, H. Aafke, F. Kuiken and R. Towell (eds) *The Interface Between Syntax and Lexicon in Second Language Acquisition* (pp. 21–44). Amsterdam: John Benjamins.

Haznedar, B. and Schwartz, B. (1997) Are there optional infinitives in child L2 acquisition? In E. Hughes, M. Hughes and A. Greenhill (eds) *Proceedings of the 21st Annual Boston University Conference on Language Development* (pp. 257–268). Somerville, MA: Cascadilla Press.

Herschensohn, J. and Arteaga, D. (2009) Tense and verb raising in advanced L2 French. *Journal of French Language Studies* 19 (3), 291–318.

Howard, M. (2005) On the role of context in the development of learner language: Insights from study abroad research. *International Journal of Applied Linguistics* 147/148, 1–20.

Howard, M. (2008) Morpho-syntactic development in the expression of modality: The subjunctive in French L2 acquisition. *Revue Canadienne de Linguistique Appliquée* 11 (3), 171–191.

Howard, M. (2012) From tense and aspect to modality: The acquisition of future, conditional and subjunctive morphology in L2 French. A preliminary study. *Cahiers Chronos* 24, 201–223.

Howard, M. (2015) At the interface between sociolinguistic and grammatical development: The expression of futurity in L2 French: A preliminary study. *Arborescence* 5, 97–125.

Izquierdo, J. and Collins, L. (2008) The facilitative role of L1 influence in tense-aspect marking: A comparison of Hispanophone and Anglophone learners of French. *The Modern Language Journal* 92 (3), 350–368.

Kupisch, T., Lein, T., Barton, D., Schröder, J.D., Stangen, I. and Stoehr, A. (2014) Acquisition outcomes across domains in adult simultaneous bilinguals with French as a weaker language. *Journal of French Language Studies* 24 (3), 347–376.

Labeau, E. (2015) Il était une fois le passé simple.... *Journal of French Language Studies* 25 (2), 165–187.

Lealess, A. (2005) En français, il faut qu'on parle bien: Assessing native-like proficiency in L2 French. MA thesis, University of Ottawa.

Leung, Y.-k.I. (2002) Functional categories in second and third language acquisition: A crosslinguistic study of the acquisition of English and French by Chinese and Vietnamese speakers. Doctoral dissertation, McGill University, Montreal.

Leung, Y.-k.I. (2005) L2 vs. L3 initial state: A comparative study in the acquisition of French DPs by Vietnamese monolinguals and Cantonese-English bilinguals. *Bilingualism: Language & Cognition* 8 (1), 39–61.

Lyster, R. (2004) Research on form-focused instruction in immersion classrooms: Implications for theory and practice. *Journal of French Language Studies* 14 (3), 321–341.

McManus, K. and Mitchell, R. (2015) Subjunctive use and development in L2 French: A longitudinal study. *Language, Interaction and Acquisition* 6 (1), 42–73.

Myles, F. (2005) The emergence of morpho-syntactic structure in French L2. In J-M. Dewaele (ed.) *Focus on French as a Foreign Language: Multidisciplinary Approaches* (pp. 88–113). Clevedon: Multilingual Matters.

Mitchell, R. and Myles, F. (2004) *Second Language Learning Theories*. London: Arnold.

Norris, J. and Ortega, L. (2015) Implicit and explicit instruction in L2 learning: Norris and Ortega (2000) revisited and updated. In P. Rebuschat (ed.) *Implicit and Explicit Learning of Languages* (pp. 443–482). Amsterdam: John Benjamins.

Prévost, P. and White, L. (2000) Missing surface inflection or impairment in second language acquisition? Evidence from tense and agreement. *Second Language Research* 16 (2), 103–134.

Rankin, T. and Unsworth, S. (2016) Beyond poverty: Engaging with input in generative SLA. *Second Language Research* 32 (4), 563–572.

Robison, R.E. (1990) The primacy of aspect: Aspectual marking in English interlanguage. *Studies in Second Language Acquisition* 12 (3), 315–330.

Robison, R.E. (1995) The aspect hypothesis revisited: A cross-sectional study of tense and aspect marking in interlanguage. *Applied Linguistics* 16 (3), 344–371.

Shintani, N. (2015) The effectiveness of processing instruction and production based instruction on L2 grammar acquisition: A meta-analysis. *Applied Linguistics* 36 (3), 306–325.

Shirai, Y. and Kurono, A. (1998) The acquisition of tense-aspect marking in Japanese as a second language. *Language Learning* 48 (2), 245–279.

Slabakova, R., Teal, T.L. and Liskin-Gasparro, J. (2014) We have moved on: Current concepts and positions in generative SLA. *Applied Linguistics* 35 (5), 601–606.

Sorace, A. (2011) Pinning down the concept of interface in bilingualism. *Linguistic Approaches to Bilingualism* 1 (1), 1–33.

Spada, N. and Tomita, Y. (2010) Interactions between type of instruction and type of language feature: A meta-analysis. *Language Learning* 60 (2), 263–308.

Yang, Y. and Lyster, R. (2010) Effects of form-focused practice and feedback on Chinese EFL learners' acquisition of regular and irregular past tense forms. *Studies in Second Language Acquisition* 32 (2), 235–263.

4 When Nonnative Speakers Show Distinction: Syntax and Task Interactions in Long-Distance Anaphoric Dependencies in French

Laurent Dekydtspotter and Charlene Gilbert

Introduction

A growing body of nonnative sentence processing research argues that the processing of target language sentences by nonnative speakers (NNSs) is characterized by under-learned lexical access and by target deviant representations that require parse revisions, as well as by the suppression of first language (L1) knowledge. These have significant downstream implications (Dekydtspotter, 2001; Dekydtspotter & Miller, 2013; Dekydtspotter *et al.*, 2006; Miller, 2015; inter alia). Nonnative sentence processing can, therefore, be partially characterized by computations that may time out and fail to complete in a target-like manner in the limit of available working memory. Under-learned lexical access induces delayed and/or diminished effects of syntactic integration (Miller, 2014, 2015) or prediction (Hopp, 2013, 2016; Kaan *et al.*, 2010; Lew-Williams & Fernald, 2010).

The domain-specificity of the representations computed by NNSs can be assessed by focusing on cyclic re-representations of displaced *wh*-constituents. Traces/copies of moved constituents in cyclic nodes – where they are not otherwise needed for thematic integration – suggest a specific grammatical architecture. Claims that nonnative sentence processing lacks detailed syntactic representations in real time as per the Shallow Structures Hypothesis (SSH) (Felser *et al.*, 2012; Marinis *et al.*, 2005; cf. Pliatsikas & Marinis, 2012) are called into question by evidence that moved *wh*-constituents are re-represented in phase-by-phase derivation during real-time processing of *wh*-movement dependencies in nonnative sentence processing (Dekydtspotter & Miller, 2013; Dekydtspotter *et al.*, 2012; Miller, 2015).

Universal Grammar-constrained nonnative grammatical development might, therefore, constitute a by-product of a deductive reflex to parse when confronted by target-language input after the grammar of the L1 has been established (Dekydtspotter, 2001; Dekydtspotter & Renaud, 2014; Truscott & Sharwood-Smith, 2004).[1] A syntactic reflex to parse seems to be a central part of grammar acquisition. Without syntactic computations, the tractability of the input seems beyond the realm of plausibility. Additionally, the facility of native speaker (NS) processing is rather fragile: peak performance can easily be degraded in ways that are reminiscent of the performance of NNSs (Frimu, 2017; Hopp, 2010, 2016; López-Prego & Gabriele, 2014; McDonald, 2006).

Roberts (2013) suggests that NNSs do not generally compute detailed structural representations; however, the task may call for the focus of attention to be placed on structure when a grammatical judgment demanding attention to details is required. Thus, if a detailed structure is advantageous in completing a grammatical task successfully, a detailed structural analysis might be recruited; otherwise it is not. This possibility might perhaps be best explained by interactive models of sentence processing that reject an automatic syntactic computation in the analysis of the input (namely, the Late Assignment of Syntax Theory, Townsend & Bever, 2001). For SSH proponents (Clahsen & Felser, 2006a, 2006b), the real-time computation of detailed morphosyntactic structures is limited by the epistemological status of nonnative representations, so that nonnative syntactic knowledge is typically not accessible within the narrow window required for real-time sentence processing. In this vein of thought followed by Roberts (2013), as well as Pliatsikas and Marinis (2012), shallow structures seem to be the default processing mode in nonnative sentence processing. Detailed syntactic processing is not completely excluded, however. It can be induced by naturalistic exposure as access to representations can be sped up (Pliatsikas & Marinis, 2012) or by the focus of the task on grammar (Roberts, 2013).

However, real-time syntactic analysis characterizes the information that must be attended to as grammatically relevant and chunks that information into manageable units (Chomsky, 2005, 2008; Rizzi, 2013). Hence, the grammatical system constitutes a dedicated lower-order attention control device for structuring linguistic input. A higher-order attention control mechanism must also monitor the coherence of the message carried by the language structures in discourse (Baddeley, 2017). Such a mechanism might naturally orient to the nature of the task at hand to focus attention on what discourse information is most relevant. In mental architecture, grammatical processing would subserve this general attention control mechanism. Thus, structure might interact with the nature of the task in determining aspects of performance. Efficiency gains linked to task differences might be qualified by structure, as an effect of the domain-specific computations that feed the general attentional system responding to the task.

We address the interplay of two systems in processing; namely, a lower-order domain-specific syntactic system and a higher-order goal-directed attention control mechanism monitoring discourse-level information. There is a strong bias in language research to characterize nonnative grammar acquisition in terms of the failures of NNSs to meet criteria established by a group of educated NS peers. Still, complex grammatical properties can be mastered by NNSs (Birdsong, 1992; Herschensohn, 1997) and NNSs do not underperform *all* NSs in every way. Indeed, age, literacy level and experience play a role in the level of performance on a typical experiment. Hence, we examine reading times (RTs) in the processing of anaphora dependent on cyclic *wh*-movement chains across two tasks with different inherent goals. The NNSs are language professionals in training who are familiar with testing. The NSs representing the educated working-age adult population are not. When NNSs distinguish themselves, we consider whether any advantage might be global or whether a syntactic reflex combines with the nature of the task.

Background

Our investigation focuses on a central distinction in grammar highlighted in Chomsky (1995), following Freidin (1986), Lebeaux (1988), who point out that (lexically selected) complements and (nonselected) modifiers engage cyclic *wh*-movement computations differently. To examine this fundamental property of language, we focus on sentences such as those in Examples (1) and (2).

(1) *Quelle décision à propos de lui est-ce que Paul a dit que* which decision at words of him is-it that Paul has said that *Lydie avait rejetée sans hésitation?*

Lydie had rejected without hesitation? 'Which decision about him did Paul say that Lydie had rejected without hesitation?'

(2) *Quelle décision le concernant est-ce que Paul a dit que* which decision him regarding is-it that Paul has said that *Lydie avait rejetée sans hésitation?*

Lydie had rejected without hesitation? 'Which decision regarding him did Paul say that Lydie had rejected without hesitation?'

In interpreting Examples (1) and (2), the speaker of French naturally construes the pronouns *lui* 'him' in Example (1) and *le* 'him' in Example (2) as anaphorically linked to the matching masculine antecedent *Paul*.[2] This similarity obtains, despite the fact that *à propos de lui* 'about him' in Example (1) constitutes a complex prepositional noun (N)-complement introduced by the preposition *à*, whereas *le concernant* 'regarding him' in Example (2) constitutes a modifying participial clause. The N-complement *à propos de lui* involves the default case form *lui* as prepositional object,[3] whereas the participial modifier *le concernant* involves the accusative clitic *le*. Both are marked for masculine gender and singular number. Crucially, these forms are also structurally distinct in deeper ways, visible in subtle referential contrasts as in Examples (3a) versus (3b).

(3a) *Quelle décision à propos du candidat$_i$ est-ce que celui-ci$_{*i,j}$ voulait révéler hier?*

'Which information about the candidate$_i$ did he$_{*i,j}$ want to reveal yesterday?'

(3b) *Quelle décision concernant le candidat$_i$ est-ce que celui-ci$_{i,j}$ voulait révéler hier?*

'Which information regarding the candidate$_i$ did he$_{i,j}$ want to reveal yesterday?'

In Example (3a) above, the candidate is disjoint from the person who wanted to reveal information, whereas the candidate could more easily be this person in Example (3b).[4] Similar contrasts have been reported for English as in Examples (3c) versus (3d) (Freidin, 1986; Lebeaux, 1988; van Riemsdijk & Williams, 1981):

(3c) Whose characterization of the typical male reviewer$_i$ does he$_{*i,j}$ resent?

(Sportiche, 2006: 63, ex. (77a))

(3d) Whose survey describing the typical male reviewer$_i$ does he$_{i,j}$ resent?

(Sportiche, 2006: 63, ex. (77b))

As Chomsky (1995) and Lebeaux (1988) note, such differences follow if complements and modifiers are treated very differently in syntactic computations. By being lexically selected, the N-complement in Example (1) qualifies its head noun *décision* at every step of computations involving the noun as in Example (4). Angled brackets indicate the moved constituent. In contrast, the noun phrase (NP)-modifier *le concernant* 'regarding him' in Example (2) needs to qualify its noun phrase *quelle décision* 'which decision' only after computations satisfying lexical requirements have applied to it as indicated in Example (5).

(4) [<quelle décision *à propos de lui*> [est-ce que [Paul$_i$ a dit [< quelle décision *à propos de lui* > [que Lydie avait rejetée < quelle décision à propos de lui$_i$ > sans hésitation]]]]]

(5) [<quelle décision> le concernant [est-ce que [Paul a dit [< quelle décision> [que Lydie avait rejetée < quelle décision > sans hésitation]]]]]

Therefore, given the structure in Example (4) for the sentence in Example (1), a pronoun in a subcategorized complement, can be syntactically bound by a matching C-commanding expression as the relevant conditions are met during the derivation. Binding condition B requires that a pronoun be free in its local domain containing the pronoun and a subject (Chomsky, 1986). It restricts binding by the matching antecedent *Paul* to the embedded clause, which includes both the pronoun *lui* and the local subject *Lydie*. In this local domain, the pronoun *lui* at the foot of the chain inside the subordinate clause in Example (4) can be bound by *Paul*, as shown by the indexing in Example (4). The pronoun receives a bound-variable interpretation at the semantic interface as soon as it is feasible to do so.[5]

With an NP-modifier as in Example (2), the syntactic computation disallows a referential chain as in Example (5), requiring coreference in discourse. As the expression *quelle décision* 'which decision' is re-represented in the subordinate clause in Example (5), the information that the referent of the pronoun is identifiable with the individual Paul, so that the decision could affect Paul, will be refreshed in discourse-semantics. This information will not be re-represented in syntax, however. In the basic organization of a generative system for language, the formation of referential chains is privileged, since referential chains reduce the processing load in the maintenance of referents in discourse-semantics (Reinhart & Reuland, 1993; Reuland, 2001; inter alia).

Hence, what role syntactic computations may play in real-time sentence comprehension in a nonnative language can be examined in terms of the degree to which efficiency gains may be obtained in the processing of interrogatives involving *wh*-constituents with N-complements in Example (1) relative to NP-modifiers in Example (2). Crucially, efficiency gains should be found at specific moments of computations associated with the re-representation of distinct *wh*-constituents in cyclic movement as in (1), given that re-representation allows for binding. The processing of Examples (1) versus (2) should bear certain fingerprints of a specific computational system enabling binding as discussed here.

A task that requires the focus of attention to include the identity of the individual directly affected by the decision in Examples (1) and (2) should influence the processing of these anaphoric dependencies differentially from a task that does not require the focus of attention to include the identity of that individual. Indeed, if the identity of the discourse referent introduced by the pronoun is significant to answer a comprehension question, the identity of the referent of the pronoun may not be left unattended. This requires committing to a value in the mental model for the discourse referent introduced by the pronoun. Undoing a commitment is costly because information must align across levels (Crocker, 1996). Theoretically, it seems necessary for the pronoun to receive a value, because for the sentence to have a value in a compositional interpretation, each subelement of interpretation must have a value (Heim & Kratzer, 1998). However, if the value of the pronoun is not central to the task, it may be disregarded (cf. Stewart *et al.*, 2007). If efficiencies are afforded both by binding as it becomes structurally available, and by not having to attend to details of referential interpretation, then these efficiencies would add up. It is, however, crucial to note that these additive effects are expected only if a value is necessarily calculated.

No such interaction in the processing of Examples (1) versus (2) will arise if structures are shallow, because the lower-order attention control system contributed by syntax will be inoperative. In the SSH, efficiency gains by advanced NNSs in a nonnaturalistic setting when the focus is on aspects of meaning rather than on grammar should not be mediated by the possibility of two processes of anaphora resolution: one in syntax (binding) and one in discourse (coreference). If there are fingerprints of structure accompanying efficiency gains due to task, this is presumably due to an autonomous syntactic reflex.

The Study

Hypotheses and predictions

Pliatsikas and Marinis (2012) observed that NNSs immersed in the target language community process language in a more target-like manner. These NNSs showed structural effects similar to those NSs. Roberts (2013) observed that sentence processing experiments with NNSs typically report finding more structural contrasts when grammatical judgments are provided. Hence, the benefits of structural processing might be sought only as a task calls for the focus of attention to be placed on grammar, presumably because the benefits of structure also come with costs. Thus, the evidence for a domain-specific reflex might be most persuasive when it is found in contexts in which the focus of attention is on aspects of the message rather than on grammatical form, and in cases in which the NNSs are not in the target-language environment.

Naturally, when NSs are also NNSs in an environment in which their second language is spoken, their processing might be affected by their active bilingualism. Such NSs might be viewed as offering better comparisons for NNSs, because they share bilingualism as a common condition. However, we propose to compare a group of advanced NNSs in a nonnaturalistic setting, but who are in an educational environment in which experimentation in various modalities is routine, to a group of educated NSs of French in France representing the working-age adult category, from 18 through 60 years of age. These NSs will not be affected by active bilingualism because the use of English is limited in their context. They are also literate, studying in educational institutions or active in their professions. However, their exposure to language research is casual, limited to what might be available in media reports and science magazines. In contrast, the NNSs are in a unit in which such research is regularly conducted, even when their own interests reside elsewhere. The advantage of a culture of language testing will, therefore, be on the side of the NNSs, although they are all linguistically naïve and unaware of the specifics of the study. The central empirical questions will be as follows: given that NNSs need not (necessarily) be disadvantaged with respect to NSs in any task in view of their experience, will their performance benefit from critical moments of sentence processing that suggest a syntactic reflex or will it be general, as they distinguish themselves from a group of adult NSs?

Sensitivity to task in sentence processing is not unique to NNSs or limited to a focus on morphosyntax. The nature of comprehension queries has been documented to reflect the depth of processing in discourse semantics, as a result of what information resides in the focus of attention. Indeed, Stewart *et al.* (2007) found that the processing of ambiguous pronouns reflected the type of comprehension questions in the task. Two self-paced reading-time experiments were conducted to determine the reading speed of ambiguous pronouns relative to unambiguous pronouns. Information queries after stimulus sentences affected the relative speed at which ambiguous pronouns were processed. When the reference of the pronoun mattered in answering the comprehension query, the processing speed of ambiguous pronouns slowed down relative to unambiguous pronouns. When the reference of the pronoun did not matter, the ambiguous pronouns were processed at the same speed as the unambiguous ones. Stewart *et al.* (2007) concluded that for the first type of questions, respondents did not immediately resolve the pronoun in shallow processing; however, if a pronoun remained valueless, the entire compositional interpretation would be valueless. Hence, this processing effect might rather reflect the inconsequentiality of the value assignment, rather than a complete lack of value. If the inconsequentiality of the value assignment to the pronoun is the right characterization, the goal inherent in the task would affect a higher-order system monitoring the coherence of the message carried by the language structures in discourse. The action of this higher-level system would not impinge on the lower-level computations of semantically interpreted categories.

The grammatical system constitutes a built-in attention system as it specifies what properties must be attended to in the input. On our working hypothesis, a syntactic computation lies at the very core of sentence processing in NSs and NNSs alike. Still, a range of individual factors superimposed on the basic linguistic computations, such as lexical retrieval in NNSs, but also familiarity with experimental practice, can also affect performance. A grammatical reflex to compute cyclic dependencies in the interpretation of anaphoric dependencies could play a role in aiding the processing of advanced NNSs of French. The interpretation of a *wh*-expression such as *quelle décision à propos de lui* 'which decision about him' relies on the fact that the masculine pronoun *lui* 'him' is syntactically re-represented as part of an N-complement. This is in contradistinction to the interpretation of a *wh*-expression such as *quelle décision le concernant* 'which decision regarding him', in which the masculine pronoun *le* 'him' is not syntactically re-represented, given that it is part of an NP modifier. Both *quelle décision à propos de lui* 'which decision about him' and have as *quelle décision le concernant* 'which decision regarding him' have anaphoric or nonanaphoric readings. With N-complements, the anaphora will be aided by syntactic chain formation, whereas with NP-modifiers, it will involve discourse anaphora. It is, therefore, predicted that processing moments during which cyclic movement computations are engaged will provide processing gains in the extraction of *quelle décision à propos de lui* 'which decision about him' in Example (1) relative to *quelle décision le concernant* 'which decision regarding him' in Example (2), owing to the help provided by syntax in processing Example (1). A task that eschews any commitment to a value for the pronoun avoids selecting a particular discourse representation in the face of referential ambiguity. As more practiced NNSs distinguish themselves from NSs, binding-related efficiencies owing to syntax should combine with efficiencies due to not having to commit to an interpretation. The location of these efficiencies should reflect the integration of N-complements versus NP-modifiers in the computation of cyclic *wh*-movement chains; namely, reflect the computation of movement traces. These specific effects are expected if syntactic processing is informationally encapsulated (Fodor, 1983, 2001), so that efficiencies in higher-order processing build on efficiencies in lower-order syntactic processing. In contrast, because a structural distinction cannot be made in real time under SSH, processing performance might be enhanced by a task requiring less effort across the two constructions.

Therefore, we ask whether a grammatical reflex enables processing efficiencies in the treatment of anaphoric dependencies, specifically at moments of processing associated with the computation of cyclic movement chains sustaining binding. It is hypothesized that the efficient resolution of anaphoric dependencies by advanced NNSs of French would build on a real-time grammar-specific structural reflex. A domain general pattern due to a focus on the identity of the pronoun referents would not have this specific character.

Stimulus and method

To advance this empirical question, we devised an experiment involving two tasks in the moving window format using Linger (Rohde, 2003). The tasks had the same items; however, distinct comprehension checks determined what information conveyed by the critical items was queried as per Stewart *et al.* (2007). This change manipulated the discourse-structure information in the focus of attention. Both tasks in the experiment were comprised of twenty critical items in a 2 × 2 (Construction * Antecedent) in a Latin square, with an additional 30 distractor items involving a range of constructions. The distractor items, however, also involved anaphora, so that the task would appear seamless from the point of view of the participants. The distractor items were also followed by comprehension queries that had the same informational orientation as in the critical items.

This design crossed NP-modifier/N-complement constructions with matching antecedents as matrix-clause/embedded-clause subjects, and then we consider whether when the exact value of the pronoun was inconsequential to answering comprehension queries. Hence, in critical items, a gendered pronoun either carried by a N-complement construction *à propos (de lui/d'elle)* 'about him/her' or by an NP-modifier construction *(le/la) concernant* 'regarding him/her' is paired with a matching antecedent either in the matrix clause or in the embedded clause. An example of a critical item is provided in Examples (6a–d).

(6a) *Quelle décision à propos de lui est-ce que Paul a dit que Lydie avait rejetée sans hésitation?*

'Which decision about him did Paul say that Lydie had rejected without hesitation?'

(6b) *Quelle décision le concernant est-ce que Paul a dit que Lydie avait rejetée sans hésitation?*

'Which decision regarding him did Paul say that Lydie had rejected without hesitation?'

(6c) *Quelle décision à propos de lui est-ce que Lydie a dit que Paul avait rejetée sans hésitation?*

'Which decision about him did Lydie say that Paul had rejected without hesitation?'

(6d) *Quelle décision le concernant est-ce que Lydie a dit que Paul avait rejetée sans hésitation?*

'Which decision regarding him did Lydie say that Paul had rejected without hesitation?'

Thus, in Example (6a) the masculine pronoun *lui* 'him' introduced in an N-complement structure is naturally understood as referring to the individual Paul, via a binding relation by hypothesis. In Example (6b), the masculine pronoun *le* 'him' introduced in an NP modifier is naturally understood as referring to the individual Paul, via a coreference relation by hypothesis. In Example (6c, d) the first subject NP is a mismatch, and the second subject NP is a potential match.

In both tasks, all experimental items, both critical and distractor items, were followed by a comprehension check in the form of a query. In one task, the answer to this query was always dependent on the value given to the pronoun. Thus, for the quadruple in Example (6a–d), the query was: *La décision est au sujet de Lydie?* 'Is the decision about Lydie?', and a negative answer was expected. The words *concernant* or *à propos de* that appeared in the critical items were never used in the comprehension queries. In a second task, every item was followed by an informational query, the answer to which was independent of the value given to the pronoun. For the quadruple in Examples (6a-d), the query was: *Paul a rejeté la décision?* 'Did Paul reject the decision?' in Examples (6a, b) or *Lydie a rejeté la décision?* 'Did Lydie reject the decision?' in Examples (6c, d). A negative answer was again expected. While the focus of attention may be extended to include beliefs about the details of the decision, beliefs about the value of the pronoun referent are not material to answering the comprehension query. The person directly affected by the decision is of no consequence to the answer; hence, the comprehension queries directly focused attention on the outcome of the pronoun resolution in one task, but not in the other task. In the training items, the focus of attention was also biased in the same way, so that the information contributed by a pronoun was in the focus of a comprehension query in one task but not in the other.

Prior to the current study, we verified our intuitions that N-complement and NP-modifier structures induce similar rates of anaphoric construal. Advanced L1-English NNSs of French ($n = 16$) with a mean age of 26 (range: 22–53) in the USA and NSs ($n = 16$) with a mean age of 22 (range: 20–31) living in France completed a 50-item interpretive judgment task, which included 20 critical items as in Example (6a, b) as part of a battery of tests. On a C-test (Renaud, 2010), these learner scores (range: 44–50) patterned like NSs (range: 42–50). These respondents accepted the anaphoric construal with the matrix-clause subject of the gendered pronouns *lui* and *le* in *à propos de lui* and *le concernant* respectively at similar rates (NNSs: 96%/96%; NSs: 91%/89%). Thus, with respect to the availability of anaphora processes, there was no difference in the availability of the anaphoric construal of *lui* and *le*. Hence, if the availability of an anaphoric construal in general affords processing efficiencies, these efficiencies would not be expected to differ significantly across the N-complement and NP-modifier constructions because an anaphoric construal seems favored to the same degree.

Questions may be used to structure discourse, but also to structure thought. Both tasks involved a context in which a series of questions were asked by a character trying to make sense of a complex situation. In one task, a character, John, was preparing for a French exam on a postmodern novel. However, he could not remember anything about the plot or the characters. Therefore, he wrote down several questions to get the details straight. Respondents were told that they were reading his notes and then answering questions about them to clarify what had happened somewhat. In a second task, a character named Benoît wanted to create a parody of primetime TV comedies. He was searching for real-life material to use. Therefore, he had been trying to remember all the crazy things that people had been saying about other people over the year. Benoît had (also) written up several questions to organize his thoughts. Respondents were told that they were going to read his notes, and answer queries about them to clarify what had happened.

The item presentations in each task were fully randomized for each subject and alternated whether subjects in each group saw the task with queries focusing on the pronoun referent first or whether they saw the task with queries not focusing on the pronoun referent first. This mitigated the order of presentation on the task. If there is an effect of task, we naturally did not want it to be due to the order of tasks. Respondents might become faster as they habituate to doing a task. On both tasks, subjects were told to read as naturally as possible, making sure that they understood what they read. Likewise, they were told to answer comprehension queries as quickly and as accurately as possible. The instruction also included finger placement for quick reading and answering.

Subjects and procedures

Given that it is not always the case that educated NNSs are in every way at a disadvantage in their nonnative language in comparison with NSs, we selected advanced NNSs and NSs of French through personal contact. We recruited advanced NNSs in a nonnaturalistic setting at an English-medium university in the USA. These NNSs were graduate students in their late 20s, and they were training to be language and literature professionals. They were engaged in teaching French at the time of testing. They are, therefore, of advanced proficiency, some with very little foreign accent and few gender errors, but they are not immersed in the target language community. They had spent one year in France on average at the time of testing.

We recruited educated NSs of French in France, so they would be working adults from 18 through 60 years of age. These NSs of French all lived in Paris, France. They all had schooling in two foreign languages including English, but without the experience of living abroad. Any use of English at the time of testing was limited to the educational context and to an occasional encounter in daily life and occasional international travel. These included students, teachers and individuals working in the professions. All individuals were therefore literate. Hence, the performance of these NSs of French will not be affected by active bilingualism. The protocol was approved by an institutional review board.

We ensured that both groups followed a matching protocol. After reviewing procedures, respondents were assigned to Task A with questions on reference or to Task B without questions on reference, they then completed a C-test (Renaud, 2010). The C-test involved two paragraphs with half of every other word missing after the first background sentence providing 50 blanks to be completed. The paragraphs had 74 and 97 words, respectively, and 25 blanks each. The blanks were balanced between open-class and close-class items. This task had to be completed in the limit of 10 minutes; 5 minutes per paragraph. Thereafter, the respondents filled out a biographical questionnaire including age, education, language background and length of exposure. Subjects were then assigned to the second computer-delivered task. The correctness scores were examined to ensure that the NNSs and NSs had the same response outcomes before their processing of the critical stimuli could be examined. We report on a group of advanced NNSs of French ($n = 14$). They have a mean age of 26, ranging from 24 to 30 years of age and a mean C-test score of 48, with a range of 46 through 50. NSs of French ($n = 14$) have a mean age of 36, ranging from 18 to 60 and a mean C-test score of 48 with a range of 46 through 50. Hence, in terms of basic language abilities as measured by the C-test, the NNSs were nondistinct from the NSs. These NNSs are clearly not intermediate learners of French: scores for intermediate learners would cluster around the midpoint under the same conditions (Renaud, 2010).

More central to our point, the NNSs could not be distinguished from the NSs of French in the experimental conditions in which they had to provide answers to questions. These NNSs were clearly not at a disadvantage in the response rates: the accuracy rate of the NNSs on all items over the two tasks (mean – 81%, SD – 4) could not be distinguished from the accuracy rate of the NSs (mean = 80%, SD = 7). The NNSs' accuracy rate on critical items (mean = 87%, SD = 8) also could not be distinguished from that of the NSs (mean = 86%, SD = 11). Across both tasks, the accuracy rate of the NNSs of French on critical items in the task with comprehension questions addressing pronoun reference (mean = 86%, SD = 12) could not be distinguished from the accuracy rate of the NSs (mean = 84%, SD = 17). Similarly, the accuracy rate of the NNSs on critical items in the task with comprehension questions in which the pronoun reference was immaterial (mean = 87%, SD = 8) could not be distinguished from the accuracy rate of NSs (mean = 88%, SD = 12). A general linear model on critical items found no effects of (NS versus NNS) Group Task or Group * Task interaction, $p > 0.4$. The results of a general linear model on all items conducted in SPSS found no significant main effect of (NS versus NNS) Group in these response patterns, $F(1, 26) = 6.446$, $p = 0.555$, nor an interaction of Group with Task, $F(1, 26) = 0.116$, $p = 0.736$. The analysis found a significant main effect of Task, $F(1, 26) = 149.035$, $p < 0.0005$. The NNSs and NSs are statistically tied.

The high rates of expected responses make it very clear that both the NNSs and NSs took these tasks very seriously. They had nondistinct outcomes in response to comprehension queries. Hence, when NNSs perform at high levels in comprehension, will NNSs' reading performance be distinguished in a way suggestive of a syntactic computation or will their performance be the result of a shallow structures processing mode?

Specifically, is there evidence that NNSs' peak reading performance will reflect processing efficiencies linked both to binding along the movement chain and to not having to commit to a value?

Analysis of reading times

The analysis of RTs requires certain procedures that address the nature of reading. It takes a certain amount of time for graphical information to be absorbed and for a word to be identified and integrated into a sentential context. Also, physical aspects such as planning the movement of eyes in normal reading are not immediate. Therefore, RTs below 250 ms were eliminated and replaced by their closest acceptable values. Likewise, RTs beyond 2 standard deviations beyond the mean were adjusted to their closest acceptable values at exactly 2 standard deviations. Both populations were crucially treated by these standards. It has been argued by some that, because NNSs show greater variability than NSs do, a different data treatment keeping values at 2.5 or 3 standard deviations beyond the mean is appropriate for NNSs. A difference in procedures for the two groups, however, contravenes the possibility of direct comparisons, since applying different standards would actually introduce variability. Data pruning and replacement by the closest acceptable values was performed for each group, each condition and each task separately.

RTs are not normally distributed, since it takes a certain amount of time to plan reading and to access lexical knowledge as eyes scan the script, and multiple layers of processing are engaged. For this reason, a Log 10 transformation of adjusted RTs was performed. The Log 10 transformation normalizes the data, so that RTs are normally distributed meeting the assumption of statistical tests, while preserving the structure of the data. A Linear Mixed Model was then performed on Log RTs for each segment, declaring Construction (N-complement/ NP-modifier), Antecedent (Matrix-clause subject match or mismatch), Group (NS versus NNS), Task (Questions requiring commitment to referential values or not), as well as all interactions: Construction * Antecedent, Construction * Antecedent * Group, Construction * Antecedent * Task, Construction * Antecedent * Group * Task as fixed effects, while declaring subjects and items as random effects.[6] This Linear Mixed Model was performed in SPSS. It should be noted that as part of the Linear Mixed Model, SPSS provides both F statistics and Bonferroni corrected pairwise comparisons, which form the basis of this report.[7]

On our working hypothesis, Construction * Antecedent * Group interactions and possibly Construction * Antecedent * Group * Task interactions are expected on the subordinator *que* 'that' (with a possible spillover on the following segment) and on the verb – with a possible spillover on the following segment. Indeed, the subordinator *que* signals a computational cycle constituted by the clausal complement. It confirms that a *wh*-dependency, which could not be resolved in the matrix clause, must now rely on a new phase of computation, so that a binding relation can now be established. Encountering the verb, which provides the central thematic information, confirms the well-formedness of the *wh*-dependency in the embedded clause and reaffirms any anaphoric dependency.

Binding can only be established if the head noun selected a complement as part of the numeration. On each phase of computation, a complement such as *à propos de lui* 'about him' is part of the syntactic representation. Hence, the pronoun can be bound derivationally. With an NP modifier such as *le concernant* 'regarding him', only the head noun is syntactically re-represented on each cycle. As the head noun (alone) is re-represented in syntax, the modification, which includes the pronoun, can be reactivated at the discourse level by its association with the syntactically refreshed head noun information.

Following Reinhart (1983), it is typically assumed that, although not cost free, syntactic binding dependencies provide cost savings with respect to coreference. This predicts efficiencies that are dependent on the availability of binding at crucial moments of the parse. This role for binding determined by cyclic movement chains is unexpected, if nonnative sentence processing involves shallow structures. Nonnative anaphoric processing would then need rely on discourse-level coreference, according to SSH. According to our hypothesis, in contrast, any efficiencies should follow a specific direction as syntax feeds discourse and higher-level processes monitoring the message contained in discourse. Efficiencies owing to not having to commit to a value will combine with efficiencies owing to syntax and will therefore be consistent with trace-theoretic computations.

Results

Figures 4.1 and 4.2 provide a visual of the RTs results for the NSs (Figure 4.1) and NNSs (Figure 4.2) on the task that required commitment to the value of the pronoun for successful completion. This is labeled Task A – questions on reference. Mean RTs for the NNSs were generally as fast as or faster than RTs for the NSs, while the groups still maintained non-distinct accuracy rates. Figures 4.3 and 4.4 provide a visual representation of the RTs results for the NSs and NNSs, respectively, on the task that did not require any commitment to the value of the pronoun for successful completion. Figures 4.3 and 4.4 are labeled Task B – not requiring commitment to a referential value. Again, RTs for the NNSs seemed as fast as or faster than RTs for the NSs, with non-distinct accuracy rates between NS and NNS groups.

It was hypothesized that NNSs' peak reading performance might be reached through chain efficiencies arising from the possibility of binding along the movement chain and from not needing to commit to a referential value in discourse. Efficiencies owing to the movement chain might be found

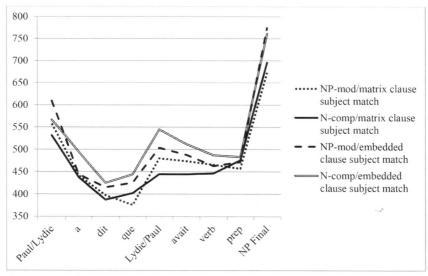

Figure 4.1 Task A – questions on reference: NS RTs

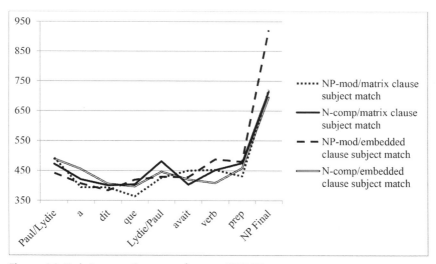

Figure 4.2 Task A – questions on reference: NNS RTs

with expressions tied to specific computational moments allowing binding along the movement chain. These computational moments are the processing of the clause-edge as the structure of the embedded clause is established and the embedded-clause verb as all grammatical relations on the chain are confirmed. Table 4.1 highlights the location of main effects of Task and also of Group in view of the theoretical issues that we have raised.

This group of NNSs was not disadvantaged with respect to the group of NSs at any point during the reading of the propositional content after

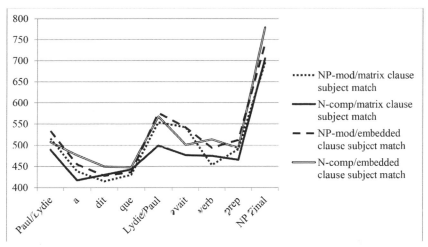

Figure 4.3 Task B – not requiring commitment to a referential value: NS RTs

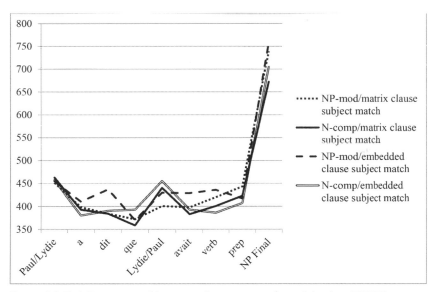

Figure 4.4 Task B – not requiring commitment to a referential value: NNS RTs

the *wh*-expression. There were no significant main effect of Group. No difference approached the statistical margin in RTs. This finding is, therefore, consistent and robust.

The NNSs are within NSs' range both in reading and in the decisions based on the information that they extracted during reading. We now turn to a possible main effect of Task. A main effect of Task was detected on the first antecedent, $F(1, 995.411) = 5.106$, $p = 0.024$, with no further effects. Comprehension queries that focused attention on the identity of the pronoun referent resulted in slower reading of the first

Table 4.1 Summary of main effects of group and task, and interactions with structure

Segments	Task main effect (sig.)	Group main effect (sig.)	Const.*Ant.* Group (sig.)	Const.*Ant. * Task* Group (sig.)
Paul/Lydie	p = 0 .024 ✓	p > 0.3	p > 0.4	p > 0.9
a (aux)	p = 0.061	p > 0.2	p > 0.2	p > 0.5
dit (say)	p > 0.1	p > 0.5	p > 0.6	p > 0.1
que (that)	p > 0.8	p > 0.2	p > 0.9	p = 0.033 ✓
Lydie/Paul	p > 0.2	p > 0.2	p = 0.070	p = 0.077
avait (had)	p > 0.9	p > 0.1	p > 0.7	p > 0.1
verb	p > 0.3	p > 0.3	p = 0.039 ✓	p > 0.1
Prep	p > 0.4	p > 0.4	p > 0.4	p = 0.017 ✓
NPfinal	p > 0.8	p > 0.8	p > 0.3	p = 0.078

Note: The symbol ✓ indicates statistical significance.

NP, which consisted either in a (matching) potential antecedent for the pronoun or not. This was not further modulated by Group; however, the log RTs revealed no main effect of Task on the rest of the sentence beyond a marginal spillover on the auxiliary ($p = 0.061$).[8] Hence, the nature of the comprehension queries distinguishing the two tasks did not generally affect reading speed after an initial effort on the matrix clause subject.

Crucially, a statistically significant Construction * Antecedent * Group * Task interaction was found on the subordinator que 'that', $F(4, 1078) = 2.627$, $p = 0.033$.[9] The mean raw RTs for the subordinator que 'that' across groups and tasks are provided in Table 4.2.

The Bonferroni-corrected pairwise comparisons of contrasts showed that the NSs read the subordinator que 'that' more slowly when the referent value did not matter than when the referent value mattered in the condition requiring coreference (NP-modifier with matching matrix-clause subject): (mean difference, 044; SE, 0.021; df, 1078.000; $p = 0.038$). The NNSs also contributed to the interaction in crucial ways. The NNSs read the subordinator que 'that' more quickly when the value of the pronoun

Table 4.2 Summary of RTs on the cyclic segment que 'that'

	NSs of French		NNSs of French	
	Task A	Task B	Task A	Task B
NP-modifier Matrix clause subject match	376 (108)	430 (184)	364 (100)	372 (121)
N-complement Matrix clause subject match	402 (164)	443 (233)	404 (163)	359 (120)
NP-modifier Embedded clause subject match	425 (173)	436 (166)	420 (201)	370 (107)
N-complement Embedded clause subject match	444 (198)	448 (222)	398 (169)	392 (161)

Note: The standard deviations are given in parentheses.

referent did not matter than when it did only in the condition enabling binding (N-complement with matching matrix-clause subject): (mean difference, 043; SE, 0.021, df, 1078.000; $p = 0.039$).[10]

On the embedded-clause subject segment, there was a Construction * Antecedent * Group interaction at the statistical margin, $F(3, 1013.416) = 2.363$, $p = 0.070$. This was due to the NSs who read the embedded-clause subject marginally more quickly in the context of N-complements with matching matrix-clause subjects than in the context of N-complements with matching embedded-clause subjects (mean difference, 0.050; SE, 0.019, df, 231.768; $p = 0.010$). The possibility of binding seemed therefore to have been distinguished from the other conditions in NSs specifically as the embedded-clause subject was considered. On the embedded clause subject, a marginal Construction * Antecedent * Group * Task, $F(4, 991.234) = 2.117$, $p = 0.077$ was also due to the NSs. NSs took marginally more time with the NP-modifier construction when the referent value did not matter than when the referent value mattered as they encountered a local match in the subordinate clause (mean difference, 0.047; SE, 0.026, df, 988.823; $p = 0.073$). In the absence of the need to commit to a value for the pronoun referent, these NSs seemed to have hesitated slightly at a time when the *wh*-expression might be syntactically reactivated.[11]

Crucially for the theory of movements, a Construction * Antecedent * Group interaction was found on the verb, $F(3, 1008.300) = 2.801$, $p = 0.039$. Table 4.3 provides mean raw RTs on the verb segment across groups and tasks. The pairwise comparisons of contrasts revealed that, when pronouns matched embedded-clause subjects, N-complements induced the NNSs to read the verb more quickly than NP-modifiers did (mean difference, 046; SE, 0.017, df, 189.009; $p = 0.008$). In addition, in the context of N-complements with pronouns matching embedded-clause subjects, the NNSs read the verb segment marginally faster than the NSs (mean difference, 074; SE, 0.042, df, 32.727; $p = 0.087$). This suggests that the N-complement structure plays a clear role in the reading ability of these advanced NNSs. This was followed by a second interaction involving

Table 4.3 Summary of RTs on the thematic verb segment

	NSs of French		NNSs of French	
	Task A	Task B	Task A	Task B
NP-modifier Matrix clause subject match	466 (214)	453 (190)	452 (234)	419 (160)
N-complement Matrix clause subject match	446 (185)	475 (226)	452 (211)	400 (142)
NP-modifier Embedded clause subject match	463 (215)	494 (254)	488 (293)	436 (162)
N-complement Embedded clause subject match	487 (232)	513 (279)	409 (139)	386 (126)

Note: The standard deviations are given in parentheses.

Table 4.4 Summary of RTs on the prepositional segment (spill-over)

	NSs of French		NNSs of French	
	Task A	Task B	Task A	Task B
NP-modifier	457	490	431	443
Matrix clause subject match	(169)	(202)	(114)	(144)
N-complement	476	465	475	423
Matrix clause subject match	(187)	(151)	(168)	(117)
NP-modifier	472	512	480	417
Embedded clause subject match	(174)	(239)	(243)	(129)
N-complement	483	493	458	407
Embedded clause subject match	(190)	(202)	(185)	(116)

Note: The standard deviations are given in parentheses.

Construction, Antecedent, Group and Task on the preposition following the verb segment, $F(4, 984.585) = 3.043$, $p = 0.017$. The mean raw RTs for the preposition across groups and tasks are provided in Table 4.4.

For NP-modifiers with the embedded-clause subject matching the pronoun in gender, the NNSs read the post-verbal preposition more slowly when the referent value mattered than when it did not matter (mean difference, 043; SE, 0.019, df, 982.958; $p = 0.026$). For N-complements with the matrix-clause subject matching the pronoun in gender, the NNSs also read the post-verbal preposition more slowly when the referent value mattered than when it did not matter (mean difference, 043; SE, 0.019, df, 982.958; $p = 0.025$). Finally, for N-complements with the embedded-clause subject matching the pronoun in gender, the NNSs again read the postverbal preposition more slowly when the referent value mattered than when it did not matter (mean difference, 041; SE, 0.019, df, 982.958; $p = 0.032$).[12] Finally, we note a marginal Construction * Antecedent * Group * Task interaction on the final noun segment following the preposition, $F(4, 987.562) = 2.110$, $p = 0.078$. This marginal effect was due to the NNSs taking marginally more time reading the final segment when comprehension queries focused on the value of the pronoun than when they did not. Specifically this occurred in the NP-modifier condition when the pronoun could corefer with the embedded-clause subject: mean difference, 055; SE, 0.031, df, 985.482; $p = 0.076$.

Discussion

In a self-paced reading experiment involving two tasks with comprehension queries focusing on distinct information units, a group of advanced NNSs of French could not be distinguished from a group of working-age educated NSs in global reading speed and in their extraction of information as measured by accuracy rates. Indeed, there was no significant overall RT difference nor was there any significant difference in accuracy rates between the two groups. However, at critical chain-theoretic processing moments in the task eliminating the need for referential commitment, the NNSs distinguished themselves from the NSs in reading speed. The effect of the syntactic mechanism is prima facie visible in reflexes of syntactic computations, most notably the availability of binding with complements such as *à propos de lui* 'about him', which are syntactically represented on every cycle along a movement chain. Hence, there is prima facie evidence supporting a syntactic mechanism in structural effects at critical chain-theoretic processing moments. These are the subordinator *que* 'that' marking the edge of the embedded clause and the embedded-clause verb. There is also prima facie evidence supporting a general attention control mechanism in effects of tasks that manipulate the focus of attention on parts of the message, in view of the information that is sought.

Main effects of Task in RTs were limited to the matrix-clause subject, but the tasks modulated structural effects that were found at crucial moments in the computation of *wh*-movement chains. Effects involving structure at the clause edge on the subordinator and the verb (and the following prepositional segment) suggest the role of a domain-specific computational system. The subordinator verifies a new cycle of computations for the embedded clause and the verb domain provides the central thematic information. As the subordinator was processed, the possibility of a syntactically mediated binding relation led to asymmetries in the NNSs. With N-complements as the matrix-clause subject matched the pronoun (enabling binding), the NNSs read the subordinator *que* 'that' more quickly when the task did not require any commitment to the pronoun value than when it did. The significance of the syntactic context allowing binding suggests efficiencies that are enabled by a domain-specific computational system in a nonnative language. Faster reading by the NNSs modulated by task suggests a superimposition of two levels of processing, in which efficiencies owing to a binding computation combined with efficiencies due to not having to either commit to this construal or reject it. With an NP-complement with a matrix-clause subject matching the pronoun (enabling coreference), the NSs read the subordinator *que* 'that' more slowly when the task required no commitment to the pronoun value than when the referent value mattered in the condition requiring coreference. Slower reading by the NSs modulated by task again suggests a superimposition of two effects, in which the need to commit to a value helped the assignment of a value, whereas the focus of attention directed away from the pronoun referent seems to have induced additional costs at the embedded clause edge, presumably as the memory system dealt with referential uncertainty in a group of NS respondents unfamiliar with this testing modality.

As the verb provides the central thematic information for the embedded clause, the possibility of a syntactically mediated binding relation led to faster reading by the NNSs. N-complements with matching embedded-clause subjects induced the NNSs to read the verb generally more quickly than NP-modifiers did. For N-complements with the matrix-clause subject matching the pronoun in gender, the NNSs also read the postverbal preposition more slowly when the focus of attention was on the pronoun referent. Finally, for N-complements with the embedded-clause subject matching the pronoun in gender, the NNSs read the postverbal preposition more slowly when the referent value mattered than when it did not matter. This is generally expected since the clause-mate binding of the pronoun within the NP domain is expected to involve a strategy in which the calculation of an NP-subject (Chomsky, 1995) allows the NP to be construed as the binding domain for the pronoun. Increased processing loads have been reported in the literature for NSs and NNSs under these conditions (Dekydtspotter *et al.*, 2012).

In sum, the location and nature of effects suggest a role for the information carried across cycles of *wh*-movement computations. The modulation by task suggests the role of attention on distinct aspects of the message. Two distinct but interacting levels of processing are in evidence. The fact that the role of task was not a constant across types of anaphoric construal, but mediated by syntax-discourse processes of anaphora, seems highly theoretically significant.

Conclusion and Perspectives

Advanced NNSs have been shown to compute detailed syntactic representations in real time (see Pliatsikas & Marinis' (2012) replication of Marinis *et al.* (2005) showing structural effects in fluent learners in conditions of naturalistic input). The strong version of the SSH, claiming shallow structures across the spectrum as a general mode of operation in nonnative sentence processing (Clahsen & Felser, 2006a, 2006b) seems to have led to a compromise position by recognizing the possibility of structural processing under conditions of naturalistic exposure (Pliatsikas & Marinis, 2012) and task focusing on grammaticality (Roberts, 2013). This compromise position still views detailed syntactic representations as a computational luxury that is only accessed under these special conditions. However, for Hopp (2015) and for Lim and Christianson (2013a, 2013b), nonnative sentence processing falls within the same model involving both semantic-heuristic and syntactical processing steps (Ferreira *et al.*, 2002).

For our part, we noted that syntax seems to provide computational benefits that should be advantageous. We argued that, in parallel processing by modules interacting in the limits of their interfaces, depth of processing might be characterized by the degree to which partial information across distinct levels align and the degree to which commitment to the specifics of the message is required. We reported on a group of NNSs of French who are of advanced language proficiency, but who were not in a naturalistic setting nor gave grammaticality judgments. However, they answered information queries about the information content associated with *wh*-movement structures at the very same rate as NSs. More to the point, patterns of NS-NNs RT differences revealed that syntax interacted with task in eking out efficiencies for these NNSs. The location of these efficiencies in part reflected the integration of N-complements versus NP-modifiers in the computation of cyclic *wh*-movement chains.

Notes

(1) There are different views. See Carroll (2002) for autonomous inductive learning and O'Grady (2013) for a view of grammatical development as parsing enhancement that rejects a calculus of domain-specific categories and operations.

(2) However, these pronouns may receive some other individual (masculine) value determined by the discourse context.

(3) The expressions *à propos/au sujet* 'about' as arguments of nouns allow extractions (i.) whereas *concernant* 'regarding' as a modifier does not.
   (i) A *propos/au sujet de qui$_i$ Lydie a-t-elle rejeté une décision ec$_i$?*
       'Who(m) did Lydia reject a decision about?'
   (ii) **Concernant qui$_i$ Lydie a-t-elle rejeté une décision ec$_i$?*
       '*Who(m) did Lydia reject a decision regarding?'

(4) An anonymous reviewer pointed out that co-reference judgments vary on these constructions.

(5) This requires that binding be the preferred mechanism for resolving anaphoric dependencies whenever possible (Reinhart & Reuland, 1993). Indeed, it is widely assumed that, if available, a binding construal is preferred over a coreference construal (Koornneet *et al.*, 2011; Reuland, 2001; Reinhart & Reuland, 1993; cf. Cunnings *et al.*, 2014).

(6) On the segments, *dit* 'said', *que* 'that' and *avait* 'had', the variance for the item parameter was null, so that the items were removed for the model.

(7) Groups appear nondistinct on most dimensions except for significant interactions group and task with structural conditions that appear in critical regions linked to *wh*-movement. As noted by an anonymous reviewer, Bayesian testing enables stronger claims about similarities between groups. This is at the cost of conclusion about differences. Exploring similarity more in depth offers an interesting and relatively unexplored line of thought to pursue in a difference-oriented field. However, the current argument is based on the significance of distinctions arising in critical regions. The lack of significance on non-critical regions does not enter into the argument except to offer a contrast to the presence of significant condition-related differences due to group and task in specific critical regions.

(8) On the auxiliary, a main effect of Antecedent was found ($p = 0.034$).

(9) On the verb *dit* 'said', the analysis only revealed a main effect of Antecedent ($p = 0.038$).

(10) On the subordinator *que* 'that', the analysis also revealed a main effect of Antecedent ($p = 0.006$).

(11) On the embedded-clause subject, the analysis again revealed a marginal main effect of Antecedent ($p = 0.089$).

(12) On the embedded-clause auxiliary, the analysis revealed main effects of Construction ($p = 0.023$) and Antecedent ($p = 0.030$).

References

Baddeley, A.D. (2017) The concept of working memory: A view of its current state and probable future development. In A. Baddeley (ed.) *Exploring Working Memory* (pp. 99–106). London: Routledge.

Birdsong, D. (1992) Ultimate attainment in second language acquisition. *Language* 68, 706–755.

Carroll, S. (2002) Induction in a modular learner. *Second Language Research* 18 (3), 224–249.

Chomsky, N. (1986) *Knowledge of Language: Its Nature, Origin, and Use.* New York: Praeger Publishers.

Chomsky, N. (1995) *The Minimalist Program.* Cambridge, MA: MIT Press.

Chomsky, N. (2005) Three factors in language design. *Linguistic Inquiry* 36, 1–32.

Chomsky, N. (2008) On phases. In R. Freidin, C.P. Otero and M.L. Zubizarreta (eds) *Foundational Issues in Linguistic Theory* (pp. 133–166). Cambridge, MA: The MIT Press.

Clahsen, H. and Felser, C. (2006a) Continuity and shallow structures in language processing. *Applied Psycholinguistics* 27, 107–126.

Clahsen, H. and Felser, C. (2006b) Grammatical processing in language learning. *Applied Psycholinguistics* 27, 3–42.

Crocker, M. (1996) *Computational Psycholinguistics: An Interdisciplinary Approach to the Study of Language.* Dordrecht: Kluwer.

Cunnings, I., Patterson, C. and Felser, C. (2014) Variable binding and coreference in sentence comprehension: Evidence from eye movements. *Journal of Memory and Language* 7 (1), 39–56.

Dekydtspotter, L. (2001) The universal parser and interlanguage: Domain-specific mental organization in the comprehension of *combien* interrogatives in English-French interlanguage. *Second Language Research* 17, 91–143.

Dekydtspotter, L. and Miller, K. (2013) Inhibitive and facilitative priming induced by traces in the processing of *wh*-dependencies in a second language. *Second Language Research* 29, 345–372.

Dekydtspotter, L. and Renaud, C. (2014) On second language processing and grammatical development: The parser in second language acquisition. *Linguistic Approaches to Bilingualism* 4 (2), 131–165.

Dekydtspotter, L., Schwartz, B.D. and Sprouse, R. (2006) The comparative fallacy in L2 processing research. In M. O'Brien, C. Shea and J. Archibald (eds) *Proceedings of the 8th Generative Approaches to Second Language Acquisition Conference* (GASLA 2006) (pp. 33–40). Somerville, MA: Cascadilla.

Dekydtspotter, L., Wang, Y.T., Kim, B., Kim H.J., Kim, H.K. and Lee, J-K. (2012) Anaphora under reconstruction during processing in English as a second language. *Studies in Second Language Acquisition* 34, 561–590.

Ferreira, F., Bailey, K. and Ferraro, V. (2002) Good-enough representations in language comprehension. *Current Directions in Psychological Science* 11, 11–15.

Felser, C., Cunnings, I., Batterham, C. and Clahsen, H. (2012) The timing of island effects in nonnative sentence processing. *Studies in Second Language Acquisition* 34 (1), 67–98.

Fodor, J. (1983) *The Modularity of Mind: An Essay on Faculty Psychology.* Cambridge, MA: MIT Press.

Fodor, J. (2001) *The Mind Doesn't Work That Way: The Scope and Limits of Computational Psychology.* Cambridge, MA: MIT Press.

Freidin, R. (1986) Fundamental issues in the theory of binding. In B. Lust (ed.) *Studies in the Acquisition of Anaphora* (Vol. I) (pp. 151–188). Dordrecht: Reidel.

Frimu, R. (2017) Non-linguistic cognitive dimensions of subject-verb agreement error detection in (L2) French. Doctoral dissertation, Indiana University.

Heim, I. and Kratzer, A. (1998) *Semantics in Generative Grammar* (Vol. 1185). Oxford: Blackwell.

Herschensohn, J. (1997) Parametric variation in French L2 speakers. In E. Hughes, M. Hughes and A. Greenhill (eds) *Proceedings of the Twenty-first Annual Boston University Conference on Language Development* (pp. 281–292). Somerville, MA: Cascadilla Press.

Hopp, H. (2010) Ultimate attainment in L2 inflection: Performance similarities between non-native and native speakers. *Lingua* 120 (4), 901–931.

Hopp, H. (2013) Grammatical gender in adult L2 acquisition: Relations between lexical and syntactic variability. *Second Language Research* 29, 33–56.

Hopp, H. (2015) Individual differences in the second language processing of object–subject ambiguities. *Applied Psycholinguistics* 36 (2), 129–173.

Hopp, H. (2016) Learning (not) to predict: Grammatical gender processing in second language acquisition. *Second Language Research* 32, 277–316.

Kaan, E., Dallas, A. and Wijnen, F. (2010) Syntactic predictions in second-language sentence processing. In J-W. Zwart and M. de Vries (eds) *Structure Preserved. Festschrift in the Honor of Jan Koster* (pp. 207–213). Cambridge: Cambridge University Press.

Koornneef, A.W., Avrutin, S., Wijnen, F. and Reuland, E. (2011) Tracking the preference for bound-variable dependencies in ambiguous ellipses and only-structures. In J.T. Runner (ed.) *Experiments at the Interfaces* (pp. 67–100). Leiden: Brill.

Lebeaux, D. (1988) *Language Acquisition and the Form of Grammar*. Amsterdam: Benjamins.

Lew-Williams, C. and Fernald, A. (2010) Real-time processing of gender-marked articles by native and non-native Spanish speakers. *Journal of Memory and Language* 63, 447–464.

Lim, J.H. and Christianson, K. (2013a) Second language sentence processing in reading for comprehension and translation. *Bilingualism: Language and Cognition* 16, 518–537, doi: 10.1017/S1366728912000351.

Lim, J.H. and Christianson, K. (2013b) Integrating meaning and structure in L1–L2 and L2–L1 translations. *Second Language Research* 29 (3), 233–256.

López-Prego, B. and Gabriele, A. (2014) Examining the impact of task demands on morphological variability in native and non-native Spanish. *Linguistic Approaches to Bilingualism* 4, 192–221.

Marinis, T., Roberts, R., Felser, C. and Clahsen, H. (2005) Gaps in second language sentence processing. *Studies in Second Language Acquisition* 27 (1), 53–78.

McDonald, J.L. (2006) Beyond the critical period: Processing-based explanations for poor grammaticality judgment performance by late second language learners. *Journal of Memory and Language* 55, 381–401.

Miller, K. (2014) Accessing and maintaining referents in L2 processing of wh-dependencies. *Linguistic Approaches to Bilingualism* 4 (2), 167–191.

Miller, K. (2015) Intermediate traces and intermediate learners. Evidence for the use of intermediate structure during sentence processing in second language French studies. *Second Language Acquisition* 37, 487–516, https://doi.org/10.1017/S0272263114000588.

O'Grady, W. (2013) The illusion of language acquisition. *Linguistic Approaches to Bilingualism* 3, 253–285.

Pliatsikas, C. and Marinis, T. (2012) Processing empty categories in a second language: When naturalistic exposure fills the (intermediate) gap. *Bilingualism: Language and Cognition* 1, 1–16.

Reinhart, T. (1983) *Anaphora and Semantic Interpretation*. Chicago: University of Chicago Press.

Reinhart, T. and Reuland, E. (1993) Reflexivity. *Linguistic Inquiry* 24 (4), 657–720.

Renaud, C. (2010) On the nature of agreement in English-French acquisition: A processing investigation in the verbal and nominal domains. PhD thesis, Rutgers University: The State University of New Jersey.

Reuland, E. (2001) Primitives of binding. *Linguistic Inquiry* 32, 430–492.

Rizzi, L. (2013) Locality. *Lingua* 13, 169–186.

Rohde, D. (2003) *Linger*. Available at: http://tedlab.mit.edu/~dr/Linger/ (accessed 3 June 2009).

Roberts, L. (2013) Sentence processing in bilinguals. In R.P.G. van Gompel (ed.) *Sentence Processing* (pp. 221–246). Hove: Psychology Press.

Sportiche, D. (2006) Reconstruction, binding, and scope. In M. Everaert and H. van Riemsdijk (eds) *The Blackwell Companion to Syntax* (Vol. 1) (pp. 35–93). Oxford: Blackwell.

Stewart, A.J., Holler, J. and Kidd, E. (2007) Shallow processing of ambiguous pronouns: Evidence for delay. *The Quarterly Journal of Experimental Psychology* 60 (12), 1680–1696.

Truscott, J. and Sharwood-Smith, M. (2004) Acquisition by processing: A modular perspective on language development. *Bilingualism: Language and Cognition* 7 (1), 1–20.

Townsend, D.J. and Bever, T. (2001) *Sentence Comprehension: The Integration of Habits and Rules*. Cambridge, MA: MIT Press.

van Riemsdijk, H. and Williams, E. (1981) NP-structure. *The Linguistic Review* 1 (2), 171–218.

5 Age Effects and Morphological Markedness in L2 Processing of Gender Agreement: Insights from Eye Tracking

Nuria Sagarra

1 Introduction

Age of acquisition has been a debatable topic for decades. Some scholars maintain that puberty establishes an insurmountable critical period to learn a second language, L2 (Representational Deficit Hypothesis, RDH, Hawkins, 2009; Interpretability Hypothesis, IH, Tsimpli & Dimitrakopoulou, 2007). In contrast, others advocate for the possibility for learners to gain native-like proficiency in the L2, and provide a myriad of explanations for adult L2 learners' errors. First, some generativist models associate L2 errors with representational problems with morphosyntax (Feature Reassembly Hypothesis, FRH, Lardiere, 2005) and inflectional morphology (Morphological Underspecification Hypothesis, MUH, McCarthy, 2008). Other generativist models attribute L2 errors to processing constraints (Missing Surface Inflectional Hypothesis, MSIH, Haznedar & Schwartz, 1997; Prévost & White, 2000; Parser-as-Language-Acquisition-Device, PLADH, Dekydtspotter & Renaud, 2009, 2014; Shallow Structure Hypothesis, SSH, Clahsen & Felser, 2006, 2017). Finally, connectionist models link L2 errors to the learners' limited experience with the L2, the nonsalience nature of bound morphemes, and cue availability and reliability (e.g. Associative Cognitive Construction-based, Rational, Exemplar-driven, Emergent and Dialectic, CREED, Ellis, 2006; Unified Competition Model, see MacWhinney, 2012, for a review; statistical learning models, such as Romberg & Saffran, 2010). This issue has been widely investigated with native speakers of genderless languages (e.g. English) acquiring gender agreement in gendered L2s (e.g. Spanish) during adulthood; however, studies on the topic are contradictory.

Critically, most studies are offline, and the ones that are online have used explicit tasks (grammaticality judgments) or noncumulative tasks (the moving windows paradigm in self-paced reading studies, or rapid serial visual presentation in event-related potential (ERP) studies).[1] This is problematic, because explicit tasks are more challenging than implicit tasks (e.g. Roberts, 2012), and noncumulative tasks are more demanding than cumulative tasks that allow readers to regress when needed (Sagarra & Seibert Hanson, 2011). These characteristics could have imposed additional cognitive demands and biased the results. Furthermore, of all the offline and online studies on the topic, only a few have examined morphological markedness explanations for L2 morphological variability, and all of them have employed explicit tasks (see Alemán Bañón et al., 2017, for a review). Because explicit tasks may be cognitively costlier than implicit tasks and the processing of markedness is associated with cognitive load (marked forms are more difficult to process than default forms; Dekydtspotter & Renaud, 2009, 2014), the results of these online studies need to be examined critically.

This chapter tests current representational and processing explanations for L2 inflectional variability. In particular, it investigates the effects of age (whether adult learners can process L2 grammatical dependencies absent in their L1 like native speakers), and morphological markednesss (e.g. whether agreement with feminine/marked nouns is more difficult than with masculine/default nouns) in Anglophones' processing of grammatical gender agreement in L2 Spanish. To overcome the methodological limitations of previous online gender studies (i.e. possible confusion of limitations owing to the learners acquiring the L2 postpuberty or to the methodology, task and dependency being too difficult), it employs the least taxing online methodology (eye tracking, Sagarra & Seibert Hanson, 2011), task type (implicit, Roberts, 2012), noun termination (transparent, Bordag et al., 2006) and dependency (adjacent, Keating, 2009).

2 The Linguistic Phenomenon

In Spanish, nouns have gender (masculine, feminine) and number (singular, plural) (Carroll, 1989). Transparent nouns are marked with the inflectional morphemes /-o/ for masculine (M) gender (vestido 'dress$_M$'), and /-a/ for feminine (F) gender (camisa 'shirt$_F$'). About 34% of singular nouns violate this rule, making the gender suffix less reliable than the number suffix. Gender is determined naturally (based on biological sex) in animate nouns, and arbitrarily in inanimate nouns (Corbett, 1991). Plurality (P) is formed by adding /-s/ to singular (S) count nouns ending in /-o/ or /-a/ (vestidos 'dresses$_{MP}$'; camisas 'shirts$_{FP}$'), /-es/ to nouns ending in a consonant (*relojes* 'clocks$_{MP}$'; *sartenes* 'pans$_{FP}$') and rarely, nothing is added to nouns already ending in /-s/ (*atlas* 'atlas$_{MS,MP}$'; *tesis* 'thesis$_{FS,FP}$') (Saporta, 1965). In Spanish, the most frequent gender is masculine (Battistella, 1990; Bonet, 1995) and the most frequent number is singular (Battistella, 1990; McCarthy, 2008), making masculine singular the default form (Harley & Ritter, 2002). Determiners, adjectives, pronouns and past participles agree in gender and number with the noun they modify (Carroll, 1989; Zagona, 2002) (*el vestido nuevo* 'the$_{MS}$ dress$_{MS}$ new$_{MS}$'; *los vestidos nuevos* 'the$_{MP}$ dresses$_{MP}$ new$_{MP}$'; *la camisa nueva* 'the$_{FS}$ shirt$_{FS}$ new$_{FS}$'; *las camisas nuevas* 'the$_{FP}$ shirts$_{FP}$ new$_{FP}$').

In English, nouns lack gender inflectional marking, there is no gender agreement, no number agreement between nouns and adjectives or past participles, and limited number agreement between nouns and some determiners (*this–these; that–those*). Thus, when acquiring Spanish, Anglophones must learn gender marking for inanimate nouns, gender agreement between nouns and determiners, and gender and number agreement between nouns and adjectives.

3 Theoretical Explanations for L2 Inflectional Difficulties

Children acquire inflectional morphology early (e.g. Carroll, 1989; Pérez-Pereira, 1991), but adult L2 learners struggle to acquire grammatical information absent in their L1. For example, in Guillelmon and Grosjean's (2001) seminal study, early English-French bilinguals showed facilitation and inhibition effects in response to congruent and incongruent gender marking, but late English-French bilinguals were insensitive to gender congruency-incongruency differences. The debate centers around whether the challenges are lasting or temporary, and on whether the nonnativelike behavior is caused by representational or processing factors.

3.1 Representational explanations for L2 inflectional difficulties

Generative approaches assume that learners build an interlanguage grammar (mental representations) based on input, an innate language acquisition device and universal language principles (for a review, see Slabakova, 2006). Linguistic knowledge involves syntactic operations whose goal is to merge and remerge lexical items, and spell out syntactic objects that can converge at the semantic and phonological interfaces. Syntactic outputs converge when all the features that the lexical items contain are interpretable at these interfaces, or are valued and deleted before being spelled out (Pesetsky & Torrego, 2004). Features can be semantically interpretable (e.g. biological gender, number) or grammatically uninterpretable (e.g. gender and number agreement). For example, a grammatical feature such as number in Spanish is interpretable in nouns, but uninterpretable in adjectives. Consequently, the interpretable number in nouns values and deletes the uninterpretable number feature in adjectives. Once this is done, a Spanish noun phrase involving a noun and an adjective can converge at the interfaces, since it does not contain any uninterpretable features. In order to comply with principles of economy and efficient computation, the syntactic operations can take place by manipulating an underspecified or default form when it comes to valuing and deleting bundle of features representing gender and number – or any other type of grammatical features. As these features are abstract when the syntax manipulates them with their lexical items, they are spelled out by the morphological component – that is, the morphological level of representation after the syntactic spell-out – by inserting the corresponding inflectional material for those features (Halle & Marantz, 1993; Harley & Noyer, 1999). Relevant to the present study, interpretable features are available through adulthood, whereas there is debate about whether uninterpretable features can be acquired postpuberty if absent in the learner's L1. Some generative models claim that adults can acquire new L2 semantic representations (e.g. biological gender, tense, aspect, number, which are interpretable features), but only L2 grammatical representations (e.g. case, grammatical gender, uninterpretable features) already instantiated in their L1 (e.g. RDH, Hawkins, 2009; IH, Tsimpli & Dimitrakopoulou, 2007). For the present study, these limited accessibility models predict that English learners of Spanish will be insensitive to N-A gender and number agreement violations, because both uninterpretable features are absent in their L1.

Other generativist models argue that adult L2 learners can acquire new grammatical representations, and that their inflectional variability is due to lack of enough consistent evidence in the input to (re)assemble new L2 uninterpretable features appropriately, typical of early stages of Second Language Acquisition (SLA) (FRH, Lardiere, 2005, 2009). Therefore, English learners of Spanish will have more difficulties processing gender than number agreement, because the interpretable feature of number, but not gender, marking is present in their L1.

The models described so far claim that L2 morphological variability is due to difficulties acquiring L2 syntactic representations absent in the L1. McCarthy's (2008) MUH argues that the problem lies in forming new *morphological* representations. Under MUH, morphological variability is due to morphological representational deficits, L2 preference for default forms in comprehension and production, and variability to forms present and absent in the L1 (MUH, McCarthy, 2008). Consequently, English learners of Spanish will accept and produce more *default errors*, also called *feature mismatch errors* (*falda nuevo* "*skirt$_{FS}$ new$_{MS}$*') than *feature clash errors* (*libro blanca* "*book$_{MS}$ white$_{FS}$*'). The distinction between these two types of errors follows from current morphosyntactic characterizations of linguistic levels of knowledge in theoretical linguistics, principles of economy and efficient computation, and cognitive costs (e.g. Carstens, 2000; Chomsky, 2000; Pesetsky & Torrego, 2004). To overcome possible default errors in output (e.g. *falda nuevo*) in which the underspecified uninterpretable gender feature of the goal is valued by the interpretable gender feature of the feminine noun, the morphology component applies a subset principle (Halle, 1997), which constrains spell-out computations inserting default forms by choosing the more specified form (*nueva*) during lexical competition. Against this background, default errors by second language learners (*falda nuevo*) are argued to be more frequent than feature clash errors since they are less cognitively costly in terms of syntactic computations, lexical insertion and working memory (cf. Dekydtspotter & Renaud, 2014) than the former. This is because feature clash errors involve extra cognitive costs as they require the application of the subset principle, an extra computational step not happening with default errors.

3.2 Processing explanations for L2 inflectional difficulties

Some scholars explore the importance of processing explanations and argue that L2 morphological variability is mostly caused by processing constraints, linguistic characteristics or language experience, and that adults can reach native-like proficiency in an L2. Processing constraints include production under time pressure (MSIH, Haznedar & Schwartz, 1997; Prévost & White, 2000), shallow processing (SSH, Clahsen & Felser, 2006, 2017), parsing restrictions (PLADH, Dekydtspotter & Renaud, 2009, 2014) and limited cognitive resources (e.g. working memory, WM).

First, the MSIH assumes that feminine and plural are fully specified (marked), but masculine and singular are underspecified (default). Although learners can acquire syntactic and morphological features, they struggle to retrieve the latter under communicative pressure, so that, for example, English learners of Spanish will erroneously produce default gender suffixes (*falda nuevo* '*skirt$_{FS}$ new$_{MS}$*'), but not marked gender suffixes (*vestido nueva* 'dress$_{MS}$ new$_{FS}$'). Second, the SSH posits that L2 learners tend to process inflected words as whole words (rather than decomposing them as monolinguals do). This is so, because L2 learners tend to attend more to semantic, pragmatic, probabilistic or other types of nongrammatical information than to morphological and syntactic information. This nonnative processing behavior is the result of a shallower L2 representation, difficulty applying some grammar violation constraints during real-time comprehension, linguistic complexity and age effects. This model predicts that English learners of Spanish will show a reduced ability to use grammatical information during processing, but it remains agnostic as to whether this impairment is permanent or not. Third, the PLADH postulates that adults can overcome L2 inflectional variability, and that such variability is caused by parsing constraints on a feature (re)assembly process guided by a universal human language parser. If true, L1 English-L2 Spanish learners should be more sensitive to feature clash errors (*vestido nueva* 'dress$_{MS}$ new$_{FS}$') than default errors (*falda* *nuevo* '*skirt$_{FS}$ new$_{MS}$'). Fourth, some scholars argue that L2 inflectional difficulties are partially due to WM limitations (higher WM span learners are more sensitive to gender agreement violations than lower WM span learners, Sagarra & Herschensohn, 2010).

Other approaches explain L2 morphological variability in terms of linguistic and language experience effects on processing. Linguistic factors include noun animacy (Sagarra & Herschensohn, 2011), salience (e.g. Jiang, 2004; Renaud, 2014; Sato & Felser, 2008; Zobl & Liceras, 1994) and linear distance between the agreeing elements (Keating, 2009, 2010). Language experience factors include L1 transfer and L2 proficiency. Most domain-specific models (e.g. Franceschina, 2005; Hawkins, 2009; Hopp, 2009; Sabourin & Stowe, 2008; Tsimpli & Dimitrakopoulou, 2007) and domain-general models (e.g. DeKeyser, 2007; Ellis, 2006; MacWhinney, 2005, 2012; Sagarra & Ellis, 2013) agree that adult learners' L1 affects SLA.

With regard to L2 proficiency, numerous studies show sensitivity to gender agreement violations at higher, but not lower, proficiency levels (see Section 4.1 below for more information). This is so because highly proficient learners have been exposed to more L2 input and are better at identifying the probabilistic patterns needed to process the L2 quickly and effectively (MacWhinney, 1987; Romberg & Saffran, 2010). Like children, L2 learners start relying on available cues based on frequency and they gradually learn to rely on reliable cues based on distributional regularities (Unified Competition Model, UCM, MacWhinney, 2012). Thus, L2 learners make gender assignment errors while speaking until they gain enough proficiency and knowledge of lexical gender (Hopp, 2013; see also Caffarra *et al.*, 2017, for evidence against this proposal).

4 Studies on Grammatical Gender Agreement

4.1 Age effects in adult L2 learners

Offline and online studies on whether adult L2 learners of genderless L1s can acquire and process grammatical gender and number agreement in L2 Spanish are as variable and inconclusive as the theoretical models described in the previous section. On the one hand, the data of some studies suggest a permanent failure to reach native-like levels in adult SLA. For example, Franceschina and colleagues' offline studies show that Italians (gendered L1) are better at perceiving (Franceschina, 2002) and producing (Franceschina, 2001; Hawkins & Franceschina, 2004) D-N and N-A gender and number agreement in L2 Spanish than Anglophones (ungendered L1), who overuse masculine singular default forms (see Franceschina, 2005, for a review). Other studies have reported similar findings in L2 Spanish learners of other L1s (e.g. Chinese: Cuza *et al.*, 2013; Brazilian Portuguese: Borgonovo *et al.*, 2006; English: McCarthy, 2008), even at near-native levels (English: Valenzuela, 2005).

These studies employ offline techniques and cannot determine whether adult L2 learners exhibit the same limitations while processing the L2 during real time. Also, L2 learners can show sensitivity to gender agreement violations in offline, but not online, measures (e.g. nominal agreement: Sagarra & Herschensohn, 2010), or the opposite, in online, but not offline, measures (e.g. nominal agreement: Tokowicz & MacWhinney, 2005). Some online behavioral studies indicate that Anglophones are insensitive to D-N gender agreement violations by L2 learners of Dutch (e.g. Meulman *et al.*, 2014; Sabourin, 2003; Sabourin & Stowe, 2008), French (Guillelmon & Grosjean, 2001) and Spanish (Foote, 2011; Keating, 2009). Because these studies are based on Anglophones, and English lacks gender, they cannot tease apart inflectional difficulties owing to the L1 or to other factors. However, studies examining gender agreement in advanced learners of gendered L1s also show inflectional variability. This suggests that L2 difficulties are due to factors besides the L1.

In contrast to the aforementioned studies, others suggest that it is possible to overcome the barriers to attain nativelikeness in adult SLA, with enough knowledge of lexical gender and increased proficiency. For instance, offline data show that highly proficient learners can acquire new grammatical structures, such as D-N and N-A gender and number agreement (Bruhn de Garavito & White, 2002; Gess & Herschensohn, 2001; Herschensohn, 2001; Herschensohn & Arteaga-Capen, 2007; Prévost, 2004; White *et al.*, 2004).

Likewise, online behavioral studies reveal that highly proficient Anglophone learners are sensitive to D-N and N-A gender disagreement (L2 French: Foucart & Frenck-Mestre, 2012; Herschensohn & Frenck-Mestre, 2005; L2 Spanish: Sagarra & Herschensohn, 2010), but lower proficiency learners are not (L2 French: Osterhout *et al.*, 2008; L2 Spanish: Alarcón, 2009; Keating, 2009; Sagarra & Herschensohn, 2010; Tokowicz & MacWhinney, 2005). Furthermore, high, but not low, proficiency L1 English-L2 Spanish learners use L2 determiners' gender to anticipate incoming nouns like Spanish monolinguals (Lew-Williams & Fernald, 2010 and Italian-Spanish learners (Dussias *et al.*, 2013).

Online neurocognitive studies offer a similar scenario. First, D-N gender agreement violations elicit a Left Anterior Negativity (LAN) and a Positive 600 (P600) effect (both effects are associated with sensitivity to grammatical violations) in higher proficiency learners (L2 Spanish: Gillon-Dowens *et al.*, 2010; Rossi *et al.*, 2006). However, D-N gender agreement violations do not produce LAN (L2 German: Hahne & Friederici, 2001), P600 (L2 English: Weber-Fox & Neville, 1996), a delayed P600 (L2 Spanish: Rossi *et al.*, 2006) or a Negative 400 (N400) (an effect linked to sensitivity to semantic anomalies, L2 Spanish: Morgan-Short *et al.*, 2010) in lower proficiency learners (Tokowicz & MacWhinney, 2005 found P600 effects, but their L1 English-L2 Spanish learner group included both beginners and intermediates). Second, particularly relevant for the current study,

N-A gender agreement violations generate a P600 effect in intermediate (Bond *et al.*, 2011; Gabriele *et al.*, 2013) and advanced (Alemán Bañón *et al.*, 2014, 2017; Gabriele *et al.*, 2013) L1 English-L2 Spanish learners, but not in beginning L1 English-L2 Spanish learners (Gabriele *et al.*, 2013). Third, in the verbal domain, gender and number agreement violations produce a P600 effect in intermediate (subject-verb agreement: Bond *et al.*, 2011) and advanced (object-clitic agreement: Rossi *et al.*, 2014) L1 English-L2 Spanish learners. For a review of other neurocognitive studies showing native-like brain activity at very high levels of proficiency, see Steinhauer *et al.* (2009). Finally, some of these ERP studies have used an additional offline task and show that L2 learners of gender-free L1s perform at ceiling (i.e. they exhibit native-like representation, e.g. Alemán Bañón *et al.*, 2014; Gabriele *et al.*, 2013; Gillon-Dowens *et al.*, 2010).

Taken together, previous offline and online studies suggest that native speakers of genderless L1s can gain representation and processing of grammatical gender agreement, provided they have knowledge of lexical gender and high proficiency. Native-like representation is measured via production errors and in processing via sensitivity to gender agreement errors. However, not all errors are alike: default errors are far more frequent than feature clash errors. Yet, only a handful of L2 studies examine morphological markedness and WM.

4.2 Morphological markedness

The Distributed Morphology (DM) model (Halle & Marantz, 1993) postulates that morphological features are organized into hierarchies: underspecified or unmarked morphemes (default) simply indicates the presence of a feature (e.g. gender, for masculine gender), and specified or marked morphemes indicates the type of feature (e.g. feminine, for feminine gender, Harley & Ritter, 2002). Default items are more frequent and have a more general meaning than marked ones, and default, but not marked, items lose some meaning specification in some contexts (Battistella, 1990). Under this markedness theory, these differences should result in an asymmetrical representation of features. Thus, default forms should be easier to acquire than marked forms, due to morphological representational deficits in comprehension and production (MUH, McCarthy, 2008), or due to computational difficulties (to reduce cognitive load) in comprehension (PLADH, Dekydtspotter & Renaud, 2014) or in production (MISH, Haznedar & Schwartz, 1997; Prévost & White, 2000; Rothman, 2007; White, 2011).

Online studies with native speakers are inconclusive. Some studies show that they process default forms more easily than marked forms. Thus, ERP data show that monolinguals are more sensitive (larger P600) to subject-predicate feature clash errors than default errors. This pattern applies to both gender agreement errors (e.g. Hebrew: Deutsch & Bentin,

2001; Spanish: Alemán Bañón & Rothman, 2016) and number agreement errors (e.g. Dutch: Kaan, 2002; English: Mehravari *et al.*, 2015; Tanner & Bulkes, 2015). In contrast, other online studies reveal that natives process marked forms more easily than default forms. For instance, López Prego and Gabriele's (2014) behavioral data reveal that monolinguals are more accurate in rejecting feature clash than default gender and number disagreement errors under time pressure. These findings suggest that morphological markedness is not limited to L2 learners and is therefore constrained by cognitive load.

This mixed scenario extends to the L2 literature. On the one hand, numerous offline L2 studies suggest that default forms are more easily acquired than marked forms (e.g. Dewaele & Veronique, 2001; Franceschina, 2001; McCarthy, 2008; Montrul *et al.*, 2008; Prévost & White, 2000; Sabourin, 2003; White *et al.*, 2004). Similarly, two behavioral studies with L1 English-L2 French learners show that they rely more on default than marked forms while processing auxiliary verbs and past participles (Dekydtspotter & Renaud, 2009; Renaud, 2011). Likewise, a recent ERP study with L1 English-L2 Spanish learners reveals that they are more sensitive to feature clash errors than default errors, that they exhibit the same type of sensitivity to morphological markedness as monolinguals (contra MUH), and that natives and nonnatives are sensitive to morphological markedness in comprehension, but not in production (contra MISH, Alemán Bañón *et al.*, 2017). Interestingly, López Prego and Gabriele (2014) reported that low proficiency learners showed no default-marked asymmetries in either a timed or an untimed task, but that, in the timed task, intermediate and advanced learners were more accurate in default than marked number errors, and, unexpectedly, *less* accurate in default than marked gender errors. Again, the results of this study point to a possible association between cognitive load (timed versus untimed task in the L2 speakers, and variation in speed in the natives) and sensitivity to morphological markedness.

Considering López Prego and Gabriele's (2014) findings, and the fact that all L1 and L2 online studies have employed explicit tasks (grammaticality judgments) presented in a noncumulative manner (doubly cognitively complex), it is necessary to examine sensitivity to morphological markedness in a cognitively simple task (implicit, cumulative). The current study aims to fill this gap.

5 The Study

The theoretical models and empirical evidence summarized in the background section show that it is still unclear whether adult L2 learners can acquire and process morphosyntactic structures absent in their L1, and what factors cause L2 inflectional difficulties. In particular, this study investigates whether adult L2 learners process grammatical structures absent in their L1 (L1-L2 qualitative differences), and if they do, whether they do it as effectively as monolinguals (L1-L2 quantitative differences). This study also examines whether morphological markedness explains L2 learners' difficulties processing new grammatical structures. For Research Question 1, based on previous studies and predominantly on Sagarra and Herschensohn (2010), it is predicted that intermediate English learners of Spanish will match Spanish monolinguals qualitatively (sensitive to adjacent N-A grammatical gender and number agreement violations in Spanish), but not quantitatively (i.e. the monolinguals will react faster and longer to the violations). For Research Question 1, it is expected that the L2 learners, but not the monolinguals, will have more difficulty processing gender agreement violations with feature clash errors than default errors.

To address these research questions, this study adopts the following linguistic and methodological conditions. Linguistically, it investigates gender agreement between inanimate MS (masculine singular), FS (feminine singular), MP (masculine plural) and FP (feminine plural) transparent nouns and adjacent adjectives. It examines N-A agreement, because most studies focus on D-N agreement, and evidence about how monolinguals and L2 learners process N-A is scant (Sagarra & Herschensohn, 2010). It focuses on transparent nouns because L2 learners have difficulty processing opaque nouns (Bordag *et al.*, 2006). It explores adjacent agreement, because long-distance agreement is cognitively more difficult (Keating, 2009) and cannot determine whether insensitivity to agreement violations is due to maturational constraints or to linguistic complexity. It includes all gender and number combinations, in order to differentiate between default errors (N_{FEM}-Adj_{MASC}; N_{PL}-Adj_{SG}) and feature clash errors (N_{MASC}-Adj_{FEM}; N_{SG}-Adj_{PL}) (McCarthy, 2008).

Methodologically, the study employs a self-paced reading implicit eye-tracking task, to ensure that cognitive demands related to the task or the methodology do not hinder sensitivity to agreement violations. Self-paced tasks are easier than timed tasks (e.g. Sabourin, 2003), implicit tasks are easier than explicit tasks (Roberts, 2012), written tasks are easier than oral tasks (e.g. Montrul *et al.*, 2008) and eye-tracking tasks are easier than ERP tasks (rapid serial visual presentation) and moving windows tasks (noncumulative self-paced reading). Eye-tracking is cognitively easier and closer to natural reading than all these tasks, because it allows participants to see the entire sentence at once and to regress as needed.

6 Methods

6.1 Participants

Twenty-four L1 English-L2 Spanish intermediate classroom learners and 17 Spanish monolinguals participated in the study in exchange for extra credit and monetary compensation. All participants were right handed (Oldfield, 1971), had normal or corrected-to-normal vision and had attained at least a high school degree. They were between 18 and 32 years old, because processing speed and WM decline after the age of 40 (Park *et al.*, 2003).

The learners were born and raised in the USA, began studying Spanish after the age of 12, had no knowledge of other foreign languages apart from Spanish and had not lived abroad for more than three months. The Spanish monolinguals were born and raised in a monolingual community in Spain, did not speak any foreign language apart from some English learned in school and had not lived in a bilingual community or abroad for more than one month. Both groups were comparable in terms of: (1) WM (SD values indicated in parenthesis) (learners: $M = 44.79$ (13.84); monolinguals: $M = 39.71$ (15.17)), $F(1, 39) = 0.116$, $p = 0.736$; (2) overall reading speed on the eye-tracking sentences (learners: 2,074.61 (370.20); monolinguals: $M = 2,326.36$ (536.63), $F(1, 39) = 0.296$, $p = 0.590$; (3) overall sentence understanding (all scored at least 88.54% on the comprehension questions); and (4) knowledge of the vocabulary and grammar used in the experimental sentences (all scored 100%). Finally, the original sample pool consisted of 43 participants, but two had to be excluded because they did not complete all of the tasks.

6.2 Materials and procedure

The participants completed six tests in a single individual session in this order: (1) a language history questionnaire (10 minutes); (2) an L2 proficiency test, or the *Diploma de Español como Lengua Extranjera* (DELE) for L2 learners, the *Test of English as a Foreign Language* (TOEFL) for Spanish monolinguals (15 minutes); (3) an eye-tracking reading task with yes/no comprehension questions (20–30 minutes); (4) a WM reading span test adapted from Waters & Caplan, 1996 (15–20 minutes); (5) a vocabulary test (5–10 minutes); and (6) a gender marking and agreement test (10–15 minutes). Participants received 1 point per correct answer and 0 per incorrect answer for all the measures except the eye-tracking and the WM test.

6.2.1 Language history questionnaire

The language history questionnaire was administered in the participants' L1, and contained questions regarding age of onset, previous and current contact with Spanish and other languages, and location and length of time living abroad.

6.2.2 L2 proficiency tests

The Spanish learners completed an adapted version of DELE, and the Spanish monolinguals an adapted version of the TOEFL. Both tests measured grammatical knowledge via a 20-item multiple choice test. The L2 learners scored between 40% and 60% (a range considered to correspond to an intermediate level), and the monolinguals below 30% (suggesting that they were not fluent in English, and that English minimally affected how they processed Spanish).

6.2.3 Eye-tracking task

The experiment was programmed with *Experiment Builder*, and the data were extracted with *Data Viewer* (both, from SR Research, Ottawa, Ontario). The eye-tracker was an EyeLink 1000 (SR Research), with sampling rate of 1k Hz, spatial resolution of 0.32° horizontal and 0.25° vertical, and averaged calibration error of 0.01°. There were 146 sentences: six practice, 100 fillers and 40 experimental sentences (20 per condition: gender agreement, gender disagreement). Each experimental condition had five sentences with MS nouns, five with FS nouns, five with MP nouns and five with FP nouns. The filler and experimental sentences were divided into 20 blocks, and each block contained five filler sentences and two experimental sentences (one per condition). Following a Latin square design, randomization occurred between and within blocks. This procedure minimized the possibility that two experimental sentences of the same condition appeared next to each other. All of the sentences were 9–15 words long, and contained fewer than 20% of cognates to minimize lexical priming effects. For each sentence, participants looked at a black calibration dot located where the sentence would begin, read a two-line sentence in Spanish at their own pace, pressed a button when ready, read a question in Spanish about the sentence they had just read, and pressed a 'yes' or a 'no' button to answer. The conditions for the experimental sentences were gender agreement and gender disagreement: *La mujer compra el vestido nuevo/*nueva para la fiesta de graduación* 'The woman buys the dress$_{MS}$ new$_{MS}$/*new$_{MS}$ for the graduation party.'

The experimental sentences were 11–13 words long, followed a fixed syntactic order and contained two to four syllable inanimate nouns and descriptive adjectives with transparent gender, selected from Spanish textbooks used in the participants' Spanish courses. The NP1 nouns consisted of animate nouns with the same transparent gender ending as the NP2 nouns, to avoid possible gender or number spillover effects from the NP1 to the NP2 nouns. Half of the NP1 and the NP2 nouns were masculine (half singular, half plural) and half feminine (half singular, half plural). Following Sagarra and Herschensohn (2010), the following types of nouns were excluded in the NP1 and the NP2. First, gender-inflected pairs (e.g. *puerto-puerta* 'seaport$_{masc}$, door$_{fem}$'), because they could prime the opposite gender noun and bias the RTs on the target nouns. And second, Spanish uncountable nouns and Spanish countable nouns that are uncountable in English they could create L1 interference or comprehension problems because mass nouns lack number marking.

The comprehension questions were based on the content of the previous sentence, instead of its grammaticality, to avoid drawing the participants' attention to the agreement violations. For example, for the sentence *La mujer compra el vestido nuevo/*nueva para la fiesta de graduación* 'The woman buys the dress$_{MS}$ new$_{MS}$/*new$_{MS}$ for the graduation party,' the question was *¿La mujer lleva los pantalones de su marido a la tintorería?* 'Does the woman take her husband's pants to the dry cleaners?' For the experimental sentences, the questions focused on the nouns of the NP1 (*mujer*), the NP3 (*hijo*) and the NP 4 (*tintorería*). The questions never focused on the target noun or the target adjective to encourage the participants to read the entire sentence for comprehension, and to divert them from concentrating on the target structure. For all the sentences, half of the questions required a 'yes' response and half a 'no' response.

6.2.4 WM test

This test was programmed with *E-Prime 2.0 Professional* (Psychology Software Tools, Sharpsburg, PA), and was adapted from Waters and Caplan's (1996) reading span test. Participants read 80 sentences in their L1 silently at a fast pace, one by one, and pressed a 'yes' or a 'no' button after each to indicate whether the sentence was semantically plausible. At the end of the set, they were asked to recall the final word of each sentence within that set. Half of the sentences were plausible and half implausible with subject-object animacy inversion. Sentences were grouped into 20 sets of sentences, divided into five groups (span sizes two to six sentences) of four sets each. For accuracy scoring, participants received one point if their plausibility judgment was accurate, their recalled word was correct, and their response time was 300–5000 ms long and 2.5 standard deviations above or below the mean. Because WM comprises *simultaneous* processing and storage, trials with a correct recall and an incorrect judgment, or correct judgment and incorrect recall, were excluded. Response times faster than 300 ms and slower than 5000 ms were omitted, because college students need 225–400 ms to process single words (Rayner & Pollatsek, 1989), and because unlimited sentence processing time would jeopardize the complexity of the test. The WM data were used for group homogeneity purposes.

6.2.5 Vocabulary test

This test evaluated the L2 learners' lexical knowledge of the target words, via a Spanish-English matching task with the experimental nouns and adjectives in masculine singular (e.g. *blanco* → *white*).

6.2.6 Grammar test

To assess learners' grammatical knowledge of gender and number marking, participants indicated the gender and number of the target nouns in isolation. This is important because lexical gender assignment affects processing of gender agreement (Hopp, 2013, 2016). In addition, learners' syntactic knowledge of gender and number agreement was assessed to ascertain that they had the prerequisite syntactic knowledge to complete the experimental task.

7 Results

Nine Generalized Linear Mixed Models (GLMMs) were conducted with Agreement (Gender Agreement, Gender Violation), Morphological Markedness of the noun (Markedness, MS, FS, MP, FP) and Group (Spanish monolinguals, Spanish L2 learners), and all of their possible interactions as fixed factors, and Subject and Item as random factors. The nine dependent variables were accuracy on the comprehension questions, gaze duration on Det, N, Adj and Adj + 1, and regression duration on Det, N, Adj and Adj+1. Gaze duration is the time spent on the target word before moving on or looking back, and regression duration is the duration of all nonfirst pass fixations on the target word (i.e. the sum of all fixations except those included in gaze duration). Gaze duration on Det and N was analyzed as a control measure, to demonstrate that the participants processed similarly across conditions up to the adjective. Regressions to Det were analyzed because Spanish monolinguals (Lew-Williams & Fernald, 2010) and English-Spanish high proficiency learners (Dussias et al., 2013) use determiners' gender to speed up processing of upcoming nouns. For all the GLMMs, accuracy data followed a binomial distribution (frequency logit link), and the rest a gamma distribution (frequency log link). For Markedness, we will focus on gender contrasts (masculine, feminine); number contrasts (as well as WM effects) are reported elsewhere. Also, owing to space limitations, only significant main effects and interactions are reported. Finally, Table 5.1 illustrates descriptive statistics.

First, the 2 (Agreement) × 4 (Markedness) × 2 (Group) GLMM on accuracy on the comprehension questions revealed no significant main effects or interactions. Second, the 2 × 4 × 2 GLMMs on gaze duration (early processing) showed a significant main effect of Agreement at Adj, $F(1, 1502) = 18.083$, $p = 0.000$, and Adj + 1, $F(1, 1112) = 17.512$, $p = 0.000$, such that all the participants seemed to process Adj and Adj + 1 more slowly in gender disagreement than agreement. However, the significant interaction of Agreement × Group in Adj, $F(1, 502) = 9.807$, $p = 0.002$, and Adj + 1, $F(1, 1112) = 7.316$, $p = 0.007$, revealed that only the monolinguals processed Adj and Adj + 1 more slowly in gender disagreement than agreement (both, $p = 0.000$). Importantly, there was a significant main effect of Markedness at Adj, $F(3, 1502) = 2.799$, $p = 0.039$, such that all participants were slower at reading the Adj preceded by MP than MS N ($p = 0.046$). Also, there was a significant main effect for gaze duration at N, $F(1, 1529) = 25.323$, $p = 0.000$, showing that the L2 learners read N more slowly than the monolinguals. Crucially, the 2 × 4 × 2 GLMMs on regression duration at Adj showed a significant main effect for Agreement

Table 5.1 Descriptive statistics for the eye-tracking task

Measure	Group	Gender and number agreement		Gender agreement violation	
		M	SD	M	SD
Acc	Monolinguals	0.9147	0.2797	0.8941	0.3081
	Learners	0.8854	0.3189	0.8563	0.3512
Gaze Dur Det	Monolinguals	243.30	86.17	252.12	104.75
	Learners	240.61	82.69	235.53	80.78
Gaze Dur Noun	Monolinguals	288.40	144.15	302.76	146.30
	Learners	411.66	212.52	421.92	225.17
Gaze Dur Adj	Monolinguals	344.61	132.55	399.41	196.98
	Learners	371.94	168.25	377.72	184.57
Gaze Dur Adj + 1	Monolinguals	233.55	74.71	275.40	123.67
	Learners	257.44	106.70	267.17	104.29
Regr Dur Det	Monolinguals	279.46	132.72	258.65	94.80
	Learners	253.99	95.85	249.64	93.11
Regr Dur Noun	Monolinguals	311.02	177.83	306.86	162.97
	Learners	322.75	175.78	338.76	175.29
Regr Dur Adj	Monolinguals	287.83	125.36	300.24	130.86
	Learners	289.21	122.90	324.36	144.61
Regr Dur Adj + 1	Monolinguals	244.76	82.49	270.02	146.58
	Learners	273.22	119.80	276.37	1121.95

at Adj, $F(1, 752) = 6.070$, $p = 0.014$, indicating that *all* participants were slower at reading Adj in gender disagreement than agreement.

8 Discussion

This study investigated age effects and morphological markedness effects on the processing of grammatical adjacent N-A agreement by Spanish natives and English learners of Spanish, via a reading eye-tracking task with comprehension questions. The results revealed that the monolinguals and the L2 learners were sensitive to gender agreement violations, but the monolinguals reacted faster to the violations than the L2 learners. Also, all participants were insensitive to morphological markedness for gender, and slightly sensitive to morphological markedness for number (longer RTs at Adj preceded by marked rather than default forms).

8.1 Age effects

The first research question (RQ1) examined whether adult L2 learners process grammatical structures absent in their L1, and if they do, whether they perform like monolinguals. The prediction that intermediate English learners of Spanish would match Spanish monolinguals qualitatively, but not quantitatively, was supported. Qualitatively, both groups showed sensitivity to gender agreement violations (with similar accuracy rates on the comprehension question); longer regressions to Adj in gender disagreement than agreement. Quantitatively, the monolinguals reacted to gender agreement violations more quickly and longer (higher difference in RTs between disagreement and agreement) than the L2 learners. First, the monolinguals were faster because they showed sensitivity to gender disagreement during the first-pass reading of Adj (the L2 learners had to wait to regress to Adj later on). Second, the monolinguals reacted more strongly because their sensitivity lasted beyond the Adj (longer gaze duration at both Adj and Adj + 1).

These results support studies and models showing that adults can process grammatical structures absent in their L1 in a native-like way. Offline studies include Bruhn de Garavito and White (2002), Gess and Herschensohn (2001), Herschensohn (2001), Herschensohn and Arteaga-Capen (2007), Prévost (2004) and White *et al.* (2004). Online studies include Foucart and Frenck-Mestre (2012), Herschensohn and Frenck-Mestre (2005), Rossi *et a*l. (2006) and Sagarra and Herschensohn (2010). Theoretical models encompass: (1) generativist models rooted in morphosyntactic (e.g. FRH, Lardiere, 2005, 2009) and morphological difficulties at the representational level (MUH, McCarthy, 2008); (2) generativist models based on processing constraints (MSIH, Haznedar & Schwartz, 1997; Prévost & White, 2000; PLADH, Dekydtspotter & Renaud, 2009, 2014; SSH, Clahsen & Felser, 2006, 2017); and (3) usage-based accounts molded by language experience with the L2, salience, and cue availability and reliability (e.g. Ellis, 2006; MacWhinney, 2012; Romberg & Saffran, 2010). The findings of the current study, however, run counter to representational theories proposing a deficit in the L2 grammar as the source of learners' inflectional difficulties (RDH, Hawkins, 2009; IH, Tsimpli & Dimitrakopoulou, 2007). The data that address the second research question further evaluate some of these models.

8.2 Morphological markedness (marked versus default markers)

The second research question explored whether L2 learners' difficulty processing new grammatical structures is related to morphological markedness. The hypothesis that the L2 learners, but not the monolinguals, would have more difficulty processing gender agreement violations with default (*vestido nueva* 'dress$_{MS}$ new$_{FS}$') rather than marked (*falda nuevo* '*skirt$_{FS}$ new$_{MS}$') adjectives was not supported. This is so because markedness did not affect L1 or L2 processing of gender agreement.

The results revealed that morphological markedness did not affect how monolinguals and learners process gender agreement/disagreement. This indicates that adult learners can acquire default and marked forms at the level of the morphology, and do not need to rely on default forms.

This applies to intermediate proficiency levels and cognitively simple tasks (implicit tasks with cumulative display with adjacent dependencies using transparent nouns). Considering López Prego and Gabriele's (2014) study showing a lack of markedness effects in low, but not high, proficiency learners, one could argue that the results of the present study could be due to the L2 learners not being sufficiently proficient. We argue this is not the case, based on three pieces of evidence. First, López Prego and Gabriele's low proficiency learners were not sensitive to gender disagreement, but ours are. Second, López Prego and Gabriele's (2014) low proficiency learners were insensitive to markedness for both gender and number, but ours are sensitive to markedness for number (longer RTs at adjectives preceded by MP than MS nouns). Third, the absence of markedness effects in our intermediate learners is in line with Alemán Bañón *et al* 's (2017) comprehension data with advanced learners.

If the absence of markedness effects for gender is not related to insufficient L2 proficiency, what can explain the null findings? Quite simply, cognitive load. As mentioned earlier, all previous L1 and L2 online studies have used explicit tasks presented in a non-cumulative manner, which consume more attentional resources than our implicit task presented in a cumulative manner that allows readers to regress to previously read text as needed. This also explains why native and non-native speakers behave alike. This explanation is in line with models advocating that the root of L2 morphological variability is processing difficulties, (e.g. PLADH, Dekydtspotter & Renaud, 2009, 2014) and WM limitations (e.g. Sagarra & Herschensohn, 2010).

Regarding why all the participants showed sensitivity to markedness in number but not gender, we argue that marked forms are more salient (and feature clash errors are more disruptive) in number than in gender. The explanation cannot be the presence of number marking, but not gender marking, in English, because both are present in the monolinguals' grammar, and the monolinguals also show sensitivity to markedness in number, but not gender. Another piece of evidence in favor of our interpretation lies in the absence of a significant interaction between markedness and agreement. The fact that markedness affects the processing of both number agreement and number disagreement suggests that markedness is guided by general salience principles during online sentence comprehension. Finally, expected markedness effects (default forms being easier than marked forms) in number, but not gender, agreement/disagreement is in line with recent behavioral (López Prego & Gabriele, 2014) and electrophysiological (Alemán Bañón *et al.*, 2017) studies.

9 Conclusion

This study investigated the causes of inflectional variability in adult L2 learners of ungendered L1s, with a focus on age effects (postpuberty learners) and morphological markedness (default versus marked forms). Eye-tracking data revealed that adult intermediate English learners of Spanish and Spanish monolinguals were sensitive to adjacent N-A grammatical gender disagreement (all regressed longer to adjectives with gender disagreement than agreement), although the monolinguals reacted more quickly and more strongly (higher difference in RTs between disagreement and agreement) to the violations than the L2 learners (the monolinguals read adjectives and the word following adjectives in gender disagreement more slowly than agreement). The data also showed that none of the groups were affected by morphological markedness when processing gender agreement/disagreement, but both groups exhibited more difficulty processing marked than default forms when processing number agreement/disagreement, probably due to number suffixes being more salient than gender suffixes. Taken as a whole, these results suggest that, in cognitively simple tasks (implicit with cumulative display) and linguistic dependencies (adjacent), intermediate adult learners can process grammatical dependencies absent in their L1 qualitatively like native speakers, and that they are affected by morphological markedness like native speakers. These findings support processing explanations to adult learners' difficulties acquiring inflectional morphology absent in their L1 and speak against proposals claiming that L2 learners have morphological or syntactic deficits.

Note

(1) *Moving-window* is a part of self-paced reading tasks and it refers to the fact that only one word is shown at each time and that pressing SPACE both advances to the next word and also hides the previous word. *ERPs* are small changes in the scalp-recorded electroencephalogram time-locked to the onset of an event such as a sensory stimulus or a motor act.

References

Alarcón, I. (2009) The processing of gender agreement in L1 and L2 Spanish: Evidence from reaction-time data. *Hispania* 92 (4), 814–828.

Alemán Bañón, J. and Rothman, J. (2016) The role of morphological markedness in the processing of number and gender agreement in Spanish: An event-related potential investigation. *Language, Cognition, and Neuroscience* 31, 1273–1298.

Alemán Bañón, J., Fiorentino, R. and Gabriele, A. (2014) Morphosyntactic processing in advanced second language (L2) learners: An event-related potential investigation of the effects of L1-L2 similarity and structural distance. *Second Language Research* 30, 275–306.

Alemán Bañón, J., Miller, D. and Rothman, J. (2017) Morphological variability in second language learners: An examination of electrophysiological and production data. *Journal of Experimental Psychology: Learning, Memory, and Cognition* 43 (10), 1509–1536.

Battistella, E.L. (1990) *Markedness: The Evaluative Superstructure of Language*. Albany, NY: SUNY Press.

Bond, K., Gabriele, A., Fiorentino, R. and Alemán Bañón, J.A. (2011) Individual differences and the role of the L1 in L2 processing: An ERP investigation. In D. Tanner and J. Herschensohn (eds) *Proceedings of the 11th Generative Approaches in Second Language Acquisition Conference* (pp. 17–29). Somerville, MA: Cascadilla Press.

Bonet, E. (1995) Feature structure of Romance clitics. *Natural Language and Linguistic Theory* 13, 607–647.

Bordag, D., Opitz, A. and Pechmann, T. (2006) Gender processing in first and second languages: The role of noun termination. *Journal of Experimental Psychology: Learning, Memory, and Cognition* 32 (5), 1090–1101.

Borgonovo, C., Bruhn de Garavito, J., Guijarro-Fuentes, P., Prévost, P. and Valenzuela, E. (2006) Specificity in Spanish: The syntax-semantics interface in SLA. *EUROSLA Yearbook, 6* (pp. 57–78), Somerville, MA: Cascadilla.

Bruhn de Garavito, J. and White, L. (2002) The L2 acquisition of Spanish DPs: The status of grammatical features. In A.T. Pérez-Leroux and J.M. Liceras (eds) *The Acquisition of Spanish Morphosyntax: The L1/L2 Connection* (pp. 153–178). Dordrecht: Kluwer.

Caffarra, S., Barber, H., Molinaro, N. and Carreiras, M. (2017) When the end matters: Influence of gender cues during agreement computation in bilinguals. *Language, Cognition, and Neuroscience* 32 (9), 1069–1085.

Carroll, S. (1989) Second-language acquisition and the computational paradigm. *Language Learning* 39, 535–594.

Carstens, V. (2000) Concord in minimalist theory. *Linguistic Inquiry* 31, 319–355.

Chomsky, N. (2000) Minimalist inquiries. In R. Martin, D. Michaels and J. Uriagereka (eds) *Step by Step: Essays on Minimalist Syntax in Honor of Howard Lasnik* (pp. 89–155). Cambridge: MIT Press.

Clahsen, H. and Felser, C. (2006) Grammatical processing in language learners. *Applied Psycholinguistics* 27 (1), 3–42.

Clahsen, H. and Felser, C. (2017) Some notes on the Shallow Structure Hypothesis. *Studies in Second Language Acquisition*, doi: 10.1017/S0272263117000250.

Corbett, G.G. (1991) *Gender*. Cambridge: Cambridge University Press.

Cuza, A., Pérez-Leroux, T. and Sánchez, L. (2013) The role of semantic transfer in clitic-drop among simultaneous and sequential Chinese-Spanish bilinguals. *Studies in Second Language Acquisition* 35, 1–33.

DeKeyser, R. (2007) Skill acquisition theory. In J. Williams and B. VanPatten (eds) *Theories in Second Language Acquisition: An Introduction* (pp. 97–113). Mahwah, NJ: Erlbaum.

Dekydtspotter, L. and Renaud, C. (2009) On the contrastive analysis of features in second language acquisition: Uninterpretable gender on past participles in English-French processing. *Second Language Research* 25 (2), 251–263.

Dekydtspotter, L. and Renaud, C. (2014) On second language processing and grammatical development: The parser in second language acquisition. *Linguistic Approaches to Bilingualism* 4 (2), 131–165.

Deutsch, A. and Bentin, S. (2001) Syntactic and semantic factors in processing gender agreement in Hebrew: Evidence from ERPs and eye movements. *Journal of Memory and Language* 45, 200–224.

Dewaele, J-M. and Véronique, D. (2001) Gender assignment and gender agreement in advanced French interlanguage: A cross-sectional study. *Bilingualism: Language and Cognition* 4, 275–297.

Dussias, P., Valdés Kroff., J., Guzzardo Tamargo, R. and Gerfen, C. (2013) When gender and looking go hand and hand: Grammatical gender processing in L2 Spanish. *Studies in Second Language Acquisition* 35, 353–387.

Ellis, N. (2006) The Associative-Cognitive CREED. In B. VanPatten and J. Williams (eds) *Theories in Second Language Acquisition: An Introduction* (pp. 77–95). Mahwah, NJ: Earlbaum.

Foote, R. (2011) Integrated knowledge of agreement in early and late English-Spanish bilinguals. *Applied Psycholinguistics* 32, 187–220.

Foucart, A. and Frenck-Mestre, C. (2012) Can late L2 learners acquire new grammatical features? Evidence from ERPs and eye-tracking. *Journal of Memory and Language* 66 (1), 226–248.

Franceschina, F. (2001) Morphological or syntactic deficits in near-native speakers? An assessment of some current proposals. *Second Language Research* 17, 213–247.

Franceschina, F. (2002) Case and phi-feature agreement in advanced L2 Spanish grammars. In F.H. Foster-Cohen, T. Ruthenberg and M.L. Poschen (eds) *EUROSLA Yearbook, 2* (pp. 71–86). Amsterdam, The Netherlands: John Benjamins.

Franceschina, F. (2005) *Fossilized Second Language Grammars: The Acquisition of Grammatical Gender.* Amsterdam/Philadelphia: John Benjamins.

Gabriele, A., Fiorentino, R. and Alemán Bañón, J. (2013) Examining second language development using event-related potentials: A cross-sectional study on the processing of gender and number agreement. *Linguistic Approaches to Bilingualism* 3, 213–232.

Gess, R. and Herschensohn, J. (2001) Shifting the DP parameter: A study of Anglophone French L2ers. In R. Camps and C. Wiltshire (eds) *Romance Syntax, Semantics, and their L2 Acquisition* (pp. 105–119). Philadelphia: John Benjamins.

Gillon-Dowens, M., Vergara, M., Barber, H.A. and Carreiras, M. (2010) Morphosyntactic processing in late second-language learners. *Journal of Cognitive Neuroscience* 22, 1870–1887.

Guillelmon, D. and Grosjean, F. (2001) The gender marking effect in spoken word recognition: The case of bilinguals. *Memory and Cognition* 29, 503–511.

Hahne, A. and Friederici, A.D. (2001) Processing a second language: Late learners' comprehension mechanisms as revealed by event-related brain potentials. *Bilingualism: Language and Cognition* 4, 123–141.

Halle, M. (1997) Distributed morphology: Impoverishment and fission. *MIT Working Papers in Linguistics* 30, 425–449.

Halle, M. and Marantz, A. (1993) Distributed morphology and the pieces of inflection. In K. Hale and J. Keyser (eds) *The View from the Building 20: Essays in Linguistics in Honor of Sylvain Bromberger* (pp. 1–52). Cambridge, MA: MIT Press.

Harley, H. and Noyer, R. (1999) Distributed morphology. *Glot International* 4 (4), 3–9.

Harley, H. and Ritter, E. (2002) Person and number in pronouns: A feature-geometric analysis. *Language* 78, 482–526.

Hawkins, R. (2009) Statistical learning and innate knowledge in the development of second language proficiency: Evidence from the acquisition of gender concord. In A.G. Benati (ed.) *Issues in Second Language Proficiency* (pp. 63–78). London: Continuum.

Hawkins, R. and Franceschina, F. (2004) Explaining the acquisition and non-acquisition of determiner-noun gender concord in French and Spanish. In P. Prévost and J. Paradis (eds) *The Acquisition of French in Different Contexts* (pp. 175–206). Amsterdam, The Netherlands: John Benjamins,.

Haznedar, B. and Schwartz, B.D. (1997) Are there optional infinitives in child L2 acquisition? In E. Hughes, M. Hughes and A. Greenhill (eds) *Proceedings of the 21st Annual Boston University Conference on Language Development* (pp. 257–268). Somerville, MA: Cascadilla Press.

Herschensohn, J. (2001) Missing inflection in L2 French: Accidental infinitives and other verbal deficits. *Second Language Research* 17, 273–305.

Herschensohn, J. and Arteaga-Capen, D. (2007) Parameters and processing: Gender agreement in L2 French. Paper presented at the 17th EUROSLA Conference, Newcastle, 11–14 September 2007.

Herschensohn, J. and Frenck-Mestre, C. (2005) Failed [ugender] features in L2 French: What ERPs reveal about L1 influence. Paper presented at the 15th EUROSLA Conference, Dubrovnik, 14–17 September 2005.

Hopp, H. (2009) The syntax-discourse interface in near-native L2 acquisition: Off-line and on-line performance. *Bilingualism: Language and Cognition* 12, 463–483.

Hopp, H. (2013) Grammatical gender in adult L2 acquisition: Relations between lexical and syntactic variability. *Second Language Research* 29, 33–56.

Hopp, H. (2016) Learning (not) to predict: Grammatical gender processing in second language acquisition. *Second Language Research* 32 (2), 277–307.

Jiang, N. (2004) Morphological insensitivity in second language processing. *Applied Psycholinguistics* 25, 603–634.

Kaan, E. (2002) Investigating the effects of distance and number interference in processing subject-verb dependencies: An ERP study. *Journal of Psycholinguistic Research* 31, 165–193.

Keating, G.D. (2009) Sensitivity to violations of gender agreement in native and nonnative Spanish: An eye-movement investigation. *Language Learning* 59, 503–535.

Keating, G.D. (2010) The effects of linear distance and working memory on the processing of gender agreement in Spanish. In B. VanPatten and J. Jegerski J (eds) *Research in Second Language Processing and Parsing* (pp. 113–134). Amsterdam: John Benjamins.

Lardiere, D. (2005) On morphological competence. In L. Dekydtspotter, R.A. Sprouse and A. Liljestrand (eds) *Proceedings of the 7th Generative Approaches to Second Language Acquisition Conference (GASLA 2004)* (pp. 178–192). Somerville MA: Cascadilla Press.

Lardiere, D. (2009) Some thoughts on the contrastive analysis of features in second language acquisition. *Second Language Research* 25 (2), 173–227.

López Prego, B. and Gabriele, A. (2014) Examining the impact of task demands on morphological variability in native and non-native Spanish. *Linguistic Approaches to Bilingualism* 4, 192–221.

MacWhinney, B. (1987) The competition model. In B. MacWhinney (ed.) *Mechanisms of Language Acquisition* (pp. 249–308). Hillsdale, NJ: Lawrence Erlbaum.

MacWhinney, B. (2005) A unified model of language acquisition. In J.F. Kroll and A.M.B. de Groot (eds) *Handbook of Bilingualism: Psycholinguistic Approaches* (pp. 49–72). Oxford: Oxford University Press.

MacWhinney, B. (2012) The logic of the unified model. In S. Gass and A. Mackey (eds) *Handbook of Second Languages Acquisition* (pp. 211–227). New York: Routledge.

McCarthy, C. (2008) Morphological variability in the comprehension of agreement: An argument for representation over computation. *Second Language Research* 24, 459–486.

Mehravari, A.S., Tanner, D., Wampler, E.K., Valentine, G.D. and Osterhout, L. (2015) Effects of grammaticality and morphological complexity on the P600 event-related potential component. *PLoS ONE* 10 (10), e0140850, https://doi.org/10.1371/journal.pone.0140850.

Meulman, N., Stowe, L.A., Sprenger, S.A., Bresser, M. and Schmid, M.S. (2014) An ERP study on L2 syntax processing: When do learners fail? *Frontiers in Psychology* 5, 1–17.

Montrul, S., Foote, R. and Perpiñán, S. (2008) Gender agreement in adult second language learners and Spanish heritage speakers: The effects of age and context of acquisition. *Language Learning* 58, 503–553.

Morgan-Short, K., Sanz, C., Steinhauer, K. and Ullman, M. (2010) Second language acquisition of gender agreement in explicit and implicit training conditions: An event-related potential study. *Language Learning* 60 (1), 154–193.

Oldfield, R.C. (1971) The assessment and analysis of handedness: The Edinburgh inventory. *Neuropsychologia* 9, 97–113.

Osterhout, L., Poliakov, A., Inoue, K., McLaughlin, J., Valentine, F., Pitkanen, I., Frenck-Mestre, C. and Herschensohn, J. (2008) Second-language learning and changes in the brain. *Journal of Neurolinguistics* 21, 509–521.

Park, D., Welsh, R., Marschuetz, C., Gutchess, A., Mikels, J., Polk, T., Noll, D. and Taylor, S. (2003) Working memory for complex scenes: Age differences in frontal and hippocampal activations. *Journal of Cognitive Neuroscience* 15 (8), 1122–1134.

Pérez-Pereira, M. (1991) The acquisition of gender: What Spanish children tell us. *Journal of Child Language* 18, 571–590.

Pesetsky, D. and Torrego, E. (2004) Tense, case, and the nature of syntactic categories. In J. Guerón and J. Lecarme (eds) *The Syntax of Time* (pp. 495–537). Cambridge, MA: MIT Press.

Prévost, P. (2004) The semantic and aspectual properties of child L2 root infinitives. In P. Prévost and J. Paradis (eds) *The Acquisition of French* (pp. 305–332). Amsterdam/ Philadelphia: John Benjamins.

Prévost, P. and White, L. (2000) Missing surface inflection or impairment in second language acquisition? Evidence from tense and agreement. *Second Language Research* 16, 103–133.

Rayner, K. and Pollatsek, A. (1989) *The Psychology of Reading*. New York: Prentice Hall.

Renaud, C. (2011) Processing gender: The case of pronouns and adjectives in L2 French. In J. Herschensohn and D. Tanner (eds) *Proceedings of the 11th Generative Approaches to Second Language Acquisition Conference* (pp. 121–134). Somerville, MA: Cascadilla Press.

Renaud, C. (2014) A processing investigation of the accessibility of the uninterpretable gender feature in L2 French and L2 Spanish adjective agreement. *Linguistic Approaches to Bilingualism* 4 (3), 222–255.

Roberts, L. (2012) Individual differences in second language sentence processing. *Language Learning* 62 (2), 172–188.

Romberg, A.R. and Saffran, J. (2010) Statistical learning and language acquisition. *Wiley Interdisciplinary Reviews Cognitive Science* 1 (6), 906–914.

Rossi, S., Gugler, M.F., Friederici, A.D. and Hahne, A. (2006) The impact of proficiency on syntactic second-language processing of German and Italian: Evidence from event-related potentials. *Journal of Cognitive Neuroscience* 18 (12), 2030–2048.

Rossi, E., Kroll, J. F. and Dussias, P. (2014) When bilinguals process gender and number: ERP evidence for the role of cross-language similarity in sentence processing. *Neuropsychologia* 62, 11–25.

Rothman, J. (2007) Sometimes they use it, sometimes they don't: An epistemological discussion of L2 morphological production and its use as a competence measurement. *Applied Linguistics* 28, 609–614.

Sabourin, L. (2003) Grammatical gender and second language processing: An ERP study. Unpublished doctoral dissertation, Rijksuniversiteit Groningen, Groningen, The Netherlands.

Sabourin, L. and Stowe, L. (2008) Second language processing: When are first and second languages processed similarly? *Second Language Research* 24, 397–430.

Sagarra, N. and Ellis, N. (2013) From seeing adverbs to seeing morphology. Language experience and adult acquisition of L2 tense. Special Issue: Eye tracking and SLA, A. Godfroid, S. Gass, and P. Winke (eds) *Studies in Second Language Acquisition* 35 (2), 261–290.

Sagarra, N. and Herschensohn, J. (2010) The role of proficiency and working memory in gender and number agreement processing in L1 and L2 Spanish. *Lingua* 20, 2022–2039.

Sagarra, N. and Herschensohn, J. (2011) Proficiency and animacy effects on L2 gender agreement processes during comprehension. *Language Learning* 61, 80–116.

Sagarra, N. and Seibert Hanson, A. (2011) Eyetracking methodology: A user's guide for linguistic research. Viewpoints section on 'technology in linguistics'. *Studies in Hispanic and Lusophone Linguistics* 4 (2), 543–555.

Saporta, S. (1965) Ordered rules, dialect differences, and historical processes. *Language* 41, 218–224.

Sato, M. and Felser, C. (2008) Sensitivity to morphosyntactic violations in English as a second language. Unpublished manuscript, University of Essex, Colchester.

Slabakova, R. (2006) Is there a critical period for semantics? *Second Language Research* 22 (3), 302–338.

Steinhauer, K., White, E.J. and Drury, J.E. (2009) Temporal dynamics of late second language acquisition: Evidence from event-related potentials. *Second Language Research* 25 (1), 13–41.

Tanner, D. and Bulkes, N.Z. (2015) Cues, quantification, and agreement in language comprehension. *Psychonomic Bulletin & Review* 22, 1753–1763.

Tokowicz, N. and MacWhinney, B. (2005) Implicit and explicit measures of sensitivity to violations in second language grammar: An event-related potential investigation. *Studies in Second Language Acquisition* 27, 173–204.

Tsimpli, I.M. and Dimitrakopoulou, M. (2007) The interpretability hypothesis: Evidence from wh-interrogatives in L2 acquisition. *Second Language Research* 23 (2), 215–242.

Valenzuela, E. (2005) L2 ultimate attainment and the syntax-discourse interface: The acquisition of topic constructions in non-native Spanish and English. Unpublished PhD dissertation. McGill University, Montreal, Canada.

Waters, G.S. and Caplan, D. (1996) The measurement of verbal working memory capacity and its relation to reading comprehension. *Quarterly Journal of Experimental Psychology* 49, 51–79.

Weber-Fox, C. and Neville, H.J. (1996) Maturational constraints on functional specializations for language processing: ERP and behavioral evidence in bilingual speakers. *Journal of Cognitive Neuroscience* 0, 231–256.

White, L. (2011) Second language acquisition at the interfaces. *Lingua* 121, 577–590.

White, L., Valenzuela, E., Kozlowska-Macgregor, M. and Leung, Y-K. (2004) Gender and number agreement in nonnative Spanish. *Applied Psycholinguistics* 25, 105–133.

Zagona, K. (2002) *The Syntax of Spanish.* Cambridge: Cambridge University Press.

Zobl, H. and Liceras, J.M. (1994) Functional categories and acquisition orders. *Language Learning* 44, 159–180.

6 Finding their Heads: How Immigrant Adults Posit L2 Functional Projections

Anne Vainikka and Martha Young-Scholten

1 Introduction

Researchers working under the assumption that the linguistic mechanisms (Universal Grammar, UG) involved in L1 acquisition remain available throughout the lifespan generally subscribe to one of two positions: (1) learners transfer the entirety of their L1 syntactic structure and then restructure their syntax and acquire L2 functional morphology (e.g. see Schwartz & Sprouse, 1996); or (2) learners transfer only verbs without an inflection, that is, lexical projections, and build functional syntax based on the input (Vainikka & Young-Scholten, 1994).[1] Included in evidence for both views is oral production data from adults who do not receive L2 instruction and hence are unlikely to consciously learn morphology. Research dating back to the 1970s shows that – much like L1 learners – uninstructed adult learners' earliest utterances lack functional morphology, there is no evidence of functional syntax and then their subsequent development of functional morphology and syntax – morphosyntax – is systematic. That is, the developmental sequences observed for the production of functional morphology maps onto the way in which syntax is represented, from lexical projections that contain no functional syntax, to functional projections responsible for increasingly more aspects of a clause.

In this chapter, we first provide an overview of the evidence and the associated claims bearing on the earliest stages in both L1 and L2 development to clarify the basis of the two views. Our ultimate focus is on the nontarget functional morphology learners sometimes produce at low/intermediate stages, which we argue is additional evidence for the structure building approach. Discussion is primarily based on existing data from uninstructed low/intermediate-stage adults, including those from Romance language backgrounds, acquiring German. In addition, we discuss new data on learners of English. We claim that when the learner tentatively posits a new functional projection, there is a period of time during which they (subconsciously) consider whether or not the language being acquired provides evidence for that particular head. Data from our and others' studies provide evidence from learners' overgeneralization of single words as well as multiword utterances of their active search in the input they hear for heads of functional projections. We end by calling for investigation of immigrant adults' early L2 production to also include analysis of multiword overgeneralizations.

2 Minimal Syntax at the Start

In L1 acquisition, the question of whether the development of mor-phosyntax is incremental has been pursued since the late 1980s, by those who support the idea of minimal syntax at the start (e.g. Guilfoyle & Noonan, 1992; Lebeaux, 1988, 2000; Radford, 1990, 1995; Vainikka, 1993/4) and those who support the idea that functional projections are present from the start (e.g. Boser et al., 1992; Ionin, 2008; Lust, 2006; Poeppel & Wexler, 1993; Weissenborn, 1990). Under the latter view, the operation of UG means that the child's syntax undergoes no changes during development such that meaning maps transparently onto syntactic structure, and the same meaning always maps onto the same structure (Interface Uniformity; see Culicover & Jackendoff, 2005 for discussion). Under the former view, the learner's steps are constrained by UG and by certain assumptions outlined below. These assumptions apply both to acquisition across the lifespan, and to L1 and L2 acquisition.

Under Organic Grammar (OG) (Vainikka & Young-Scholten, 2007), Interface Uniformity is replaced by the idea of a Master Tree as the back-bone of syntactic structure. The Master Tree (Assumption 1 of 10 Organic Grammar Assumptions) provides the mechanism for positing functional syntax which, we further assume, differs across languages, contra Cinque (1999); for recent ideas on this, see Chen et al. (2015) on the application of OG to Mandarin. The second assumption comes from the idea that inflectional morphology mirrors syntax, that it represents functional pro-jections. This allows for differences in projections' headedness, making explicit the idea that there must be evidence in the input for the learner to posit a functional projection (Baker, 1985; Fukui & Sakai, 2003; Giorgio & Pianesi, 1997; Grimshaw, 1986, 1997). The third assumption simply notes the involvement of UG, and the fourth assumption clarifies the process, accounting for the long-observed and highly systematic stage-like development in both first and second language acquisition.

Assumption 1: Each language has a Master Tree that includes all possible projections occurring in the language.
Assumption 2: All and only those projections occur in the Master Tree for which there is evidence in the language.

Assumption 3: UG provides the tools for acquiring the Master Tree, based on input.
Assumption 4: The Master Tree is acquired from the bottom up.

As far as the acquisition process in concerned, under Organic Grammar, UG organizes functional projections into the VP-group (verb phrase), the IP-group (inflectional phrase), and the CP-group (Vainikka & Young-Scholten, 2013). Within each group, UG provides an ordered list of potential heads that the learner either adopts or discards, depending on the input, and there is a set of possible grammatical features that can be realized as specific functional projections. If there is no evidence in the input (or the language learner cannot find it), the projection is not posited. The VP-level projections might involve the following functional heads: (1) accusative/absolutive; (2) object clitic; (3) object agreement; (4) aspect; (5) negation and (6) voice. Note that the negation head would need to be an option both at the VP-level and at the IP-level, given the cross-linguistic negation patterns (see Miestamo *et al.*, 2015).

The oral production data which drove the idea that L1 and L2 learners incrementally build up syntactic structure comes from the acquisition of German, to which we now turn.

2.1 German morphosyntax

In German, verbal suffixes mark agreement with the subject, as shown in Table 6.1 for the regularly inflected verb *trinken*, the nonfinite form. Some verbs involve irregular forms where the stem vowel changes in second and third person singular. In spoken German, first and second person singular can involve phonologically shortened forms, as shown. Note also that *Sie* is the polite form of address for both second person singular and plural. Although German is a relatively richly inflected language, unlike some Romance languages (e.g. Italian, Portuguese and Spanish), pronominal subjects cannot be dropped but must be phonologically realized.

The agreement paradigm in Table 6.1 applies in modified form to modals in the present tense (first person singular is not marked with an -*e* and third person singular is not marked with -*t*). There are suppletive

Table 6.1 The subject-verb agreement paradigm for *trinken* 'drink'

Person/pronoun	Singular	Person/pronoun	Plural
First: *ich* 'I'	*trink-e*/Ø	*wir* 'we'	*trink-en*
Second: *du* 'you'	*trink-s(t)*	*ihr* 'you'	*trink-t*
Third: *er, sie, es* 'he' 'she' 'it'	*trink-t*	*sie, Sie* 'they' 'you'	*trink-en*

Table 6.2 The forms of *haben* 'have' and *sein* 'be'

Person	Singular		Plural	
First	*habe/(e)*	*bin*	*haben*	*sind*
Second	*has(t)*	*bist*	*habt*	*seid*
Third	*hat*	*ist*	*haben*	*sind*

forms, as shown in Table 6.2 for auxiliary verb *haben* 'have' (which also functions as a main verb) and *sein* 'be' (which also functions as a copula). German does not grammatically mark aspect.

The position of the verb in German involves: (1) the finite verb in so-called second position or V2; (2) the nonfinite verb in final position in a matrix clause; (3) the nonfinite verb in final position in an embedded clause; and (4) inversion of the main verb and subject in matrix clause questions.

(1)   a. *Bettina trinkt Tee.*
        Bettina drinks tea
        'Bettina drinks tea.'

   b. *Tee trinkt Bettina.*
        tea   drinks Bettina
        'Tea is what Bettina drinks.'

Reference to past events in spoken German involve use of an auxiliary verb in second position with the main verb with the prefix *ge-* and the suffix *-t* (regular verbs) or the suffix *-n* (irregular verbs); modal verbs also follow this pattern, albeit with the nonfinite main verb.

(2)   a. *Bettina hat Tee getrunken.*
        Bettina has tea drunk
        'Bettina drank tea.'

   b. *Bettina will   morgen   Kaffee trinken.*
        Bettina wants tomorrow coffee to drink.
        'Bettina wants to drink coffee tomorrow.'

In embedded clauses, the finite verb appears at the end of the sentence:

(3)   a. *Andreas fragt Bettina, warum sie selten Kaffee trinkt.*
        Andreas asks Bettina why   she seldom coffee drinks
        'Andreas asks Bettina why she seldom drinks coffee.'

   b. *Bettina trinkt immer den Tee, der nicht viel kostet.*
        Bettina drinks always the tea   that not much costs
        'Bettina always drinks tea that doesn't cost much.'

In German, questions can involve auxiliary and modal verbs as well as main verbs:

(4)   a. *Hat Bettina Tee getrunken?*

        has Bettina   tea drunk

        'Did Bettina drink tea?

      b. *Trinkt Bettina Kaffee?*

        drinks Bettina coffee?

        'Does Bettina drink coffee?

      c. *Was   trinkt   Bettina?*

        what drinks Bettina?

        'What does Bettina drink?'

This entails the following tree:[2]

(5)

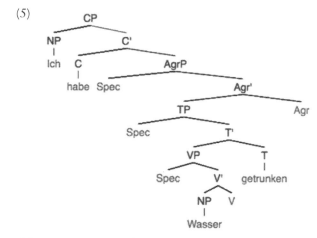

In addition to positing functional projects, the learner's development of German morphosyntax also involves raising the thematic verb from the head-final VP to second position in declaratives, and to final position (owing to a head-final AgrP) in embedded clauses.

2.2 Minimal syntax in the L1 acquisition of German

We now turn to the syntactic architecture of German verbal syntax and to the L1 acquisition data which motivated the account of L2 acquisition; (Vainikka & Young-Scholten, 1994, the basis of Organic Grammar; Vainikka & Young-Scholten, 2007).

The VP in German has long been argued to be head final (e.g. Webelhuth 1984/5), where complements such as the direct objects precede the nonfinite verb, as shown in Example (6); see examples above, especially (2a), (2b) and (4a).

(6)

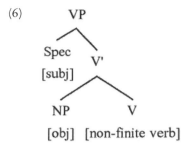

When young children start producing multiword utterances, their utterances typically consist of nonfinite verbs in which pronominal subjects are optional, regardless of whether they are obligatory in the adult language, as they are in German (e.g. utterances from Meike at age 1;10 in Mills, 1985). Following Rizzi (1993/4), the structure of the child utterances in Example (7) would be equivalent to the tree above in Example (6), albeit with no subject in Spec, VP.[3]

(7)   a. *hause gehen*
      home go-INF
      [Ich gehe nach Hause.]
      '(I) go home.'

   b. *teddy holen*
      teddy get-INF
      [Ich hole den Teddy.]
      (I) get the teddy.'

2.3 Organic Grammar and L2 acquisition

Organic Grammar assumes that the younger or older L2 learner's earliest grammars also lack all functional projections and consist of the bare VP shown in Example (1), either head-initial or head-final. This minimal syntactic tree is influenced by the learner's first language VP in terms of the head-complement order. The claims made here are based on studies shown in Table 6.3 (Vainikka & Young-Scholten, 2011).

Like children acquiring their first language, the verbs produced by L2 learners are nonfinite and pronominal subjects are optional. There is little, if any other evidence for functional syntax. In the L2 acquisition of the head-final German VP, speakers of languages with head-initial VPs (e.g. English, Italian, Portuguese and Spanish) start with the non-German word order shown in Example (8), while speakers of languages with head-final VPs (e.g. Korean and Turkish) start with what is the correct VP word order for German (longitudinal data from ZISA (Zweitspracherwerb italienischer, portuguesischer und spanischer Arbeiter) and from Vainikka

Table 6.3 Studies of uninstructed adult learners of German

Study/researcher/seminal publication	L1 and L2	Subjects	Type of study
Heidelberger Pidgin Projekt (Becker et al., 1977)	L1 Spanish L1 Italian	48	Cross-sectional
ZISA (Zweitspracherwerb italienischer, portuguesischer und spanischer Arbeiter) (Clahsen et al., 1983)	L1 Spanish L1Portuguese L1 Italian	45 12	Cross-sectional 2 year longitudinal
European Science Foundation (ESF) (Klein & Perdue, 1992)	L1 Turkish L1 Italian	4	2 ½ year longitudinal
LexLern (Lexikalisches Lernen) (Clahsen et al., 1991)	L1 Korean L1 Turkish	17	Cross-sectional
Von Stutterheim (1987)	L1 Turkish	10	Cross-sectional
Dimroth (2002)	L1 Russian L1 Croatian L1 Turkish	40	Cross-sectional
Vainikka & Young-Scholten's Americans (VYSA) (Vainikka & Young-Scholten, 2011)	L1 English	3	1 year longitudinal

& Young-Scholten, 2011; cross-sectional data from LexLern, Vainikka & Young-Scholten, 1994, 1996).

(8)   a. *Peter   lernen   die Buch.*   Paul, month 2 (L1 English)
         Peter learn-INF   the book.
         [*Peter liest das Buch.*]
         'Peter reads the book.'

      b. *Eine Katze Fisch alle essen.*   Changsu (Korean L1)
         a   cat   fish all   eat-INF
         [*Eine Katze hat den ganzen Fisch gefressen.*]
         'A cat ate the whole fish.'

With further exposure – and if required – the learner switches their L1 VP headedness to the correct L2 headedness. Example (9) shows one of the 8-year-old Italian learners of German studied by Pienemann (1981) and an adult Italian learner (from the ZISA study) both of whom switch VP headedness to the correct German complement-head order yet whose German syntax still allows nonfinite verbs and empty subjects.

Referring to Pienemann's 62-week study of three Italian 8-year-olds (who were somewhat delayed to due limited exposure to German), Prévost and White (2000a, 2000b, 2000c) conclude that these L2 children's earliest multiword utterances represent an incomplete or truncated syntactic structure. It can be argued that in early L2 German development, the vast majority of utterances (up to 90%) are analyzed as bare VPs (see also Dimroth, 2002 on L2 German and Vainikka &

Young-Scholten, 2013 on adoption of Paradis & Crago's (2001) root default account of bare VPs for L2 acquisition, as well as typical and atypical L1 acquisition).

(9)   a. *Nicht lessen*   Concetta, month 12.4 (L1 Italian)
           not   read-INF
           [*Ich lese nicht.*]
           'I don't read.'

       b. *Vielleicht Schule essen.*   Salvatore, session 6 (L1 Italian)
           maybe   school eat-INF
           [*Vielleicht isst sie in der Schule.*]
           'Maybe she eats at school.'

If we allow a stage in children's acquisition of English or German or any language that involves less than full syntactic structure, we either need to invoke maturation or propose a mechanism which is responsible for the acquisition of functional projections. If we find the same sort of stage in L2 acquisition, regardless of age (child or adult L2 acquisition), the possibility of invoking maturation is removed, and the need for such a mechanism increases. Such a mechanism is proposed in Vainikka and Young-Scholten (2013). Under Organic Grammar, it is UG that provides the L1 or L2 learner with a set of potential syntactic heads (presumably as an ordered list). The learner (subconsciously) considers each head in turn, determining whether the ambient language provides evidence for that head. If evidence is detected, the learner posits the head (along with the rest of the projection); if no evidence is found, the learner does not posit that particular head for the language. This process is reflected in a gradual acquisition of functional projections, from the bottom up, resulting in the adult tree shown above in Example (5).

3 Further Development

The continued operation of UG during the acquisition process helps the L2 learner incrementally build up syntactic structure and posit functional projections that fit within the set shown in Table 6.4, with examples in English.

As in English, in German, pronominal subjects are obligatory and verbs are raised from the VP to a higher position and marked with suffixes which agree with the subject. Verbs are marked for past with auxiliary *haben* and past participle forms which comprise the prefix *ge-* and the suffix *-t* or *-en*.

(10)   a. *Ich trinke   Wasser.*
            I drink-1SG   water
            'I drink/I am drinking water.'

Table 6.4 Common functional projections (Vainikka & Young-Scholten, 2011)

Full name	Abbreviation	Sample contents
Tense phrase	TP or TnsP	Past tense (-*ed* suffix); *When did the action take place?*
Negation phrase	NegP	The morpheme *not*; *Did the action take place or not?*
Agreement phrase	AgrP	Subject-verb agreement; the suffix -*s* in 'he walks'; *Who did something?*
Aspect phrase	AspP	Progressive aspect (-*ing* suffix); *Is the action on-going?*
Inflection phrase	IP	All of the above combined.
Complementizer phrase	CP	Question information (wh-phrase or yes/no question); other information about sentence type.

> b. *Ich   habe   Wasser   getrunken.*
>   I   have-1SG   water   drink-past.participle
> 'I have drunk water' or 'I drank water.'

Under previous work on the morphosyntax of uninstructed L2 adult learners of German, we have argued that their acquisition follows basically the same course as in L1 acquisition (Vainikka & Young-Scholten, 1994, 2006, 2007, 2011, 2013). This is not surprising if adults have access to UG. We have also argued that adult L2 learners do not rely further on their L1 morphosyntax.

We now turn to a closer examination of the low-intermediate stages of development, when learners are beginning to posit functional projections. We consider oral production data from earlier studies involving adult migrant workers and immigrants in Germany from various language backgrounds, including several Romance languages. As discussed above, under the structure building of Organic Grammar, learners identify heads in the ambient input to posit the associated functional projection. Learners' successful production of a head relevant in that language is an indication that structure is being built. It is their non-target production of functional elements – which we refer to as placeholders (for these heads) – we are interested in as this has the potential to reveal learners' (subconscious) search to identify heads in the ambient input.

4 Monomorphemic Forms as Placeholders

Before turning to the multiword strings we will consider further below, we note what researchers are familiar with the overgeneralization of single words in L1 acquisition. This has long been observed in children when they are in the process of acquiring morphological rules which they first apply to irregular forms such as the marking of plural and past tense in English (e.g. Berko, 1958). In L2 acquisition, Wagner-Gough (1978) reported on a slightly different sort of overgeneralization by a young L2 English learner who overused -*ing* forms with verbs regardless of their function. Researchers have also observed the use of 'is' to replace a main verb in L2 acquisition. For example, Lakshmanan (1993/4; Lakshmanan & Selinker, 2001), in her longitudinal study of L1 Spanish/L2 English children attending nursery school, concludes that in the earliest samples, 'is' functions as a placeholder so the contents of INFL can be discharged onto it before lexical verbs emerge in INFL later, around samples 6 to 10. For more on nontarget use in oral production of 'is' in L2 English and *ist* in L2 German by Italian and French speakers, see also Ahrenholz (2005), Hendriks (2005) and von Stutterheim and Lambert (2005). While Romance language speakers have knowledge of copula 'be' from their native languages upon which they can draw during L2 acquisition, transfer seems not to be the only contributing factor. Despite the dissimilarity of Turkish to German and Hmong to English in terms of the copula, Haberzettl (2003) observed similar nontarget use of *ist* in her study Turkish children in Germany and Huebner (1983) observed 'is' in his study of Hmong speaker Ge in the USA.

The results from a recent study by Julien *et al.* (2015) provide further evidence of use of single morphemes as placeholders during learners' search for heads. The simple present in Dutch is like that in German; lexical verbs raise and are marked by suffixes for agreement with the subject. Forms of the auxiliary *zijn* 'be' is used for the imperfective with a past participle, as in *Peter is angekomen* 'Peter has arrived' and to indicate something happening not in the vicinity of the speaker and used with intransitive verbs as in *zijn* + INF: *Moeder is werken* 'Mother is off somewhere working.' Forms of the auxiliary *gaan* 'go': *Ik ga koffie drinken*. 'I am going to drink coffee' with the infinitive mark progressive aspect ('is going to').

Julien *et al.* (2015) looked at the oral production of Dutch by 40 adults with varying levels of home language literacy (0–12 years), whose native languages were Arabic, Tarifiyt Berber and Turkish, and confirmed learners' assignment of meaning to the function words studied with a comprehension task. (For similar work, see Jordens & Dimroth, 2006; Starren, 2001; van de Craats, 2009; van de Craats & van Hout, 2010; van Kampen, 1997; Zuckerman, 2001, 2013.) In terms of possible L1 influence, Moroccan Arabic has an imperfective construction with an auxiliary similar to *gaan*: *ġādi*. There are no such similarities between Dutch and Turkish or Tarifiyt; however, the only L1-based pattern that Julien *et al.* (2015) detected in nontarget use (which they refer to as 'dummy' use) was Arabic learners' increasing use of the target Dutch *gaan* + INF. They observe that regardless of their L1, after nine months of exposure to Dutch in classes for immigrants, there is pervasive use of forms of *gaan* 'go' and *zijn* 'be', which they describe as semantically vacuous finiteness markers. Moreover, the use of these is more frequent with noninverted utterances and subjectless utterances, indicating little projection of relevant functional syntax. After roughly nine more months of Dutch classes, the learners studied by Julien *et al.* (2015) showed evidence of acquisition of verb raising, and of agreement, tense and aspect marking. This coincides with learners' decreased use of dummy auxiliaries, albeit with a greater decrease for *zijn* than *gaan*.

The L2 learners are involved in investigating how the verbal morphosyntax of Dutch works and as they take a 'structural step in the acquisition of finiteness' (Julien *et al.*, 2015: 54), they use dummy auxiliaries while they are tentatively positing TP and AgrP. Julien *et al.* (2015) refer to these L2 learners as following a process of UG-guided discovery during which rather than raising the relevant lexical verb, they instead directly retrieve and insert elements into the head, following the Economy Principle (Chomsky, 1995).

5 Learners Finding their Heads under an Organic Grammar Approach to L2 German

5.1 Previous research

For functional projections that involve a bound morpheme such as subject-verb agreement on raised verbs in German, we expect that actually 'finding' the evidence will be more difficult for adult L2 learners than for children (see Vainikka & Young-Scholten, 1998, 2011), given the difficulties phonology poses for older learners' access to bound versus free morphemes). Given this difficulty, the low-intermediate stage during which the learner has tentatively posited a projection, but has not yet confirmed it, could be a protracted one for adults. And if their exposure is as migrants whose acquisition may be taking place outside the classroom, but with little regular interaction with native speakers of the L2, we might expect to see a relatively long period during which such adult learners use placeholders.

In the previous work on Organic Grammar (Vainikka & Young-Scholten, 1994, 1996, 2011), on the L2 acquisition of German by naturalistic adult speakers of English, Korean, Italian, Portuguese, Spanish and Turkish, we have argued that their early acquisition of syntax follows basically the same course as in L1 acquisition. Assuming full access to UG (e.g. White, 1989), adult L2 learners use the same mechanisms as children for positing functional projections. Recent work on instructed learners of two other L2s corroborates this: Chen *et al.* (2015) on English-speaking adults' production of L2 Mandarin over two years, and Kahoul *et al.*'s (2018) cross-sectional study of Arabic and Mandarin adults' production, perception and processing of TP and AgrP in English.

As noted above, acquisition of functional structure in German involves raising the thematic verb from the head-final VP to second position in declaratives, and to final position in embedded clauses. With L2 structure building guided by UG (X'-theory), we expect no differences across learners from languages whose grammars differ in their functional features. There is evidence that once learners begin to posit functional projections in L2 German, they are appropriately head-initial for all learners regardless of the headedness of their native language functional projections. It is difficult to tell whether speakers with across-the-board L1 functional projections (e.g. English, Italian, Portuguese and Spanish), rely on these projections or posit German projections solely by relying on X′-theory. However, if speakers of consistently head-final languages, such as Korean and Turkish, display the same acquisition patterns as those with consistently head-initial projections (and they do), we can conclude that L1 transfer is not involved, as in Example (11) where *brau* 'need' appears to the left of the object and the nonfinite verb *fragen* 'ask' in final position (Vainikka & Young-Scholten, 1994):

(11) *Jetzt brau   Wohnungsamt   fragen.* (Sevinc/Turkish L1)
       now   need-0/1SG housing.authority ask-INF
       [*Jetzt brauche ich das Wohnungsamt fragen.*]
       'Now (I) need to ask (the) housing authority.'

In previous work on L2 German, we looked at the nontarget elements which learners use to mark syntactic positions, and in Vainikka and Young-Scholten (2009), we argued that learners fill an empty specifier position (see Vainikka & Levy, 1999 for a related account for patterns of empty subjects in Finnish and Hebrew). What we termed the Full House Principle accounts for learners' tentative positing of an AgrP without having acquired the full subject-verb agreement paradigm in German. The learner's UG-constrained grammar leads to filling the head of AgrP with a verb, but the specifier position is not filled with an obligatory subject but rather other material.

As one would predict under a UG-driven approach to acquisition, the same holds for heads. The learner searches the input for what might qualify as a head. There is a clear evidence that at the post-bare-VP stage, thematic verb forms are a possible occupant of the head of TP, but the forms learners produce vary from bare stems (as in Sevinc's production in the example above) to target-like forms to the more common default (*-n*) form (see Vainikka & Young-Scholten, 2011), as shown in Examples (8) to (10). Joan's acquisition was rapid due to her receiving a high quantity of input. She was a secondary school student on a year-long exchange living with a host family who received minimal explicit instruction in German and had no regular contact with other English speakers. Migrant workers Maria and Kemal display the same use of *-n* forms as Joan, but owing to much less exposure to German, they remained at this stage of development far longer than she did.

(12) *Ich trinken Tee immer morgen.* (Joan/L1 English)
       I   drink   tea always morning
       [*Ich trinke morgens immer Tee.*]
       'I always drink tea in the morning.'

(13)   *Und dann nachher   kommen   die Sonne nochmal wieder.*
                                                    (Maria/L1 Spanish)

And then afterwards come-INF the sun   yet   again

[*Und dann nachher kommt die Sonne nochmal wieder.*]

'And then afterwards the sun comes out again.'

(14)   *Ich sehen   Schleier.* (Kemal/L1 Turkish)

I   see-INF veil

[*Ich sehe den Schleier.*]

'I see the veil.'

We find these developmental patterns regardless of learners' native languages. If UG pushes the learner to posit a new layer of syntactic structure before the morphological content of the new layer has been acquired, we might also see learners using alternative, nontarget material, to fill the head of a given projection. And if we consider that the native languages of the learners whose L2 German data we examine here employ suffixation for verbal inflection, and that the morphology of Romance languages in particular shares some surface characteristics with German, we might observe a transparency effect. That is, if phonologically similar morphemes exist in the L1 and the L2, the learner will find it easier to detect these in the ambient input. But as mentioned above, for functional projections that are headed by a bound morpheme (such as AgrP in German with its paradigm of agreement suffixes), we expect that finding the evidence for the AgrP will be more difficult for adults than for children, and that adults will prefer free morphemes (Vainikka & Young-Scholten, 1998, 2011). Given adult L2 learners' greater challenges in identifying the correct target material for the head, the intermediate stage during which a projection has been tentatively posited but not yet confirmed, is expected to be protracted for adults, resulting in a relatively long period of using a placeholder.

We can now state the following predictions for the use of placeholders at the intermediate stage of acquisition when the learner is positing the IP-level projections in German, which are NegP, TP and AgrP:

(15)   Predictions for German placeholders:

NegP: Little use of placeholders expected because NegP only involves the verbal negator *nicht* 'not' and the nominal negator *kein* 'no', with no further morphology.

TP: Both an auxiliary verb (in T) and a matching participle form of the verb must be acquired, which makes this a difficult projection, morphologically speaking. We would therefore expect to find learners producing placeholders. One early placeholder might be a raised verb (with no special morphology, i.e. *-n*); see examples above. The best placeholder that doesn't involve verb raising would be an INFL-element that is common and not very complex morphologically, such as the modal *muss* or *will* (1sg and 3sg same form).

AgrP: The learner must both raise a thematic verb to this position and must acquire the agreement paradigm to correctly realize its head. We therefore expect a lengthy period of place holding. For AgrP, as well as TP, raising an unmarked verb is also an option here. In addition, if the learner does not raise the verb, an easy option would be the copula. In German, the common IP-related verb forms that exhibit the agreement paradigm are the auxiliary *haben* and the copula (and auxiliary) *sein*. Of these, the copula *sein* is the grammatically simplest one, as it does not require matching with a participle form of the main verb; nevertheless, the copula *sein* represents the full agreement paradigm of German. Here use of the copula may be facilitated by phonological similarities across languages, for example, for Spanish speakers who recognize third person singular *ist* (often realized by native speakers as [Is] 'is' in German on the basis of *es* 'is' in Spanish.

5.2 TP placeholders

The first study of naturalistic adults was the cross-sectional Heidelberg project of what the researchers expected would be development of a pidgin among migrant workers in Germany (Becker *et al.*, 1977). Despite large numbers at the time (267,000 from Italy; 104,000 from Spain; 169,000 from Greece; 377,000 from Yugoslavia; 516,000 from Turkey), no evidence of a pidgin was found. The study instead was one of the first to propose that L2 adults 'do not behave idiosyncratically but rather stages of acquisition are more or less common for all learners, and they pass through them in a well-defined path' (Becker *et al.*, 1977: 45). Data were from the oral production of 24 Italian and 24 Spanish manual workers speakers over the age of 18. Learners were categorized by years of residence, and for those with under 4 years in Germany, there were almost no auxiliaries, modals or copulas. After 4 years, there was a substantial increase of these functional elements along with subjects (see Vainikka & Young-Scholten, 1996, 2011 for further details). Results point to learners gradually – and slowly – projecting INFL-level syntax and using place holders. Tomá, with under four years' residence in Germany, rather than using an -*n* form, using *habe*, or a raised main verb, uses a modal and participle to mark tense:

(16) *Ich muss gesehen* (= *yo lo he visto* – 'I have seen it')

$\qquad\qquad\qquad\qquad\qquad\qquad$ Tomá A, L1 Spanish

$\quad$ I   must see-past

$\quad$ [*Ich habe das/es gesehen./Ich sah das/es.*]

$\quad$ 'I saw that/it.'

While Becker *et al.* (1977) speculate that such usage had to do with the frequency of *muss* on the factory floor where Tomá and others in the study worked, we now have a more principled explanation involving a placeholder for T as Tomá searched for the target-like material for the head.

5.3 AgrP placeholders

Following the Heidelberg study of naturalistic adult learners was the ZISA study of speakers of Italian, Portuguese and Spanish (L2 adults over two years; 45 adults in a cross-sectional design; Clahsen *et al.*, 1983). Interestingly, while the researchers established a common route of acquisition for all learners, they divided them into two groups: those who supplied functional morphology and those who omitted it. This suggests variation – perhaps based on level of education or other external influences – along the lines of the learner's search in the input for the heads of projections.

There are three verb forms in the data from Romance language learners in the ZISA study which do not mark agreement: *-n*, the nonfinite form in German, and *-e*, and zero/a bare stem. At the earliest stage of development for Italian (Salvatore and Bongiovanni) and Spanish (Jose and Rosalinda) learners of German, there are basically no auxiliaries or modals produced. Rosalinda, however, produces three instances of *wolle = will* 'want' (*wollen* nonfinite) that we can construe as a placeholder as she tentatively posits TP. In addition, she produces five instances of the copula *ist*. Jose – whose longitudinal data reveal very rapid acquisition – produces 39 instances of *ist* (and one *bin* 'am') in the earliest recordings. For Jose, the overused *ist* might be a placeholder for either T or Agr. There is no such pattern in the Italian data. At this point in their development, there is no evidence of any of the learners having acquired the agreement paradigm of suffixation on main verbs. There is some verb raising (two examples each) as shown by placement of the verb relative to adverbs and to subjects, and given that the verbs are not marked for finiteness. Moreover, placement of the verb relative to negation indicates the verb has not been raised. We suggest a role here for the transparency of *is(t)* → *es* from Spanish because the element is related in all three ways (phonologically, syntactically and semantically). However, the Italian equivalent *e* is only related syntactically and semantically. That is, *ist* functions – tentatively – as a placeholder for the head of AgrP. What makes it difficult to definitively conclude that the German copula is a placeholder for AgrP is lack of clear evidence at this point that the projection below the AgrP, the TP, has been acquired.

5.4 Multiword sequences as placeholders

In the earliest samples from Spanish children learning English, Lakshmanan (1993/94) also observed them using the prepositions *with* and *for* rather than the copula form *is* as a main verb. Categories that function as placeholders do not invariably involve INFL material and, as we shall see, placeholders do not invariably involve singe target words and can also be multiword sequences which the learner appears to be deploying as unanalyzed chunks.

Acquisition researchers have long examined the nontarget oral production of multiword sequences. These sequences are also those used in a target-like manner, for example, formulaic language, defined as 'a whole sentence or a group of words or it may be one word [...] but it must always be something which [...] cannot be further analyzed or decomposed' (Jesperson, 1924/1976: 88). That is, they function like single 'big words' (Ellis, 1996: 111). Wray (2002) lists over 50 terms that have been used to refer to the multimorphemic strings she refers to as formulaic language or formulaic sequences, neutral terms.

5.4.1 Placeholders in L2 English

Data from a recent study expand our view of what second language learners recruit as place holders. Vainikka *et al.* (2017) found that among 14 adult immigrants whose native languages were Arabic, Urdu and related Dari, Punjabi and Pahari, and who had varying levels of native and second language literacy, it was the nonliterates who produced the most instances of placeholders, and these included multiword sequences. As was the case in other studies, the learners produced these at a pre-AgrP stage. These learners are of interest in the context of discussion of children's use of formulaic sequences. Uninstructed learners are faced with the same task as young children who 'capture [from the speech stream] some pieces in order to determine their meaning' (Peters, 1983: 5). Without literacy and concomitant weak or no meta-awareness of language and its units as an object, young children may treat multiword sequences as single words without analyzing the function morphemes in these sequences 'since they have no discrete referential meaning' (Wray, 2002: 137).

Both L1-literate and nonliterate adult L2 learners follow the path of development for English predicted by Organic Grammar, and both literate and nonliterate learners recruit elements from the input as placeholders while working on the functional projections TP and AgrP. The syntactic structure assumed for English is shown in Example (17):

(17)
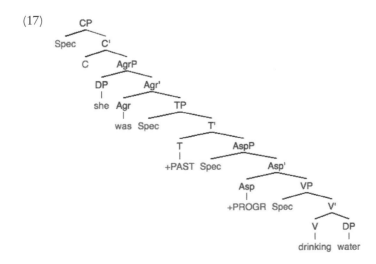

Wray remarks that for uninstructed adult L2 learners, the amount of formulaic language produced 'seems subject to considerable variation' (Wray, 2002: 148). Indeed, these data reveal variation in use of specific placeholders where nonliterates are more likely to recruit multiword placeholders that are not verbs, yet which nonetheless contain functional elements.

This occurs after the VP stage, when the learner is in the process of attempting to posit the projections shown in Example (18), along with NegP:

(18)   Predictions for English place holders:

AsP will be easy to acquire with *-ing* (without auxiliary *be*) as a straightforwardly identifiable head.

NegP in English is more difficult than the German NegP due to agreement forms of do, so we expect placeholders to surface. For T and Agr, we might possibly expect verb raising of an unmarked form to fill T or Agr even though the target language does not involve this.

TP: For T, the learner needs to figure out past regular and irregular morphology, and because this is a challenge, we expect place holders such as uninflected modals or forms of copula *be*. If the learner is paying attention to suffixes, *-s* with its three functions may be recruited as a placeholder.

AgrP: the 3SG *-s* is the greatest challenge given the confusion the three functions of *-s* cause and the impoverished agreement paradigm in English, so we predict a placeholder; again, this might be a modal or a copula *be* form.

The participants recruited for the study had all moved to the UK after puberty and had had no exposure to English prior to immigration. As with the Dutch L2 learners studied by Julien *et al.* (2015), these adult immigrants were all enrolled in English as a second language classes at the time of testing. Data were oral production, in response to a series of tasks with pictures designed to prompt utterances intended to reveal morphosyntax relating to negation and to various functional projections through their production of utterances with copula, auxiliary and main verbs in simple present, present progressive and past tenses.

We observe several of these learners at an early post-VP stage using various placeholders. For NegP, Dari speaker Sultani uses 'is don't' rather than 'not' in the negation task. For the task that sought to elicit data to examine the TP projection, Panjabi speaker Zabila produced no auxiliary verbs and few tense or copula *be* forms. However, she pervasively overgeneralized *-s*, and not only to main verbs in all persons, both singular and plural, but she also attached *-s* to other content words. The first example was produced during a task which required her to describe a picture in which a girl was reading a book. The second involved two girls depicted stirring a single pot:

(19)   a. *reads books ladies*

b. *girls this cookens ... foods this cookens.*

Arabic speakers Amro and Awad overuse 'I'm' in one of tasks in which single individuals and two or more individuals are depicted engaged in various activities.

(20)   a. *two guys I'm reading message.*

b. *three guys I'm washing ... washing in dishes.*

Mohammad S overuses items as INFL-level placeholders which are not from the same word class, for example, 'in the'. The prompt in Example (21a) was a picture of a woman reading a newspaper and in Example (21b) of a boy setting the table. The words in brackets were given as prompts:

(21)   a. *[afterwards] this woman in the book in the writing.*

b. *[every day, this boy] in the cook in the spoon in the fish.*

As far as AgrP-level place holders, the L1 Arabic speaker Rawdha is more advanced than the above learners, and seems to be using the nominative pronoun 'he' as a place holder for AgrP:

(22)   a. *the woman he shower the dog.*

b. *[every morning] the boy he get up and drink coffee.*

The individual variation in learners' use of placeholders is twofold. First, there are differences in the words and/or sequences they recruit. Some seem to be borrowing head material from other functional projections, and this might be because they are further along in acquiring these or they are recruiting functional elements which have been the focus of classroom instruction. Of note is that even when words and words in sequences produce belong to a different category than is required, these are nonetheless closed class elements. Learners' recruitment of these words and sequences is systematic; they do not simply use content words which would be frequent in their classroom input, such as 'desk' or 'door' or 'bus'. These data provide compelling evidence that learners subconsciously know and use closed class elements, that is, function words, after identifying them in the L2 input they are receiving. Since input does not come labeled, this alone is evidence for the post puberty operation of UG.

Second, placeholders are not used by all learners. Echoing Julien *et al.*'s (2015) results, those who used place holders are beyond the

VP and NegP stages and not yet at the CP stage. In this group are the slow-progressing nonliterate learners, but the group also includes those literate in their native languages. As already noted, those not literate in their native language are more likely to use placeholders not directly related to the actual verbal head, and this may be due to over-reliance on auditory input when lack of literacy precludes the use of visual memory for written text.

6 Discussion and Conclusion

Researchers have profitably examined nontarget use in adults' oral production of single morphemes or stem + unanalyzed suffix and concluded that these function as placeholders during the development of morphosyntax in an L2. There has also long been discussion about the role that the learning of multiword sequences in the target language might play; that is, acquisition could be driven by learning of multiword sequences which the learner then analyzes (see e.g. Myles *et al.*, 1999 and Myles, 2004). Decades ago, Krashen and Scarcella (1978) reviewed existing evidence and rejected such an account, and more recently, so did Bardovi-Harlig and Stringer (2017), on the basis of experimental evidence. Bardovi-Harlig and Stringer (2017) concluded that the learning of formulae in the target language does not act as some sort of catalyst for the acquisition of morphosyntax and that morphosyntax shows evidence of being acquired before the internal analysis of formulae involving the same morphosyntax. We find their evidence convincing; however, there seems to be a useful role for multiword sequences in the acquisition of morphosyntax. Overuse of such sequences may point to an input frequency effect relating to reduction of processing effort (Becker, 1975), particularly for the shorter sequences to which Wray (2002) refers as dummy fillers. If we find more evidence of multiword sequences functioning as placeholders, we cannot say they do not contribute to acquisition. We have not yet searched for such sequences in any other L2 data, but we predict that once oral production data are more closed examined – particularly data from adults similar to those discussed – we will find comparable patterns.

During the process of positing functional projections in response to primary linguistic data, it is UG that prompts the learner to fill the head of a projection, but because it takes some time for learners to figure out exactly what fills that head, they could well recruit nontarget functional elements, including multiword sequences not internally analyzed in the same or in another functional category. We suspect that there is much more evidence of the search for heads in oral production data from adult immigrant learners, but we have ignored the data because – until now – it has not fit into our own categories of data analysis.

Notes

(1) Additional accounts that fall on the one hand under Schwartz and Sprouse's (1996) Full Transfer/Full Access include Feature Reassembly (Lardiere, 2009) and Valueless Features (Eubank, 1996), and on the other hand, those which fall under structure building include Modulated Structure Building (Hawkins, 2001).

(2) *Wasser* 'water'.

(3) Some experimental evidence suggests that infants comprehend grammatical morphemes before they produce them, supporting the idea that functional projections are posited early, for example, when children produce single words. A more nuanced picture indicates that this conclusion is premature. For example, Orfitelli and Hyams (2008) found that 2 to 3½-year-old children acquiring English optionally or exclusively comprehended adult imperatives such as 'Eat a cookie' as a finite clauses referring to ongoing action. This supports our claim that at the early stages of development, children have a different mental grammar than adults, and is further evidence for children's projection of only a VP at the start of their development of morphosyntax.

References

Ahrenholz, B. (2005) Reference to persons and objects in the function of subject in learner varieties. In H. Hendriks (ed.) *The Structure of Learner Varieties* (pp. 19–64). Berlin: Mouton de Gruyter.

Baker, M. (1985) Incorporation: A theory of grammatical function changing. PhD dissertation, Massachusetts Institute of Technology.

Bardovi-Harlig, K. and Stringer, D. (2017) Unconventional expressions: Productive syntax in the L2 acquisition of formulaic language. *Second Language Research* 33, 61–90.

Becker, J. (1975) The phrasal lexicon. In R. Shank and B.L. Nash-Webber (eds) *Theoretical Issues in Natural Language Processing* (pp. 60–63). Cambridge, MA: Bolt, Baranek and Newman.

Becker, A., Dittmar, N., Gutmann, M., Klein, W., Rieck, B-O., Senft, G., Senft, I., Steckner, W. and Thielicke, E. (1977) *Heidelberger Forschungsprojekt 'Pidgin-Deutsch spanischer und italienischer Arbeiter in der Bundesrepublik': Die ungesteurerte Erlernung des Deutschen durch spanische und italienischer Arbeiter. Eine soziolinguistische Untersuchung.* Beihefte 2. Osnabrücker Beiträge zur Sprachtheorie (OBST): Osnabrück.

Berko, J. (1958) The child's learning of English morphology. *Word* 14,150–177.

Boser, K., Lust, B.C., Santelman, L.M. and Whitman, J. (1992) The syntax of CP and V-2 in early child German (ECG): The Strong Continuity Hypothesis. In K. Broderick (ed.) *Proceedings of the North East Linguistic Society Annual Meeting/NELS 22* (pp. 51–65). Amherst, MA: GLSA.

Chen, D., Vainikka, A. and Young-Scholten, M. (2015) Functional projections in L2 Mandarin. Paper presented at the ISOCTAL Inaugural Conference, Newcastle, 11 December.

Chomsky, N. (1995) *The Minimalist Program.* Cambridge, MA: MIT Press.

Cinque, G. (1999) *Adverbs and Functional Heads. A Cross-linguistic Perspective.* New York: Oxford University Press.

Clahsen, H., Meisel, J. and Pienemann, M. (1983) *Deutsch als Zweitsprache: Der Spracherwerb ausländischer Arbeiter.* Tübingen: Narr.

Clahsen, H., Vainikka, A. and Young-Scholten, M. (1991) Lernbarkeitstheorie und lexikalisches Lernen. *Linguistische Berichte* 130, 466–477.

Culicover, P. and Jackendoff, R. (2005) *Simpler Syntax.* Oxford: Oxford University Press.

Dimroth, C. (2002) Topics, assertions, and additive words: How L2 learners get from information structure to target-language syntax. *Linguistics* 40, 891–923.

Ellis, N.C. (1996) Sequencing in SLA: Phonological memory, chunking and points of order. *Studies in Second Language Acquisition* 18, 91–216.

Eubank, L. (1996) Negation in early German-English interlanguage: More value-less features in the L2 initial state. *Second Language Research* 12, 73–106.

Fukui, N. and Sakai, H. (2003) The visibility guideline for functional categories: Verb raising in Japanese and related issues. *Lingua* 113, 321–375.

Giorgio, A. and Pianesi, F. (1997) *Tense and Aspect: From Semantics to Morphosyntax.* Oxford: Oxford University Press.

Grimshaw, J. (1986) A morphosyntactic explanation for the mirror principle. *Linguistic Inquiry* 17, 745–749.

Grimshaw, J. (1997) Projection, heads, and optimality. *Linguistic Inquiry* 28, 373–422.

Guilfoyle, E. and M. Noonan. (1992) Functional categories in language acquisition. *Canadian Journal of Linguistics* 37, 241–272.

Haberzettl, S. (2003) 'Tinkering' with chunks: Form-oriented strategies and idiosyncratic utterance patterns without functional implications in the IL of Turkish speaking children learning German. In C. Dimroth and M. Starren (eds) *Information Structure and the Dynamics of Language Acquisition* (pp. 45–64). Amsterdam: Benjamins.

Hawkins, R. (2001) *Second Language Syntax. A Generative Introduction.* Malden, MA: Blackwell.

Hendriks, H. (ed.) (2005) Structuring pace in discourse: A comparison of Chinese, English, French and German L1, and English, French and German L2 acquisition. In H. Hendriks (ed.) *The Structure of Learner Varieties* (pp. 111–156). Berlin: Mouton de Gruyter.

Huebner, T. (1983) *The Acquisition of English. A Longitudinal Analysis.* Ann Arbor, MI: Karoma Publishers.

Ionin, T. (2008) Progressive aspect in child L2-English. In B. Haznedar and E. Gavruseva (eds) *Current Trends in Child Second Language Acquisition: A Generative Perspective*, Language Acquisition and Language Disorders (Vol. 46, pp. 17–53). Amsterdam: John Benjamins.

Jesperson, O. (1924/1976) Living grammar. In *The Philosophy of Grammar* (pp. 17–29). London: George Allen and Unwin, London. Reprinted in Bornstein, D.D. (ed.) *Readings in the Theory of Grammar* (pp. 82–93). Cambridge, MA: Winthrop Publishers.

Jordens, P. and Dimroth, C. (2006) Finiteness in children and adults learning Dutch. In N. Gagarina and I. Gülzow, I. (eds) *The Acquisition of Verbs and their Grammar: The Effect of Particular Languages* (pp. 173–200). Dordrecht: Springer.

Julien, M., van Hout, R. and van de Craats, I. (2015) Meaning and function of dummy auxiliaries in adult acquisition of Dutch as an additional language. *Second Language Research* 32, 49–73.

Kahoul, W., Vainikka, A. and Young-Scholten, M. (2018) Solving the mystery of the missing surface inflections. In C. Wright, T. Piske and M. Young-Scholten (eds) *Mind Matters in SLA* (pp. 93–116). Bristol: Multilingual Matters.

Klein, W. and Perdue, C. (1992) *Utterance Structure: Developing Grammars Again.* Amsterdam: John Benjamins.

Krashen, S. and Scarcella, R. (1978) On routines and patterns in language acquisition and performance. *Language Learning* 28, 283–300.

Lakshmanan, U. (1993/4) 'The Boy for the Cookie': Some evidence for the non-violation of the case-filter in child L2 acquisition. *Language Acquisition* 3, 51–97.

Lakshmanan. U. and Selinker, L. (2001) Analyzing interlanguage: How do we know what learners know? *Second Language Research* 17, 393–420.

Lardiere, D. (2009) Some thoughts on the contrastive analysis of features in second language acquisition. *Second Language Research* 25, 173–227.

Lebeaux, D. (1988) Language acquisition and the form of the grammar. Unpublished PhD thesis, University of Massachusetts.

Lebeaux, D. (2000) *Language Acquisition and the Form of the Grammar.* Amsterdam: Benjamins.

Lust, B.C. (2006) *Child Language – Acquisition and Growth.* Cambridge: Cambridge University Press.

Miestamo, M., Tamm, A. and Wagher-Nagy, B. (2015) *Negation in Uralic Languages*. Amsterdam: Benjamins.

Mills, A. (1985) The acquisition of German. In D.I. Slobin (ed.) *The Cross-linguistic Study of Language Acquisition* (pp. 141–254). London: Erlbaum.

Myles, F. (2004) From data to theory. *Transactions of the Philological Society* 102, 139–168.

Myles, F., Hooper, J. and Mitchell, R. (1999) Interrogative chunks in French L2: A basis for creative construction? *Studies in Second Language Acquisition* 21, 49–80.

Orfitelli, R. and Hyams, N. (2008) An experimental study of children's comprehension of null subjects: Implications for grammatical/performance accounts. In H. Chan, H. Jacob and E. Kapia (eds) *Proceedings BU Conference of Child Language Development (BUCLD) 32* (Vol. 2) (pp. 335–346). Somerville, MA: Cascadilla Press.

Paradis, J. and Crago, M. (2001) The morphosyntax of specific language impairment in French: Evidence for an extended optional default account. *Language Acquisition 9*, 269–300.

Peters, A. (1983) *Units of Language Acquisition*. Cambridge: Cambridge University Press.

Pienemann, M. (1981) *Der Zweitspracherberb ausländischer Arbeiterkinder*. Bonn: Bouvier Verlag Herbert Grundmann.

Poeppel, D. and Wexler, K. (1993) The Full Competence Hypothesis of clause structure in early German. *Language 69*, 1–33.

Prévost, P. and White, L. (2000a) Missing surface inflection or impairment in second language acquisition. Evidence from tense and agreement. *Second Language Research* 16, 103–134.

Prévost, P. and White, L. (2000b) Finiteness and variability in SLA: More evidence for Missing Surface Inflection. In A. Greenhill, H. Littlefield and C. Tano (eds) *BUCLD 23 Proceedings* (pp. 575–586). Somerville, MA: Cascadilla Press.

Prévost, P. and White, L. (2000c) Accounting for morphological variation in second language acquisition: Truncation or missing inflection? In M.A. Friedman and L. Rizzi (eds) *The Acquisition of Syntax: Studies in Comparative Developmental Linguistics* (pp. 202–235). London: Longman.

Radford, A. (1990) *Syntactic Theory and the Acquisition of English Syntax*. Oxford: Blackwell.

Radford, A. (1995) Children: Architects or brickies? In D. MacLaughlin and S. McEwen (eds) *BUCLD 19 Proceedings* (pp. 1–19). Somerville, MA: Cascadilla Press.

Rizzi, L. (1993/4) Some notes on linguistic theory and language development: The case of root infinitives. *Language Acquisition 3*, 371–393.

Schwartz, B.D. and Sprouse, R. (1996) L2 cognitive states and the Full Transfer/Full Access model. *Second Language Research* 12, 40–72.

Starren, M. (2001) The second time: The acquisition of temporality in Dutch and French as a second language. Unpublished PhD, Tilburg University, the Netherlands.

Vainikka, A. (1993/4) Case in the development of English syntax. *Language Acquisition 3*, 257–325.

Vainikka, A. and Levy, Y. (1999) Empty subjects in Hebrew and Finnish. *Natural Language and Linguistic Theory* 17, 613–671.

Vainikka, A. and Young-Scholten, M. (1994) Direct access to X'-Theory: Evidence from Korean and Turkish adults learning German. In T. Hoekstra and B.D. Schwartz (eds) *Language Acquisition Studies in Generative Grammar – Papers in Honor of Kenneth Wexler from the 1991 GLOW Workshops* (pp. 265–316). Amsterdam/Philadelphia: John Benjamins.

Vainikka, A. and Young-Scholten, M. (1996) The early stages in adult L2 syntax: Additional evidence from Romance speakers. *Second Language Research* 12, 140–176.

Vainikka, A. and Young-Scholten, M. (1998) Tree growth and morphosyntactic triggers in adult SLA. In M.L. Beck (ed.) *The L2 Acquisition of Morphology* (pp. 89–113). Amsterdam: Benjamins.

Vainikka, A. and Young-Scholten, M. (2006) The roots of syntax and how they grow. Organic Grammar, the basic variety and processability theory. In S. Unsworth, A. Sorace, T. Parodi and M. Young-Scholten (eds) *Paths of Development in L1 and L2 Acquisition* (pp. 77–106). Amsterdam: John Benjamins.

Vainikka, A. and Young-Scholten, M. (2007) Minimalism vs. Organic Syntax. In S. Karimi, V. Samiian and W. Wilkins (eds) *Clausal and Phrasal Architecture: Syntactic Derivation and Interpretation. Papers in Honour of Joseph Emonds* (pp. 319–338). Amsterdam: Benjamins.

Vainikka, A. and Young-Scholten, M. (2009) Successful features: Verb raising and adverbs in L2 acquisition under an Organic Grammar approach. In N. Snape, I.Y-K. Leung and M. Sharwood Smith (eds) *Representational Deficits in SLA. Studies in Honour of Roger Hawkins* (pp. 53–68). Amsterdam: Benjamins.

Vainikka, A. and Young-Scholten, M. (2011) *The Acquisition of German. Introducing Organic Grammar*. Berlin/Boston: Mouton de Gruyter.

Vainikka, A. and Young-Scholten, M. (2013) Universal minimal structure: Evidence and theoretical ramifications. *Linguistic Approaches to Bilingualism* 3 (2), 180–212.

Vainikka, A., Young-Scholten, M., Ijuin, C. and Jarad, S. (2017) Literacy in the development of L2 English morphosyntax. *Proceedings of the 12th Annual Low-educated Second Language and Literacy Acquisition Conference* (pp. 239–250). Granada, Spain, 8–10 September 2016.

van de Craats, I. (2009) The role of IS in the acquisition of finiteness by adult Turkish learners of Dutch. *Studies in Second Language Acquisition* 31, 59–92.

van de Craats, I. and van Hout, R. (2010) Dummy auxiliaries in the L2 acquisition of Moroccan learners of Dutch: Form and function. *Second Language Research* 26, 473–500.

van de Craats I and Verhagen, J. (eds) (2013) *Dummy Auxiliaries in First and Second Language Acquisition*. Berlin: De Gruyter Mouton.

van Kampen, J. (1997) *First Steps in wh-Movement*. Delft: Eburon.

von Stutterheim, C. (1987) *Temporalität in der Zweitsprache*. Berlin: de Gruyter.

von Stutterheim, C. and Lambert, M. (2005) Cross-linguistic analysis of temporal perspectives in text production. In H. Hendriks (ed.) *The Structure of Learner Varieties* (pp. 203–230). Berlin: Mouton de Gruyter.

Wagner-Gough, J. (1978) Comparative studies in second language learning. In E. Hatch (ed.) *Second Language Acquisition. A Book of Readings* (pp. 155–174). Rowley, MA: Newbury House.

Webelhuth, G. (1984/5) German is configurational. *The Linguistic Review* 4, 203–246.

Weissenborn, J. (1990) Functional categories and verb movement: The acquisition of German syntax reconsidered. *Linguistische Berichte Special Issue* (3), 190–224.

White, L. (1989) *Universal Grammar in Second Language Acquisition*. Amsterdam: Benjamins.

Wray, A. (2002) *Formulaic Language and the Lexicon*. Cambridge: Cambridge University Press.

Zuckerman, S. (2001) The acquisition of 'optional' movement. Unpublished PhD thesis, University of Groningen, The Netherlands.

Zuckerman, S. (2013) Dummy auxiliaries in Dutch first language acquisition. In E. Blom, I. van de Craats and J. Verhagen (eds) *Dummy Auxiliaries in First and Second Language Acquisition* (pp. 39–74). Berlin: De Gruyter Mouton.

7 The Acquisition Environment for Instructed L2 Learners: Implementing Hybrid and Online Language Courses

Bridget Yaden

1 Introduction

Given the many ways in which online course offerings can be compatible with missions of academic excellence and student access, as well as being able to meet the goals of language courses, colleges may be encouraged to develop online courses in a targeted, intentional way. A two-year pilot project for developing blended and online Spanish courses at a small residential liberal arts college will be described below. I will describe how I transformed a face-to-face first-year Spanish curriculum, with a communicative approach to language learning, into a fully online summer course. The communicative approach (Lee & VanPatten, 2003) includes the key theoretical concepts of comprehensible input, negotiation of meaning and information exchange, among others. These areas can all be addressed through effective uses of various technologies. The goals of the first-year curriculum are for students to develop basic communicative proficiency in listening, speaking, reading and writing, using Spanish meaningfully from the first day of instruction in order to aid acquisition. In the first-year courses, the students learn Spanish vocabulary, pronunciation and structures, and read and listen to a fair amount of authentic oral and written Spanish. Written and oral student work, assessed using performance indicators for language proficiency that align with the American Council on the Teaching of Foreign Languages (ACTFL) Proficiency Guidelines, demonstrated that all students exiting the first year program through the online offerings were at least at the program's goal of novice high proficiency, if not higher.[1]

2 Literature Review

An increasing number of students in higher education are taking online courses. 'Online enrollments have continued to grow at rates far in excess of the total higher education student population, with the most recent data demonstrating no signs of slowing' (Allen & Seaman, 2008: 1) However, it is not uncommon for small, residential liberal arts colleges to resist developing or providing online courses for students, as many faculty and administrators consider online teaching as being incompatible with the mission of their institution. Faculty in the humanities and in world languages, in particular, may hold the strong belief that their courses would not work in an online format. Blake writes that many language educators 'harbor deep-seated doubts as to whether a blended course, much less a completely virtual learning experience, could ever provide L2 learners with an accepted way to gain linguistic proficiency' (Blake, 2008: 102). Pannapacker challenges this notion by writing, 'online courses developed within an institutional context can preserve rather than under-mine our unique missions as liberal-arts colleges' (Pannapacker, 2014). The question, therefore, is two-fold: (1) how can hybrid/blended (partially online) or fully online courses serve the mission of a traditionally residen-tial liberal arts college; and (2) how specifically can world language course content be delivered online in such a way that achieves similar goals as face-to-face courses? As Hermosillo describes blended courses, 'the most common structure of a hybrid language course combines face-to-face (F2F) time with an instructor and the use of an online platform; it may also incorporate experiential learning in a language lab or in a real or virtual community of native speakers' (Hermosillo, 2014: 2).

There are many ways in which blended and fully online courses can support the mission of any institution, but particularly small liberal arts colleges that are historically residential with primarily face-to-face instruction. Pannapacker (2014) describes how online courses can support the mission and values of a liberal arts institution and the benefits include helping to improve the 4-year graduation rate, meeting the needs of students with extremely tight schedules in professional programs, and keeping credits and tuition dollars at the home institution. Students with limited time and money may choose to take advantage of summer courses, but this is often at community colleges or other institutions from which students transfer credits back to their home institution. Providing online courses in the summer allows a small, liberal arts college to keep more oversight on the curriculum and the student experience 'by making it less necessary for students to transfer credit for entire courses from outside parties' (Pannapacker, 2014). In a 2008 report (Allen & Seaman, 2008: 6), researchers found that 'both chief academic officers and online teaching faculty said that flexibility in meeting the needs of students was the most important motivation for teaching online.' If universities offer a discount for their online courses, this allows for increased access and is another way to meet students' needs. As Wang (2015) found in a study of 103 institutions, schools tend to heavily discount their online courses compared to on-campus courses, and smaller and private institutions set significantly lower prices when compared to online course costs at public and larger institutions. Sanders (2005) describes a 2-year project developing blended beginning Spanish courses that had the positive effects of increasing enrollments by 85% and lowering costs to students by 29%, with a reduction in class size from 30 to 25 students per section. In these and many other ways, small colleges can benefit from online course offerings.

Language programs can also reap these access benefits, while at the same time provide high-quality instruction. The technology tools available to educators and students in the 21st century allow for online courses that meet the needs of both traditional (grammar-based) and modern (communicative) language teaching methodologies. The experience will, by definition, be different from a face-to-face course, but similar language goals can be achieved in an online course. Computer-mediated communication (CMC) can provide opportunities for 'increasing the input (students) receive and the interaction in which they engaged in electronic form' (Ensslin & Krummes, 2013: 23). Despain's (2003) 2-½-year study comparing first year university level Spanish students who were in face-to-face classrooms and those who were taking the same course via an internet-based option, found that the two groups had similar overall achievements in the course. However, attrition rates were higher in the online course and the author in part attributes this to the lack of appropriate screening of students and orientation to the tools needed to be successful. Blake (2009) describes several empirical studies where online students outperform students in traditional face-to-face courses (Blake, 2009: 112–113), suggesting that 'online language learning can be effective' but noting that 'more research is needed to substantiate these initial observations.' In addition, for students with high anxiety about taking a language course, a phenomenon described in detail in Horwitz *et al.* (1986), as well as for students who need self-paced coursework, online courses can be extremely beneficial. For example, Payne (2004) found that students' anxieties are lower in computer-mediated chat exchanges and that students have more processing time than they in face-to-face interactions.

3 Institutional Context

In this section, the institutional context for a 2-year pilot of online and hybrid beginning Spanish courses will be described and I will argue that the benefits described here can be achieved at any kind of institution. Pacific Lutheran University (PLU) is a small, private liberal arts college in the Pacific Northwest, just minutes from the center of Washington State's second largest city (Tacoma). It is part of the New American Colleges and Universities consortium (http://newamericancolleges.org/), as an institution that has a liberal arts core through the College of Arts and Sciences, integrated with the professional schools of Business, Education, Nursing and Communications. Historically, PLU has been a residential college, with first- and second-year students in particular encouraged to live on campus. The university has a robust campus life, with successful residential halls that increasingly offer a variety of living-learning opportunities. In fact, the seven language programs within the Department of Languages and Literatures have benefited from years of collaboration with Residential Life, and can boast the development of the first living-learning community on campus, Hong International Hall, over a dozen years ago. However, in recent years, the number of commuter students (even among first-year students) has increased. The reasons are many – including costs, work schedules, family life and other factors. Campuses such as PLU are always looking for ways to improve the links between commuter students and the university. In addition, pressures of student retention, in particular at institutions that depend heavily on tuition, are ever-present, even in the best of financial times. Graduation rates are receiving tighter scrutiny from financial aid providers, so keeping students on track to graduate within four years is another priority.

Like many college and universities, our student population continues to change as we enroll more diverse groups, such as first-generation college students, veterans and students of color. Increasingly, our students have part- or full-time jobs, as well as family obligations and other situations that limit their schedule flexibility. In addition, students in professional programs with a tight curriculum that is restricted by external accrediting agencies and heavy curricular requirements find little flexibility in their class schedules. Online and hybrid courses provide additional choices to all students. For language programs in particular, we can attract students by offering first-year language courses in nontraditional formats through high-quality hybrid and online courses developed and taught by full-time language faculty.

With considerations of recruitment, retention, access (both cost and time) and on-time graduation rates, liberal arts institutions should explore the possibilities that technology-supported classes can offer. Given the benefits outlined above, I developed a 2-year pilot to experiment with hybrid and fully online beginning Spanish language courses. The courses, described below, were each successful in their own ways. In the future, the program will focus primarily on summer fully online courses to meet the specific needs of access and retention.

4 Faculty Development in Course Design

When institutions take the leap to move all or parts of a course to an online delivery model, they will find that 'many teachers tend to simply transfer what they've always done in the onsite classroom to the online environment', a move that 'is insufficient to realize our learners' potential in the 21st century' (Stein & Graham, 2014: 11). At PLU, academic leaders knew this could be a problem and turned this into an opportunity to design hybrid and online courses from the ground up. Through a cohort model, creatively named PLUTO (PLU Teaching Online), faculty apply to be a part of an extended workshop on developing technology-enhanced courses. The goals of PLUTO include developing blended and online courses that will meet the diverse needs of students, keep students connected to campus, improve retention, provide low-cost offerings and help students graduate on time. The workshops provide in-depth learning on pedagogy (technology-based and otherwise), accessibility and thoughtful course design.

As we are mainly a residential campus, our institution is currently limiting the blended and online courses so that they will only be offered in summer and January (J-term – interim term) only. During summer and interim sessions, students often return home or travel away from campus and take courses online or in person at other institutions such as state or community colleges, then transfer the credit back to PLU. If they can take courses from our own faculty, regardless of their physical location in the interim term and summer term, we hope they will be more likely to return to campus the next full semester. In addition, we can keep these tuition dollars in house as well as have quality control over the course content.

How can an institution encourage faculty participation and ensure high-quality technology offerings? Stipends or course releases for course development can be offered, and in-depth, high-quality training must be provided. At PLU, the PLUTO 'team' of faculty, administrators and tech staff offers extended cohort-based workshops twice a year – one to assist faculty in developing hybrid/blended courses, and the second for designing fully online courses. Faculty who complete the program earn an extra stipend, in addition to their course pay. The workshops are led by instructional technologists, faculty who have participated in previous workshops, and invited guests who present in-person or virtually. In addition, the workshops include a student panel, so that faculty can hear directly from students their hopes and fears regarding online learning.

The workshop included a variety of topics that are important to consider when redesigning a course for blended or fully online modes. Introductions include an overview of blended/online course development and research-based elements of good course design, with examples from other institutions as well as our own colleagues. Dedicated-technology training is provided as needed, so that faculty can effectively maneuver the tools that will help their students the most. Some institution-specific examples include Sakai (a learning management system), videoconferencing tools (such as Zoom) and tools for creating instructional videos (such as Camtasia). These tools will be described in more detail below. Other important training topics include backward planning with the focus on end learning objectives, assessment plans that include formative and summative assessments, and tools for interaction and engagement. Accessibility and accommodations are just as important online as face-to-face, so our training included how to make Word and PowerPoint files accessible to students, using headers and alt tags, and providing transcripts for videos.

Some faculty fear that they will eventually be replaced by technology and online courses, but Blake (2008: 14) argues that technology can 'complement what can be done in the L2 classroom, if used wisely' and that 'teachers who use technology will probably replace teachers who do not.' In fact, the instructor's role in online courses is just as important as it is in face-to-face learning, for both educational outcomes as well as retention. Our institution prides itself on individualized attention and personal connections with students, so this must be duplicated as much as possible in the online offerings. Class sizes are intentionally kept small (10–15 students or smaller) and the faculty presence must permeate the course. Therefore, much of the faculty training involves transferring this campus experience to the online experience, through tools for engagement such as facilitating student-student and faculty-student interaction in online discussions, dynamic experiences and personalized, timely feedback.

To ensure quality and as a tool for peer feedback on course design, faculty used the Quality Matters (QM) rubric (https://www.qualitymatters.org/). QM is a leader in setting standards for online courses, and provides a detailed rubric with eight sets of standards describing quality in areas such as learning objectives, assessment, instructional materials, learner support and accessibility/usability. Courses can go through official QM program review, for a fee, to achieve QM certification. At PLU, QM is used as a peer review process. Each course was reviewed by at least two colleagues using the QM tool, and faculty had time to integrate this valuable feedback before finalizing their courses. In addition, instructional technologists guided faculty and gave feedback every step of the way during the course design process.

When considering a language course redesign, Blake (2008: 107) argues that 'many hybrid-course teachers tend to view the computer components of this format as only suitable for drill-and-kill, or mechanical grammar practice, so as to free up the classroom meetings for more communicative activities', a view 'tied to a pedagogy spawned in the 1980s, with roots in behaviorism.' With the increasingly interactive nature of technology, technology-supported world language course content can be delivered in such a way that achieves similar goals as face-to-face courses. Comprehensible input, authentic materials and interactive communicative tasks can be provided through a variety of 21st century technology tools, as will be described below.

How do we ensure that students are ready to take these courses so that our course retention and successful completion is high? Despain

(2003) suggests vetting students prior to enrolling in the online course and describing what technical skills will be needed to complete it. To accomplish this, we first were very clear in the course description about the blended or online nature of the course. Then, we developed a student self-survey where students could assess their online course readiness. Finally, in the course introduction, we explicitly describe what prior knowledge, including technology experience, is required for the course. For example, for the Hispanic Studies101/102 (Beginning Spanish I and II) fully online courses, in the syllabus and on the landing page for the course website, I posted 'To be successful in this course, you should: have little to NO previous experience with Spanish – this course is for true beginners!; work consistently (no cramming!) and be willing to make mistakes!; and have access to the Internet to access Sakai and the online textbook and workbook.' Immediately following this note on the landing page, the students were taken through a tour of the course materials and resources, both by text but also a tutorial video that I created showing step-by-step where to find each resource and how to engage with the resource.

5 Blended Spanish Course Implementation

The first course developed for this 2-year pilot was a hybrid Spanish 101 course designed through participation in the first of its kind professional development cohort on campus (described above). Blended is not simply taking part of the course and moving it online while keeping a face-to-face component, but rather involves an intentional redesign of the course, to take 'the best of onsite and online to create a new learning environment' for students (Stein & Graham, 2014: 9). Through intentional course redesign, I built on over 20 years of experience teaching traditional university-level first-year Spanish courses to develop an effective course that shifted the focus from a teacher-centered to a more student-centered learning experience. Hermosillo (2014: 4) writes that 'well-designed hybrid programs can offer students concrete opportunities to appreciate language learning by helping them realize that they can produce their own learning outcomes and become autonomous learners of the Spanish language.' This is a release of control that some faculty might find uncomfortable at first but has enormous benefits for the students and was central in my thinking around designing this course and the fully online courses that followed.

The course was offered to first-year students in the January term, which is a 1-month intensive term between fall and spring semesters when students focus on one course only. The course capacity was 20 students, but owing to demand, 22 were accepted onto the course, and all 22 students successfully completed the course. The course (101) is designed for true beginners of the language, but as is common in our program, there were a handful of false-beginners in the class who have previous experience with Spanish but, for a variety of reasons (such as desire for review, insecurities in their abilities) opt to start at the beginning again. In addition, there was one heritage speaker, a student who came from a Spanish-speaking background and had good receptive skills, but was not used to producing Spanish. The self-paced online portion of the course was especially useful to deal with the differentiated instruction needed to meet the needs of such a diverse group.

The course syllabus had an additional piece in the course description in order to highlight the hybrid nature of the course: 'The class will be conducted almost exclusively in Spanish and in a blended format of face-to-face (f2f) and online learning activities.' In the most practical terms, the course met daily for 4 weeks (as is typical for a January interim course), but instead of 3 hours of class time, we met for 2 hours. The additional hour each day was moved, strategically, to the online portion of the course that students were to complete before coming to class.

The learning management system (LMS) utilized at our institution is Sakai, an open-source program that provides the basic tools available in most LMS products. These tools include file management, forum boards, quizzes, announcements and a gradebook. Students accessed the online portion of the course through the LMS as well as through the digital textbook and workbook that was required for the course. Sakai also has a statistics feature, so I could see how often students were logging in, which resources they opened, and other information that helped gauge participation and interaction with the course resources (see Figure 7.1).

Students previewed the course material each evening by completing a variety of interactive resources, watching instructional videos that I developed, then completing a formative assessment to check their understanding of the material before coming to class. The instructional videos were comprised of adapted PowerPoint presentations with language and culture content that was captured using screencasting tools, and students could hear and see me as I presented the material. The screencasts were created using Camtasia, which were then saved in MPEG 4 video format.

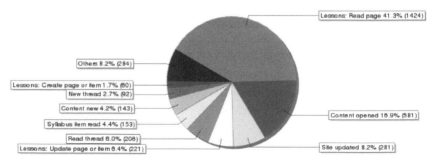

Figure 7.1 Sample of statistics tool in the learning management system (LMS)

Las universidades

- Explora las diferencias y las cosas similares entre universidades en los Estados Unidos y algunas universidades hispanas – pp. 44-45 del texto.

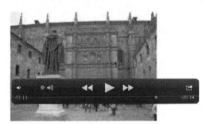

Figure 7.2 Sample screencast

A free tool that provides similar capabilities is Screencast-O-Matic (https://screencast-o-matic.com/home). In line with a communicative approach to teaching, these videos provided comprehensible input, in Spanish, to the students on a daily basis (Figure 7.2).

After the students viewed these instructional videos, they completed formative assessments in the form of online quizzes that contained mainly fill-in-the-blank and multiple choice, with automatic feedback as well as discussion boards with more open ended interactions. The quizzes were in English or Spanish, depending on whether they were more comprehension checks (e.g. ensuring the students had read the course objectives, as shown in Figure 7.3) or language production with students using the new vocabulary and grammar.

The text that was used in this course was *Sol y viento: Beginning Spanish*, 3rd edition (VanPatten *et al.*, 2012) with a communicative approach that provides comprehensible input and scaffolds language to support student output. At the time the platform for accessing the digital resources in the workbook and textbook was through *Centro*, an online platform that has since changed format to *Quia*. Students accessed interactive activities that allowed for multiple attempts and automatic instructive feedback. For open-ended activities, I could give feedback through the *Centro* system. This system also had a gradebook to track student progress. This textbook is based on a feature film that provides a context for language and culture. The students watch the episodes of the film on their own, through *Centro*, and complete online activities to assess their

1 I can work ahead, but each of my learning module assignments are due by _____ on the due date.

   ○ A. 5pm
   ○ B. 10pm
   ○ C. midnight

2 There is/are _____ written composition(s) in this course.

   ○ A. 3
   ○ B. 2
   ○ C. 1

3 There are 6 live conversations during this course, and I have to have them with the instructor.

   ○ True
   ○ False

Figure 7.3 Sample online formative assessment

comprehension. Then, the film provides a vehicle for great discussions and expansion activities in class.

The online work allowed for more face-to-face time for authentic communication. During class and group time, students worked in groups and as an entire class to use the language for real communication through polls, interviews and communicative games. For example, we had weekly 'speed dating' activities, where students had 1 minute with a partner to introduce themselves and discuss a specific topic in Spanish, then move to another partner when the 1-minute timer rang. Samples of conversation topics included introducing yourself and your hobbies (present-tense verbs and *gustar* 'to like' constructions), describing what you did the past weekend (preterit) and talking about what you were planning to do after class (future). Students gave their opinions about different topics using multimedia polls, including Polleverywhere (www.polleverywhere.com) and Kahoot (getkahoot.com) (Figure 7.4).

We also had more in-person time to engage with authentic texts, both written and multimedia. The course centered on the theme of Language: Time, Place and Identity, so materials included bilingual poems, short fiction texts in Spanish and nonfiction texts in Spanish on linguistic minorities, the indigenous languages of Oaxaca, language variation and language policies. Students were required to watch, in groups, three films from a suggested list and write a reflection on how each film connected to the course theme.

After designing and implementing this blended course, what eventually resulted was a flipped classroom, which Stein and Graham (2014: 38) describe as follows: 'Lectures are no longer done onsite, but recorded, and put online where students can watch them in their own time, at their own pace, and as many times as needed', which allows students and faculty to focus 'onsite time on the kinds of activities that benefit

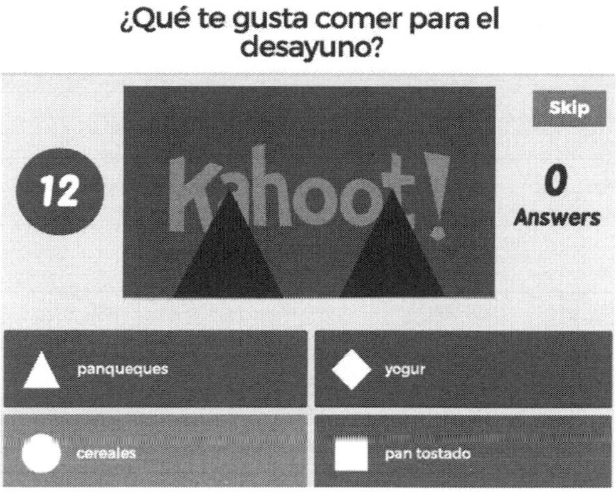

Figure 7.4 Sample of in-class communicative poll using Kahoot.it

from individually responsive and fluid interactions.' Students interacted with new material through the online format in their own time, then came to class daily for practical application of the material – namely, conversation practice and discussion of the cultural material. Flipping the classroom in this way is increasingly common in higher education. In fact, a recent student shows that the majority (55%) of faculty surveyed responded that 'they are somewhere along the spectrum of flipping all or some of their courses, in which they ask their students to view videos or some other digital matter online before coming to school and then use class time for other activities, such as hands-on and team projects or discussions' (Schaffhauser, 2016: 26). As will be described below, based on the feedback and positive learning outcomes, this course will continue to have a flipped element every time it is taught, even during regular full-semester on-campus courses.

6 Fully Online Spanish Course Implementation

After the success of the first blended beginning Spanish course, I continued to develop the course into a fully online format, as well as extend the materials to the second semester beginning Spanish course (102). The courses were developed to be offered during summer sessions, and each session is 4 weeks in length. Therefore, like the blended course, a 14-week semester's worth of material needs to be covered in four weeks. Spanish 101 was developed for the month of June and Spanish 102 for the month of July, and each course was taught two summers in a row for the pilot. Students could take either or both of the courses, and the tuition was approximately a quarter the cost of a regular on-campus course. The course built on the materials from the blended course and used the same

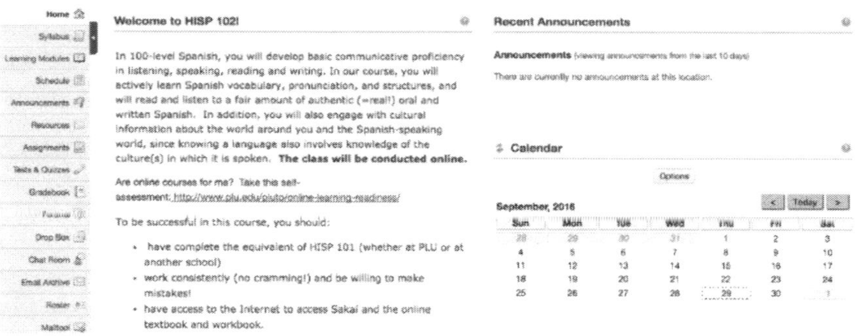

Figure 7.5 Learning management system landing page

LMS tools in Sakai. In addition, several technology tools were added to support students in this fully online course (Figure 7.5).

For the online course to work with students' schedules in the summer, and based on guidelines developed by the PLUTO group, the courses were designed to be completely asynchronous – in other words, there was no required time when students had to be online to complete the coursework. There were specific deadlines for each activity and assessment, but as long as students met the deadlines, they could work at any time of the day or night. Even the orientation to the course had to be conducted online, so I developed several tutorial videos (using the screencasting tools mentioned above) to walk students through all of the tools and resources (Figure 7.6).

An important consideration for fully online courses that stems from accreditation needs, financial aid requirements and general best practices is that all of the campus resources that are available to on-campus

Figure 7.6 Instructional video on how to navigate course site

students must be made available to students taking courses online. This includes resources such as student services, the library and tutoring. To accomplish this, our Language Resource Center provided on-call language consultants, who are peer tutors. Students could schedule appointments via email and use GoogleHangouts for help. Interestingly, no students took advantage of this resource either summer, possibly owing to the fast-moving intensive nature of the 4-week courses and the amount of on-demand help I provided.

For each course (101 and 102), I developed 18 learning modules, which were created and organized using the 'lessons' tool in Sakai. This allowed for an organization where students could find all of the materials needed for each module or task. Each module started with explicit learning objectives, then had links to an instructional video, textbook pages to study, other resources to read or view, interactive formative assessments through the online work-book and finally a short Sakai quiz on the content of the module. Each step of the daily learning module is explained in more detail below.

6.1 Learning objectives

The objectives for each learning module were written in English, in student-friendly language that focused on performance-based objectives. In other words, the objectives outlined what students should be able to do in Spanish by the end of the module. Some examples include: After completing this module, you will be able to describe foods you like to eat; talk about things you used to do as a child.

6.2 Instructional video

I created one instructional video for each of the 18 modules, using a PowerPoint presentation with slides and visuals and then a screencasting tool to record my voice and video as I presented each slideshow. The slideshows started with the performance-based objective for the module, written in English but spoken in Spanish, then a preview of vocabulary and grammar with examples and models. I would highlight areas that I knew, from experience, students might find challenging.

6.3 Textbook and other resources

The first iteration of the fully online course continued to use the McGraw-Hill text *Sol y viento* (VanPatten *et al.*, 2012). Directly in the learning module in Sakai, there is a note of the specific pages in the digital textbook that the students needed to review. The digital textbook is inter-active, and students are encouraged to click on all of the interactive pieces, such as buttons to hear audio recordings of vocabulary as well as contextualized activities that gave students automated feedback. In this section,

I would also link to other resources such as authentic materials (websites, YouTube videos, etc.) that gave students more language and culture input around the topic of the module. For example, for the clothing and shopping module, I linked directly to some department store websites from Spanish-speaking countries (such as *El Corte Inglés*), and for the lesson on school subjects, I linked to the websites of several universities. The second summer I taught this course, our program switched to using the text *Panorama* (Blanco & Redwine Donley, 2013) after convening a textbook review committee that conducted a thorough review of our program goals and curriculum. We found that this text better met our program's needs and offered more digital options.

6.4 Conversations

Students had conversation cards for each lesson, and twice a week they had to meet with a partner or with me, at a time that worked for them, to practice and record their conversation. These conversations allowed for students to negotiate meaning and exchange information in the target language, two important aspects of communicative language teaching (Lee & VanPatten, 2003). We used the web conferencing program, Zoom (https://zoom.us/), which was easy and free to use. This program allowed for students to see and hear each other, and the video pans to the student talking. Students recorded their conversation and saved it as an MPEG 4 video, which they then uploaded to their Dropbox in the LMS Sakai. I could then watch and listen to the video to give feedback, ensure students participate equally and observe whether students were reading a script or obviously using notes. Here is a sample prompt with instructions for the regular conversations:

> Conversation #1 instructions: Schedule a time with another student in the course to record a conversation via Zoom. (Watch the instructional video on Zoom below if you are new to using this program.) You can use the 'Mailtool' in the left-hand tool bar to email classmates in order to find a partner. Groups of 3 are fine, too! Be sure to have your video on. Save the conversation with a file name that has each of your names in it, and upload your recorded conversation to your DropBox. Instructions: Have a 1–2 minute conversation, unscripted – that means, don't use notes or a script. Ask and answer questions about your daily routine, using the vocabulary on *Contextos* pp. 210–211.

The first time the online course was taught, students seemed to prefer having their conversations with me rather than with other students. However, I assumed that this was because students were anxious about reaching out to other students to make the first contact. The next time I taught the course, I made an effort to invite students in the first conversation to meet with me via Zoom all together, so that I could introduce the students to each other. During that course, after the first conversation, all of the students chose to complete conversations with a partner, which in turn encouraged more peer to peer interactions.

6.5 Forum

Approximately once a week, students had tasks to complete in the forum tool, which is a discussion board. The first week, they had prompts to introduce themselves through text (and images or videos, if they would like) so that all of the participants could begin to get to know each other. As the course continued, students had more in-depth discussion topics, sometimes in English, sometimes in Spanish. For example, students read the chapter *No Speak English* (from *The House on Mango Street* by Sandra Cisneros) and then had to respond in English to the questions: How would you describe the tone of the reading? Give evidence from the text on the roles of language in the reading. Think of both the author's use of language as well as what happens 'linguistically' to the characters. What is the double meaning of 'No speak English.'? Another discussion topic was for students to read the bilingual poem 'Where you from' by Gina Valdés, and reflect on these questions: What is the main idea of the poem? Why does the author use two languages? How can 'Crossing borders' have both a literal and figurative meaning? Other forum topics, for which students needed to respond in Spanish, included topics of 'celebrations of independence' and descriptions of what students did over the weekend. For these forums to be interactive, students were required to post one original post and respond to at least two other student posts to receive full credit. In addition, each course had a 'General Course Questions' forum, where students could post questions about anything in the course, and other students and/or I could answer them.

6.6 Composition

Students wrote one formal essay for each of these 4-week courses. As with traditional courses in the curriculum, students had the opportunity to write a first (graded) draft and then revise for a higher grade based on my feedback. The LMS offered two tools that are very helpful for this task. First, students could upload their composition through the 'assignments' tool for which I could set a due date and time and where all of the students' compositions would be housed for me to assess. Secondly, the Turnitin application (http://turnitin.com/) is a tool that checks for originality and helps prevent academic integrity violations. Just having the students know that I used the tool seems to help prevent cheating and plagiarism from the beginning, but then the tool allows me to catch any suspected violations through an originality report.

6.7 Formal assessments

For the first two online courses (summer 2015), I developed multimedia exams using the 'quizzes' function of the LMS. For the second summer (2016), I used the lesson tests provided by the publisher of the textbook through the digital platform (Vista Higher Learning SuperSite for *Panorama*, 4th edn, Blanco & Redwine Donley, 2013). In both the LMS and the publisher's platform, the quizzes contained matching, multiple-choice and fill-in-the-blank questions based on written and oral prompts (that could be automatically graded by the system), as well as short answer, essay and speaking activities that I would need to assess. I provided feedback to individual students both through written and oral (recorded) notes that were delivered in-line to the students.

7 Outcomes of the Two-Year Pilot

The results of this pilot show that retention was steady, attrition was extremely low, and access to Spanish courses increased, supporting the goals of the two-year pilot. All students who began the courses completed them (with one student taking an incomplete but then finishing it within the appropriate extension timeline). For the courses' enrollment details, see Table 7.1.

This did not reduce the number of students taking the traditional face-to-face courses during the regular academic year. In other words, students who would or could not normally take a Spanish course during the school year because of time and/or cost, were able to experience Spanish online in the summer. Table 7.1 also shows that retention numbers, both for the institution generally and the Spanish program in particular, were promising. The online courses help keep students connected to the university over extended breaks (such as summer), when students often move home to work or to get ahead on credits by taking courses at their local community college or online elsewhere.

Student comments from the blended course, through regular university evaluation forms completed in class and with a 100% response rate,

Table 7.1 Enrollment and retention

Term	Enrollment	Institutional retention (continued at institution the following semester)	Spanish program retention (continued into next course in sequence)
January 2015 (101 blended)	22	22 (100%)	13 (59%)
Summer 2015 (101 online)	9	9 (100%)	6 (67%)
Summer 2015 (102 online)	10	9 (1 graduated) (90%)	1 (10%)
Summer 2016 (101 online)	6	6 (100%)	3 (50%)
Summer 2016 (102 online)	9	*6 (2 graduated, 1 transfer) (67%)	3 (33%)

*One student was taking the PLU course to transfer back to another university.

were quite positive with respect to the blended nature. All 22 students either 'agreed' or 'strongly agreed' that the course was effective. Several student comments point directly to the issue of flexible pacing as well as automatic feedback. For example, one student wrote 'I really liked the blended set-up. I was able to work at my own pace.' Another wrote 'The blended format and modules are very well planned and thought out.' 'Having lecture online so that we could focus on practicing the language more in class' helped one student learn the most.

There is not as much student feedback for the online courses compared to the blended course. Unlike the blended course, which had face-to-face time during which I could make sure that all students completed the evaluation, the fully online asynchronous classes depended on online evaluations. The institution currently does not require that students complete the online evaluations and there are no solutions to ensuring they complete them. In the future, faculty will encourage the university administrators to require students to complete them before they can receive credit, a grade or their transcript, or consider some other measure that will essentially require completion and increase the response rate. These measures could include having students bring devices to class and complete the evaluations during class time. However, through emails and the few evaluations I did receive, there is some helpful feedback below that indicates student satisfaction.

As described in the literature review above, fully online course can meet the needs of students who are anxious about studying a language, and feedback from students corroborated this. One student in the first 101 online course wrote in an email to me,

> Language has always been a struggle for me. At first I was a little hesitant about an online course, but it's working surprisingly well for me! I really like that I can go back and play the module videos that you upload as many times as I need to while working to complete the online exercises. So despite my previous language experience, this is going quite well and I am very pleasantly surprised!

For the full online courses, evaluations were as positive as the blended course results. In the first summer, 101 had a response rate of 0% (despite numerous reminders to complete the evaluations) and 102 had a response rate of 30%. For those students who did complete the 102 evaluations, all students either agreed or strongly agreed with all of the positive statements in the evaluation rating both the professor and the course. When asked what they liked about the course, a student wrote 'The online workbook. It gave immediate feedback.' Another wrote, 'there were clear instructions for each assignment.' In the second summer, 101 had a response rate of 0 and 102 had a response rate of 50%. The 102 written comments were particularly helpful and promising, as we move forward past this pilot project. 'The instructor challenged me to learn constantly by speaking Spanish in the learning module videos, providing us with links to practice quizzes, and having our homework be a mix of videos, speaking, listening, and writing'. Several students commented that 'the learning module videos are great', which validated the amount of work and planning that went in to developing them. Another student thoughtfully wrote,

> I am so happy with how (the professor) approached this course. She was so well organized. There were never any surprises. Each day was set up exactly the same, objectives were made clear, the intended flow for the module was spelled out, and quizzes were occasionally given to make sure we were engaged in the material. I felt prepared every day and able to complete each task without being uncertain about whether or not I completed what was expected of me. She recorded instructional videos everyday that were interactive and so helpful. I appreciated that she was very responsive whenever I asked her a question, being an online course there was some fear going into this that I was not going to be able to communicate with my teacher and would be forced to tackle the course on my own, that was certainly not the case. She gave feedback early on some assignments, which was reassuring knowing that she was actually looking at the material we were creating and was able to provide an opinion on them. I was so impressed with how she created this course and maintained a level of communication that was more than adequate.

In addition to the goals of access and retention that were studied in this pilot, language programs are concerned with the learning outcomes of the students. The main question to answer is: Do students learn the same amount of language and culture in the blended or online format as they would in a traditional face-to-face course? Based on assessment evidence from this 2-year pilot, the answer to this question would be 'yes'. The same course assessment content (oral assessments, formative and summative written assessments, and written essays) were used in the blended, online and face-to-face course by the same professor and the results are comparable. For future study, now that the online summer courses are part of our regular course rotations, a more formal study that would confirm the statistical significance of comparison will be needed. As the instructor for both online and face-to-face versions of these courses, I observed that the average course grades were similar, and the amount of material covered was the same. In addition, the technology allowed for other kinds of feedback to me to gauge student engagement with the content. Statistics gathered through the LMS showed that there were, for example, 1220 visits over 4 weeks by 10 students in 101, summer 2016. This is an average of 122 visits per student. The digital platform for the text (*Panorama*, Blanco & Redwine Donley, 2013) allows instructors to track how much time students spend engaging with the workbook material, and the average per student was 26 hours.

As described above, the institution's Spanish program has the goal that students will exit the first year with at least Novice High proficiency. For interpersonal speaking, descriptors of students at Novice High include 'I can communicate and exchange information about familiar topics using phrases and simple sentences, sometimes supported by memorized language. I can usually handle short social interactions in everyday situations by asking and answering simple questions' (National Council of State Supervisors for Languages (NCSSFL)-ACTFL (2017) Can-Do Statements). Towards the end of the second semester course online, all students in the online pilot demonstrated Novice High in interpersonal speaking through their recorded but unrehearsed 1–2 minute conversations in pairs on the topics of household chores (their likes and dislikes, and who in their home does which chores) and everyday technology use and habits. For presentational writing, Novice High language users 'can write short messages and notes on familiar topics related to everyday life' (NCSSFL-ACTFL (2017) Can-Do Statements). This was assessed for students exiting the second semester online course through a 250-word essay entitled 'Un viaje inolvidable' (an unforgettable trip), where students were prompted to think about an unforgettable trip they took in the past and to use the preterit and imperfect to narrate in the past, describing the trip. The results showed that students could string short, simple sentences together to write about this familiar topic.

8 Conclusion

Based on the results of the 2-year pilot described above, the Spanish program plans to continue offering 101 and 102 full online in the summer sessions. The blended course, offered in January (interim term), will continue as a traditional face-to-face course with some flipped elements to support student learning yet take advantage of the intensive, daily class interactions. The initial course development takes dedicated time and training. As Vai and Sosulski (2011: 24) explain, 'generally speaking it takes more time (teaching online) than the onsite equivalent', but that the flexible and portable nature of the work is appealing. In addition, once the course is designed and taught at least one time, future iterations of the course will be quicker and easier to develop and improve

In the future, the program will look at ways to recruit students for these courses. Opportunities for partnerships across the curriculum will be explored. For example, students in professional programs (nursing, education, etc.) could be encouraged to take Spanish as a resume booster.

Faculty in language programs at a variety of institutional settings should explore ways in which online offerings can support their mission and program goals. As Durán-Cerda describes (2010: 111), current technology tools can allow educators to 'overcome challenges in distance, space, time, and human and economic resources that limit access to language learning opportunities in cultural, literary, historical, geographical, and cross-cultural frames.' In fact, she says that it is our responsibility as language educators to use everything available to us, including technology, to maximize the opportunities for our students. Hermosillo (2014) outlines some of the past and current research in blended language course offerings. Blake (2008), Sanders (2005) and others have contributed to the body of research on effective online language instruction. Future research must continue to test the effectiveness of blended and fully online language courses.

Note

(1) Novice high speakers and writers generally depend heavily on formulaic language, mainly at the word and phrase level, but moving toward sentence-level as they progress toward the next major level of intermediate.

References

Allen, I.E. and Seaman, J. (2008) Staying the Course: Online Education in the United States. See http://www.onlinelearningsurvey.com/reports/staying-the-course.pdf (accessed 8 July 2018).

ACTFL Proficiency Guidelines. See https://www.actfl.org/publications/guidelines-and-manuals/actfl-proficiencyguidelines-2012 (accessed 8 July 2018).

Blake, R.J. (2008) *Brave New Digital Classroom: Technology and Foreign Language Learning*. Washington, DC: Georgetown University Press.

Blake, R.J. (2009) The use of technology for second language distance learning. *Modern Language Journal* 93, 822–835.

Blanco, J.A. and Redwine Donley, P. (2013) *Panorama: Introducción a la lengua Española*, 4th edn. Boston: Vista Higher Learning.

Cisneros, S. (1989) *The House On Mango Street*. New York: Vintage Books.

Despain, J.S. (2003) Achievement and attrition rate differences between traditional and internet-based beginning Spanish courses. *Foreign Language Annals* 36 (2), 243–257.

Durán-Cerda, D. (2010) Language distance learning for the digital generation. *Hispania* 93 (1), 108–112.

Ensslin, A. and Krummes, C. (2013) Electronic interaction and resources. In J. Herschensohn and M. Young-Scholten (eds) *The Cambridge Handbook of Second Language Acquisition*, 1st edn. Cambridge: Cambridge University Press,

Hermosilla, L. (2014) Hybrid Spanish programs: A challenging and successful endeavor. *Hispania* 97 (1), 2–4.

Horwitz, E.K., Horwitz, M.B. and Cope, J. (1986) Foreign language classroom anxiety. *The Modern Language Journal* 70 (2), 125–132.

Lee, J.F. and VanPatten, B. (2003) *Making Communicative Language Teaching Happen*, 2nd edn. Boston: McGraw-Hill.

NCSSFL-ACTFL (2017) *NCSSFL-ACTFL Can-do Statements*. See https://www.actfl.org/publications/guidelines-and-manuals/ncssfl-actfl-can-do-statements (accessed 8 July 2018).

Pannapacker, W. (2014) Taking the liberal arts online in the summer: New ways of delivering courses can be compatible with small-college values. See http://www.chronicle.com/article/Taking-theLiberal-ArtsOnline/146371/ (accessed 8 July 2018).

Payne, J.S. (2004) Making the most of synchronous and asynchronous discussion in foreign language instruction. In L. Lomicka and J. Cooke-Plagwitz (eds) *The Heinle Professional Series in Language Instruction: Teaching with Technology* (Vol. 1) (pp. 79–93). Boston: Heinle.

Sanders, R.F. (2005) Redesigning introductory Spanish: Increased enrollment, online management, cost reduction, and effects on student learning. *Foreign Language Annals* 38 (4), 523–532.

Schaffhauser, D. (2016) Teaching with tech: A balancing act. *Campus Technology* 29 (8). See http://pdf.1105media.com/CampusTech/2016/701920958/CAM_1608DG.pdf (accessed 8 July 2018)

Stein, J. and Graham, C.R. (2014) *Essentials for Blended Learning: A Standards-Based Guide*. New York: Routledge.

Vai, M. and Sosulski, K. (2011) *Essentials of Online Course Design: A Standards-Based Guide*. New York: Routledge.

VanPatten, B., Michael Leeser, M. and Keating, G.D. (2012) *Sol y viento: Beginning Spanish*, 3rd edn. New York: McGraw-Hill.

Wang, S. (2015) Online vs. on-campus: An analysis of course prices of U.S. educational institutions. *Online Journal of Distance Learning Administration* 18. See https://www.westga.edu/~distance/ojdla/summer182/wang182.html.

Conclusion

Deborah Arteaga

Introduction

L2 acquisition has been an important focus of theoretical research in the last two decades. One topic of debate has been whether or not adult L2 learners have access to Universal Grammar (UG), meaning that their linguistic knowledge – the grammatical representation – can eventually mirror that of native speakers, with Hawkins (*inter alia* Hawkins & Chan, 1997; Hawkins & Hattori, 2006), taking the view that they do not, and others (e.g. Lardiere, 2007; White, 2003) arguing the opposite. Related to the access to UG is the Shallow Structure Hypothesis (Clahsen & Felser, 2006), according to which the syntax of adult L2 learners never reaches the syntactic complexity of L1 learners.

With respect to ultimate attainment by L2 speakers, the influence of the L1 remains relevant. Some scholars have argued for direct L1 transfer to the grammar of the L2 (e.g. Chrabaszcz & Jiang, 2014; Mayo, 2009), along the lines of contrastive analysis first proposed by Lado (1957), while others have maintained that the L1 plays no significant role in L2 acquisition (Ellis, 2017; Hui, 2010).

Directly linked to grammatical knowledge is another aspect of L2 research, processing, with some scholars proposing that the grammar of adult L2 learners is constrained by processing (e.g. Lew & Fernald, 2010; Shantz & Tanner, 2016), while others hold the opposing view (*inter alia* Hopp, 2016; Marull, 2017). Hopp's (2007) Fundamental Identity Hypothesis addresses both processing and transfer, stating that L2 learners only at first rely on semantic and lexical cues, and any later divergence from the grammar of L1 speakers is a function of transfer and processing load.

In L2 research, both longitudinal studies and point-in-time studies (although fewer of the former), have been conducted, often showing opposing conclusions (see Orteaga & Iberri-Shea, 2005 for a meta-review). Another aspect of theoretical studies is whether they investigate heritage speakers (Montrul, 2016; Santos & Flores, 2016), immigrants (Backus & Ya mur, 2017; Kristen *et al.*, 2016), instructed learners (Derwing, 2017; Gotseva, 2017) or naturalistic learners (Benson, 2011; Birdsong & Vanhove, 2016). Finally, there has been research proposing various pedagogical models based on theoretical aspects of L2 acquisition (see contributions in Cenoz *et al.*, 2017; Loewen & Sato, 2017).

Findings in this Volume

The present volume continues these traditions, yet it has several unique features. One, the chapters do not subscribe to one particular theoretical approach (cf. Mendola & Scott, 2017; Miller *et al.*, 2012). The chapters in this volume, all written by experts in the field, present new research that touches on several current theoretical debates and presents a rich range of new empirical data.

The question of ultimate attainment is addressed by Dekydtspotter and Gilbert (Chapter 4) and Arteaga and Herschensohn (Chapter 2). Several of the contributions (Achinova & Déprez, Chapter 1; Dekydtspotter & Gilbert, Chapter 4; Sagarra, Chapter 5; Vainikka & Young-Scholten, Chapter 6), take up the issue of L1 transfer, presenting data that show that L1 transfer cannot account for L2 grammar.

Other authors argue that processing must be considered in order to properly assess the interlanguage grammars of L2 learners (Achimova & Déprez, Chapter 1; Dekydtspotter & Gilbert, Chapter 4). Three of the studies are longitudinal (Arteaga & Herschensohn, Chapter 2; Ayoun, Chapter 3; Yaden, Chapter 7). L2 learners at various stages are discussed, from beginning learners (Vainikka & Young-Scholten, Chapter 6; Yaden, Chapter 7), to intermediate learners (Sagarra, Chapter 5), to advanced learners (Ayoun, Chapter 3; Dekydtspotter & Gilbert, Chapter 4; Arteaga & Herschensohn, Chapter 2), with one study investigating all three levels (Achimova & Déprez, Chapter 1).

The students investigated in the studies range from heritage speakers (Ayoun, Chapter 3), to naturalistic learners (Arteaga & Herschensohn, Chapter 2), to instructed learners (Achimova & Déprez, Chapter 1; Dekydtspotter & Gilbert, Chapter 4; Sagarra, Chapter 5; Yaden, Chapter 7), to immigrants (Vainikka & Young-Scholten, Chapter 6). Another distinctive feature in this book includes the fact that some chapters make pedagogical recommendations based on L2 research (Achimova & Déprez, Chapter 1; Ayoun, Chapter 3; Arteaga & Herschensohn, Chapter 2; Yaden, Chapter 7).

In their chapter, Asya Achimova and Vivian Déprez (Chapter 1) consider whether the grammar of L2 learners shows evidence of the Article Choice Parameter (Ionin *et al.*, 2004), concluding that determiner choice, which is affected by specificity, is instead a function of processing load.

Deborah Arteaga and Julia Herschensohn (Chapter 2), in a longitudinal study of two advanced L2 learners of French (L1 English), argue that neither subject has mastery of both the informal and formal registers. Based on their data, the authors present a pedagogical framework that supports the sociolinguistic development of L2 learners.

Dalila Ayoun (Chapter 3) investigates acquisition of TAM (tense, aspect, mood/modality) by advanced L2 speakers of French (including L1 speakers of English and bilingual heritage speakers of French or Spanish), finding that despite focused input provided at various intervals, performance varied according to L1, task type and tense effects.

Laurent Dekydtspotter and Charlene Gilbert (Chapter 4) provide evidence from L2 learners of French, which shows that syntax plays a role in the speed of processing of pronouns such as *à-propos-de-lui/elle* 'about-him/her' and *le/la-concernant* 'regarding-him/her. Their study shows that in contexts where the pronouns are bound, students process the utterances more quickly.

Taking up the questions of ultimate attainment and L1 transfer, Nuria Sagarra (Chapter 5) teases apart gender and number agreement in L2 learners of Spanish, both absent in English. By using deficit and accessibility approaches to processing in an eye-tracking task, she shows that both intermediate learners and L1 speakers are more sensitive to number agreement than to gender, and that cognitive load impairs L2 speakers.

Bridget Yaden (Chapter 7) discusses instructed learners who in a traditional classroom setting reach the level of Novice High (American Council on the Teaching of Foreign Languages) after two years of Spanish taught through communicative methodologies with targeted input. In a study of hybrid and online language courses, she shows through assessment data that students reach the same level of acquisition regardless of the method of delivery.

Anne Vainikka and Martha Young-Scholten (Chapter 6) note that beginning immigrant L2 learners do not show evidence of producing complex morphosyntax, although they do use 'placeholders' for syntactic heads. Through a study of intermediate immigrant L2 learners, they argue that the subjects' morphology supports the existence of functional projections that do not stem from their L1. They attribute the difference between L1 and L2 speakers to the latter's phonological difficulties.

Implications for the L2 Classroom

All too often, there can be a gap between L2 research and pedagogical considerations. All of the contributions in this volume have direct implications for the L2 classroom, which makes it important reading, for both researchers and teachers alike.

Achimova and Déprez (Chapter 1) tackle the question of whether semantic features transfer between the L1 and the L2. Their work showed that while definiteness seems to transfer, learners are affected by specificity effects. This means that there is a pragmatic factor at play for L2 speakers, in the sense that because of an increased processing load, speakers do not take into account both perspectives, that of the hearer and that of the listener. This is relevant for the L2 classroom, as article choice is oftentimes problematic. Instructors may choose to spend more time on articles representing a dual perspective.

Arteaga and Herschensohn (Chapter 2) investigate the longitudinal acquisition of register in L2 French by two advanced L2 learners, basing their analysis on the difference between the informal/formal subject pronouns, *tu* and *vous*, the omission of the negative particle *ne*, and the use of *on* for *nous*. They recommend that L2 teachers in beginning and intermediate classes model the use of *on* and also focus on the difference between *tu* and *vous* by input flooding and through the use of materials, such as film. As native speakers do not drop *ne* for formal speech, students should be exposed to both registers in classroom exercises.

Ayoun's chapter (Chapter 3) is directly relevant to L2 teaching, because it addresses the oftentimes problematic acquisition of the morphosyntax of French. Her subjects included heritage speakers of both French and Spanish, which is not typically the case with L2 studies, although many instructors teach heritage speakers. All of the students were in classes which had the same curriculum organized in the same way. Input was also controlled, which did not appear to help the learners. The most accurate form that the learners produced was indicative present, and they were more accurate with states. Finally, the use of a cloze test was problematic, indicating that instructors may wish to avoid them.

Dekydtspotter and Gilbert's chapter (Chapter 4) has implications for L2 teaching. Their study showed that there was no performance difference between L2 speakers (graduate students who have not been in lengthy immersion settings) and educated Parisians. L2 teachers can incorporate the findings into the classroom, by presenting their students with far more advanced syntactic structures. An implication of their study is that teaching an L2 is far different from teaching other school subjects, as L2 speakers possess innate computational mechanisms underlying processing.

Sagarra (Chapter 5) investigates the effects of age and the use of non-default forms (i.e. feminine) on learners' reaction to gender and number agreement errors (noun/adjective). An eye-tracking task tested the reaction time for L1 and L2 speakers of Spanish. Sagarra's data showed that L1 speakers reacted more quickly and spent more time when the gender agreement was ungrammatical, although both groups were sensitive to the violations. Her study supports the notion that L2 speakers, even those whose L1 lacks a grammatical feature, can process it like L1 speakers, and errors are attributable to cognitive load.

The pedagogical application of Sagarra's work would be for instructors to take the processing load into consideration when designing exercises and tests. This could be in the form of allowing students more time when forms are morphologically marked, or allowing them to refer back to the text on exams or on-line exercises.

Vainikka and Young-Scholten (Chapter 6) present further evidence that supports their Organic Grammar model, which postulates a Master

Tree (from Universal Grammar) for all speakers, L1 or L2. They show that L2 speakers look for syntactic elements to fill the heads of projections (i.e. AgrP, TP). The pedagogical application of Vainikka and Young-Scholten is that their work shows the necessity of a great deal of L2 input to speed up L2 speakers' acquisition of syntactic heads. A combination of classes taught largely in the L2 and contact with native speakers of the L2 will increase the amount of input that L2 speakers receive, and, in turn, will spur the syntactic development of L2 speakers.

Finally, Yaden's piece (Chapter 7) has several pedagogical implications. As she notes, there has been reticence among L2 instructors toward online delivery of language classes, although many institutions are emphasizing the importance of this format. If instructors use a variety of technologies, such as Zoom or Camtasia, Yaden shows students can reach the same level of L2 competence through hybrid or online courses. She makes the important point that instructors will need training in these technologies. One interesting conclusion reported by online students is that they found classes less stressful, indicating the need for technology even in face-to-face classrooms.

References

Backus, A. and Yağmur, K. (2017) Differences in pragmatic skills between bilingual Turkish immigrant children in the Netherlands and monolingual peers. *International Journal of Bilingualism* 21, 1–14.

Benson, P. (2011) Language learning and teaching beyond the classroom: An introduction to the field. In P. Benson and H. Reinders (eds) *Beyond the Language Classroom* (pp. 7–16). Palgrave Macmillan.

Birdsong, D. and Vanhove, J. (2016) Age of second language acquisition: Critical periods and social concerns. In E. Nicoladis and S. Montanari (eds) *Lifespan Perspectives on Bilingualism*, (pp. 163–182). Berlin: de Gruyter.

Cenoz, J., Gorter, D. and May, S. (eds) (2017) *Language Awareness and Multilingualism*. Amsterdam: Springer.

Chrabaszcz, A. and Jiang, N. (2014) The role of the native language in the use of the English nongeneric definite article by L2 learners: A cross-linguistic comparison. *Second Language Research* 30, 351–379.

Clahsen, H. and Felser, C. (2006) Grammatical processing in language learners. *Applied Psycholinguistics* 27, 3–42.

Derwing, T.M. (2017) L2 fluency development. In S. Loewen and M. Sato (eds) *The Routledge Handbook of Instructed Second Language Acquisition* (pp. 245–259) New York: Routledge.

Ellis, N. (2017) Implicit and explicit knowledge about language. In J. Cenoz, D. Gorter and S. May (eds) *Language Awareness and Multilingualism* (pp. 113–124). Amsterdam: Springer.

Gotseva, M. (2017) The lexical stage of expressing temporality by Bulgarian L2 instructed learners. *Journal of Second Language Teaching & Research* 5, 176–201.

Hawkins, R. and Chan, C.Y-h. (1997) The partial availability of Universal Grammar in second language acquisition: The 'Failed Functional Features Hypothesis.' *Second Language Research* 13, 187–226.

Hawkins, R. and Hattori, H. (2006) Interpretation of English multiple wh-questions by Japanese speakers: A missing uninterpretable feature account. *Second Language Research* 22, 269–301.

Hopp, H. (2007) *Ultimate Attainment at the Interfaces in Second Language Acquisition: Grammar and Processing*. Groningen: Grodil Press.

Hopp, H. (2016) Learning (not) to predict: Grammatical gender processing in second language acquisition. *Second Language Research* 32, 277–307.

Hui, Y. (2010) The role of L1 transfer on L2 and pedagogical implications. *Canadian Social Science* 3, 97–103.

Ionin, T., Ko, H. and Wexler, K. (2004) Article semantics in L2 acquisition: The role of specificity. *Language Acquisition* 12 (1), 3–69.

Kristen, C., Mühlau, P. Schacht, D. (2016) Language acquisition of recently arrived immigrants in England, Germany, Ireland, and the Netherlands. *Ethnicities* 16, 180–212.

Lado, R. (1957) *Linguistics Across Cultures: Applied Linguistics for Language Teachers*. Ann Arbor, MI: University of Michigan Press.

Lardiere, D. (2007) *Ultimate Attainment in Second Language Acquisition: A Case Study*. Mahwah, NJ: Lawrence Erlbaum.

Lew-Williams, C. and Fernald, A. (2010) Real time processing of gender-marked articles by native and non-native Spanish speakers. *Journal of Memory and Language* 63, 447–464.

Loewen, S. and Sato, M. (eds) (2017) *The Routledge Handbook of Instructed Second Language Acquisition*. New York: Routledge.

Marull, C. (2017) Second language processing efficiency: Experience and cognitive effects on L2 morphosyntactic integration and anticipation. In M. LaMendola and J. Scott (eds) *Proceedings of the 41st Annual Boston University Conference on Language Development* (pp. 466–480). Somerville, MA: Cascadilla Press.

Mayo, M.P. (2009) Article choice in L2 English by Spanish speakers. In M.P. Mayo and R. Hawkins (eds) *Second Language Acquisition of Articles: Empirical Findings and Theoretical Implications* (pp. 13–37). Amsterdam: John Benjamins.

Mendola, M. and Scott, J. (2017) *Proceedings of the 41st Annual Boston University Conference on Language Development*. Somerville, MA: Cascadilla Press.

Miller, R.T., Martin, K.I., Eddington, C.M., Henery, A. Marcos Miguel, N., Tseng, A.M., Tuninetti, A. and Walter, D. (eds) (2012) *Selected Proceedings of the 2012 Second Language Research Forum: Building Bridges between Disciplines*. Somerville, MA: Cascadilla Press.

Montrul, S. (2016) *The Acquisition of Heritage Languages*. Cambridge: Cambridge University Press.

Orteaga, L. and Iberri-Shea, G. (2005) Longitudinal research in second language acquisition: Recent trends and future directions. *Annual Review of Applied Linguistics* 25, 26–45.

Santos, A.L. and Flores, C. (2016) Comparing heritage speakers and late L2-learners of European Portuguese. *Linguistic Approaches to Bilingualism* 6, 308–340.

Shantz, K. and Tanner, D. (2016) Are L2 Learners pressed for time? Retrieval of grammatical gender information in L2 lexical access. In J. Scott and D. Waughtal (eds) *Proceedings of the 40th Annual Boston University Conference on Language Development* (pp. 331435). Somerville, MA: Cascadilla.

White, L. (2003) *Second Language Acquisition and Universal Grammar*. Cambridge: Cambridge University Press.

Index